More praise for *Super Nutrition for Babies*

"With *Super Nutrition for Babies* (and young children), at last I finally have a book that I can wholeheartedly recommend to my patients, my students, and the physicians whom I lecture about nutrition. Someone finally got it right and I applaud the authors for their research and their willingness to tell the truth."

— **David J. Getoff, C.C.N., C.T.N., F.A.A.I.M.,** vice president, Price-Pottenger Nutrition Foundation

"You only get one chance to grow a child's body, mind, and spirit, and with our traditional food cultures in shreds, parents have been cut adrift in a sea of conflicting advice. Using clear common sense and basic nutritional concepts, Katherine Erlich and Kelly Genzlinger have written a book that can be an anchor, and then a safe harbor, for parents and babies everywhere."

— **Lierre Keith,** author of *The Vegetarian Myth: Food, Justice, and Sustainability*

"A clear, practical, and nontrendy guide for parents on how to best feed babies and toddlers, backed by the trifecta of common sense, ancestral wisdom, and sound science. The recommendations accord with Weston A. Price Foundation principles, and are exactly what's needed to get our children off to a good start and to empower their health for life."

— **Kaayla T. Daniel, Ph.D., C.C.N.,** vice president, Weston A. Price Foundation, and author of *The Whole Soy Story: The Dark Side of America's Favorite Health Food*

"*Super Nutrition for Babies* by Katherine Erlich and Kelly Genzlinger is something that every expectant and new mother and father should read! It gives the correct information for parents on how to bring up healthy, intelligent, and robust children. In a world where parents are constantly bombarded by wrong and harmful information, this book is a rare treasure! I congratulate the authors, who write with authority based on solid clinical and practical experience and their work as a medical doctor and a nutritionist—all supported by thorough research and references. I warmly recommend it."

— **Natasha Campbell-McBride, M.D.,** author of *Gut and Psychology Syndrome*

"Erlich and Genzlinger have compiled a wealth of knowledge and experience into a book that is so basic on one hand and so complete and thorough on the other that readers will understand—without difficulty—the concepts and be able to apply them easily. This is a grand reference book that can be used for many years of a child's life."

— **Nancy Appleton, Ph.D.,** author of *Lick the Sugar Habit*

This book is dedicated to babies. You deserve a fair chance to be fully healthy. You are designed that way, down to your very cells. You are perfect.

And to parents. While joyous, having a baby these days is also scary. We hope you are encouraged that this information affords you ways to safeguard your child and improve his odds in favor of health—traditional ways to nourish him that will likely ring true on a deep level. By providing the purest, most nutritious, and least toxic foods, you have the power to give your baby a solid foundation in health. With the guidance provided in this book, you will learn how to help him be the most resilient, strongest, happiest, and healthiest child possible.

And to pediatricians, especially those of you who have ever felt frustrated or helpless in caring for a child suffering with chronic or recurrent illness. We hope that this book will be an additional resource in assisting you in treating your patients.

Inspiring | Educating | Creating | Entertaining

Brimming with creative inspiration, how-to projects, and useful information to enrich your everyday life, Quarto Knows is a favorite destination for those pursuing their interests and passions. Visit our site and dig deeper with our books into your area of interest: Quarto Creates, Quarto Cooks, Quarto Homes, Quarto Lives, Quarto Drives, Quarto Explores, Quarto Gifts, or Quarto Kids.

First Published in 2018 by Fair Winds Press,
an imprint of The Quarto Group,
100 Cummings Center, Suite 265-D, Beverly, MA 01915, USA.
T (978) 282-9590 F (978) 283-2742 QuartoKnows.com

Fair Winds Press titles are also available at discount for retail, wholesale, promotional, and bulk purchase. For details, contact the Special Sales Manager by email at specialsales@quarto.com or by mail at The Quarto Group, Attn: Special Sales Manager, 100 Cummings Center, Suite 265-D, Beverly, MA 01915, USA.

22 21   3 4 5

ISBN: 978-1-59233-840-5

Digital edition published in 2018
eISBN: 978-1-63159-517-2

Originally found under the following Library of Congress Cataloging-in-Publication Data

Genzlinger, Kelly.
Super nutrition for babies : the right way to feed your baby for optimal health / Kelly Genzlinger, Kathy Erlich
p. cm.
Includes bibliographical references and index.
ISBN 978-1-59233-503-9 (pbk.) -- ISBN 1-59233-503-9 (pbk.)
1. Infants--Nutrition. I. Erlich, Kathy. II. Title.
RJ216.G3745 2012
641.5'6222--dc23
2011041666

Design: Megan Jones Design
Cover Image: Alison Bickel Photography and Shutterstock
Page Layout: Megan Jones Design
Photography: Alison Bickel Photography

Printed in China

The information in this book is for educational purposes only. It is not intended to replace the advice of a physician or medical practitioner. Please see your health care provider before beginning any new health program.

Some of the views expressed in this book are controversial and not widely accepted by the medical community. Some of the information in this book may be considered functional, complementary, alternative, or integrative medicine and may not be endorsed by governmental or academic institutions. Some of the supplements and recommendations described may not have received approval by the Food and Drug Administration or other regulatory agencies for the purpose for which they are suggested. Readers are encouraged to consult other sources and make independent judgments about the issues discussed.

SUPER NUTRITION
for babies

REVISED EDITION

The Best Way to Nourish Your Baby
from Birth to 24 Months

KATHERINE ERLICH, M.D., and
KELLY GENZLINGER, M.Sc., C.N.C., C.M.T.A.

FAIR WINDS

CONTENTS

BABY FEEDING FUNDAMENTALS

Nutrition Is Necessary for Health

MOM'S DIET DOES MATTER

Critical Feeding Information for Pregnant and Nursing Mothers and Babies

(0 TO 6 MONTHS)

DRUGSTORE FORMULA DOESN'T CUT IT

Better Options Than Commercial Alternatives

FROM FAKE FLAKES TO REAL FOOD

Meeting Nutrient Needs with First Foods

(6 TO 8 MONTHS)

5

OH-SO-MUCH-BETTER THAN CEREAL O'S

Taking the Toxins Out

(8 TO 10 MONTHS)

6

RECONSIDER BABY FOOD JARS AND NOODLE STARS

Bolstering Immunity with Nutrients and Foods

(10 TO 12 MONTHS)

7

SHAPE UP SWEETS AND SHIP OUT SUGAR

Getting Back to Nature's Basics

(12 TO 18 MONTHS)

8

THINK OUTSIDE THE BOX OF MAC 'N' CHEESE

Convenience Foods Can Cost You Your Child's Health

(18 TO 24 MONTHS)

FOREWORD

Super Nutrition for Babies is a much-needed book. Parents are confused about food and often do not have the appropriate knowledge to make the best food choices for their children. Now they have a book that guides them toward making good food decisions.

Conventional medicine makes little mention of the importance of educating parents about how to properly feed their children. Simple dietary changes that emphasize eating nutrient-rich foods would do more than any medicine or vaccine to improve a child's ability to reach their potential. In fact, educating parents about the optimal way to feed their children should be the first item discussed in the prenatal visit. *Super Nutrition for Babies* provides the optimal dietary advice that gives children the best chance to reach their true potential.

Health care for children is a disaster. What is health care for children? Conventional medicine spends untold amounts of moneys vaccinating children for numerous illnesses. And yes, many childhood illnesses have declined due to vaccinations. However, epidemic numbers of children are suffering from a host of chronic illnesses such as autism, cancer, obesity, and ADHD.

In the United States, for instance, far more money is spent on health care than any other Western country. Currently, more than 16% of the United States' gross domestic product is spent on health care. Unfortunately, spending large sums of money on health care has not provided better health indices. As compared to other Western countries, the United States ranks at the bottom of nearly every health indicator. There is more chronic illness, more heart attacks, and generally poorer health when compared to other Western countries. However, it is not just children in the United States who are suffering. All Western countries are seeing dramatic increases of chronic childhood diseases such as autism, ADD/ADHD, and cancer.

Is there an underlying theme behind the declining health of our children? It is not as simple as spending more money. Every country in the world is under strain due to budgetary constraints. In the case of children's health needs, one inexpensive way to improve the health of children is to feed them nutritious food. This would go a long way to helping the world overcome its health care crises. This process can be started by following the healthy dietary principles outlined in *Super Nutrition for Babies*.

I have been practicing holistic medicine for nearly twenty-five years. I have seen the consequences of feeding children a poor diet full of refined and devitalized foods. Feeding children a devitalized diet leads to devitalized children who will not reach their potential and suffer from myriad health issues.

My experience has clearly shown that the pathway to optimal health for us all is to eat a healthy diet. The pathway to raising a child who can achieve her full potential is to provide the child with a diet that supplies all of the valuable nutrients needed to help optimize their brain function. A healthy diet can also help the child optimize her immune and hormonal systems as well as all the other organs of the body.

Katherine Erlich, M.D., and Kelly Genzlinger, M.Sc., C.N.C., C.M.T.A, have written a must-read book for everyone who has children and for those who are thinking of starting a family. There is no doubt that the younger your child is when you begin optimizing his/her diet, the greater the tools he or she will have to succeed. These tools include vitamins, minerals, enzymes, and fatty acids. The Western diet is lacking in each of these vital items. For over twenty years, I have been testing children (and adults) for various nutritional levels. Eating a devitalized diet, full of refined foods, leads to multiple nutritional deficiencies and poor brain function.

We can and should do more for our children. It starts with mothers eating healthier diets. Erlich and Genzlinger discuss this in chapter 2. They point out that eating refined sugar and soy is not a good idea for mothers.

I see the benefits of properly feeding children. These children have fewer allergies, behavioral problems, chronic illness, depression, fatigue, and digestive problems. Furthermore, children fed a whole foods program as outlined in *Super Nutrition for Babies* have stronger immune systems.

It makes sense. If you supply the body with the correct nutrients it can do wonderful things. Just as you fuel your car with appropriate gas in order to optimize its function, we need to fuel our children with appropriate food. Children should eat whole food that is nutritious and supplies the body with the appropriate nutrients to maintain optimal function. In addition, educating children about which foods are healthy and which are not will help future generations. Erlich and Genzlinger have provided us with a blueprint for feeding our children the perfect diet. I highly recommend this book for everyone interested in improving their family's health.

David Brownstein, M.D., *is a board-certified family practitioner and medical director of the Center for Holistic Medicine (West Bloomfield, Michigan). He is the author of twelve books, including* Iodine: Why You Need It, Why You Can't Live Without It *and* Overcoming Thyroid Disorders. *To learn more, visit www.drbrownstein.com.*

INTRODUCTION
Children's New Health Concerns

We are so excited for you—new parents! There isn't a more magical time than when you're welcoming your little one into your life and cultivating a family dynamic around your newest member. Time passes quickly in the first 2 years, each day bringing fresh wonders as his abilities to smile, coo, clutch, crawl, walk, and speak all continue to develop.

We wish you congratulations during this life-changing and memorable chapter in your life. During this time of early parenthood, you too will develop new abilities—those of mother or father, protector, provider, and caregiver. Feeding is one of the most critical aspects of how you will care for your baby, and this book will provide you with the best guidance available in terms of when, how, why, and what to feed, as well as environmental and lifestyle information that can significantly impact your child's hormonal, nutritional, and overall health status.

New Concerns: The 3Cs

All parents want their children to have optimal health. But today we have more to fear in terms of pediatric health than parents did just two or three generations ago. In fact, back when your great-grandparents were giving birth to your grandparents, the general public had never heard of autism, celiac disease was incredibly rare, and peanuts were synonymous with baseball games and springtime, not *life-threatening* allergies. Cancer, type 2 diabetes, heart disease, arthritis, and obesity were diseases of the *aged*. Just a few generations ago, children, by and large, were healthy, strong, and robust. They were able to climb trees, ride bikes without helmets, and play sports without extensive concern for concussions, due to brittle, weak bones built on diets that do not support bone strength.

We see children's health getting worse with each subsequent generation, each with less robust and rather fragile children. Our children today are at grave risk, and parents' worries are many and valid. Tragically, the most recent generation of babies is slated to have *shorter* life spans than their parents. *This is unacceptable!*

Many of the conditions kids face today are new, so parents can no longer call upon the wisdom of mothers or grandmothers (who have no experience with "stimming" or EpiPens or nebulizers). Parents, perhaps even you, are turning to other parents in support groups and online communities and are becoming researchers, analysts, and metabolic "specialists" themselves in their quest to find help for their children.

As such, we recognize the following illnesses as being *Contemporary Chronic Childhood* conditions—the "3Cs":

- Autistic spectrum disorders
- Allergies, eczema
- Asthma
- Attention deficit disorders and learning disabilities
- Recurrent pain disorders (headaches, abdominal pain, joint pain)
- Emotional, mood, and behavioral disorders (anxiety disorders, depression, bipolar disorder)
- Digestive and gastrointestinal disorders (irritable and inflammatory bowel disorders, gastroesophageal reflux, eosinophilic esophagitis, and constipation)
- Autoimmune conditions (celiac disease, diabetes, thyroid disorders, arthritis)
- Overweight, obesity, metabolic syndrome, fatty liver, and type 2 diabetes
- Tooth decay and orthodontic conditions
- Cancer

Many of the 3C conditions are directly *caused* by our modern world, which is full of toxins and nutrient-poor foods (that are themselves a source of toxins). These toxins and deficiencies cripple many areas of the body, causing multiple symptoms and resulting in a veritable puzzle for modern medicine. Often, highly specialized conventional medical models fail to see the whole, for their strict focus on each of the parts. Looking at the *whole* child through a *holistic* perspective is often necessary to piece all the symptoms together when it comes to the 3Cs.

Though conventional medicine claims most of the 3C conditions are incurable, this isn't the last word. The good news is that most children with 3C conditions can improve. But more important, by following a program of Super Nutrition—the program you're holding in your hands—these problems can be *prevented and often cured.*

It boils down to this: Poor health comes from poor foods. Undernourished children are more vulnerable to infection, more susceptible to toxins and cancer, and more likely to develop learning, attention, and behavioral problems.

Because you're reading this book, we know that you want more for your child than what today's statistics promise. Instead of worrying about the bad and just hoping for good, you are taking control of your child's health destiny. Food is one of the most powerful tools you have to protect, preserve, and ensure your baby's health and well-being. In the coming chapters, we'll introduce the concept of Super Nutrition and explain how providing foods that are rich in critical nutrients, as well as reducing toxins, will enable your baby's body to function optimally. We'll focus on what you can proactively *do* to create a fundamental base of good health for your baby and significantly increase the odds of your baby living a long, happy, and *healthy* life.

A Better Way

When researchers and anthropologists study non-industrialized cultures from around the world and throughout history, they find that they are often free of heart disease, cancer, infertility, emotional and behavioral disturbances, birth defects, diabetes, autism, life-threatening allergies, dental anomalies, and other afflictions that are commonly accepted in our culture today. Even in just the last generation, we have seen a marked statistical increase in these conditions that experts believe is not attributable to better testing, awareness, or diagnosis. In fact, the 3Cs were so rare in pre-industrialized cultures that these relatively new conditions are often called *Diseases of Civilization*.

This is significant. Research corroborates that when we modernize and "industrialize" our foods (and our environment), Diseases of Civilization increase with each generation. This is very important when you consider what to feed your baby because food is the most significant "environmental" component in his life. Diet can make a significant positive impact on your baby's health and development—or it can be a major detriment to his health.

Though many attest that life was much shorter "back then," it is actually true that many primitive cultures, such as the Russian Georgians, Pakistani Hunza, and Ecuadorian Vilcabamba peoples, heralded healthy octo-, nono-, and even centenarians. It was once believed that cancer and diabetes developed only because "modern man" was living longer. We've since learned, however, that these are not just "adult-onset" diseases (that are inevitable with aging), but rather are diseases of industrialization—as now even our young suffer with them.

Many pre-industrialized cultures held certain indigenous foods sacred; science proves these to be particularly nutritious foods. We'll show you which foods these are and how to prepare them. Many of our grandparents and great-grandparents also recognized the power of food, feeding their families organ meats and spooning out cod liver oil. Somehow this knowledge has slowly faded away, while the convenience of processed foods has taken center stage.

Even as recently as when our parents were children, they had far fewer toxic exposures. They did not have genetically modified foods or high fructose corn syrup; they had fewer pesticides and far fewer antibiotics given to their food animals (and themselves); they were given significantly fewer vaccines, had no bromine in their bread, less radiation in their skies, fewer chemicals on their skin, no cell phones or laptops, and far more sun exposure, cleaner air, and daily exercise. Their diets were fresher, more local, purer, less processed, and substantially more nutritious.

Traditional wisdom, passed down through countless generations, directed parents to feed their babies the most nutrient-rich foods available, which included the meat, fat, and organs from poultry (including ducks and geese), red meat (including lamb and wild game), and fish and shellfish. Eggs, milk, raw dairy, bone broths, and even insects were also commonly found in pre-industrialized diets. These foods were accompanied by select *seasonal* fruits, veggies, nuts, seeds, and occasionally specially prepared grains and beans.

In the early decades of the twentieth century and before, babies were rarely fed industrialized "baby" food; they were fed based on your grandmother's grandmother's advice and wisdom, passed down by generation. These were decades in which deathly allergies, asthma, autism, attention problems, cancer, depression, diabetes, and even obesity were extremely rare in children.

DEEP DIVE INTO NUTRIGENOMICS AND EPIGENETICS

Individualized medicine is thought to be the way of the future for medical treatment, made possible by the understanding that genetics are not hard-coded, but are rather influenced significantly by our environment (what we ingest, absorb, or inhale, as well as our stress and physical activity levels). The chemicals we are exposed to, consume, or create (think stress chemicals) can turn *on* bad genes and can turn *off* good genes. Most experts now agree that at least 75% of our health destiny rests not with our genes, but with the environmental influence on our genes—known as epigenetics.

In addition to individualized medicine, there is a strong case for individualized nutrition and nutrient therapies. Personalized nutrition stands in stark contrast to the currently accepted practice of one-size-fits-all nutrition, as seen, for example, in the American RDA (recommended daily allowances for vitamins and minerals).

As stated in *Frontiers in Genetics* in 2011, nutrition plays a highly critical role in "promoting health, preventing or delaying the onset of disease, optimizing performance, and assessing benefits and risks." Further, as stated in 2011 in *Epigenomics*, "Importantly, emerging evidence strongly suggests that consumption of dietary agents can alter normal epigenetic states as well as reverse abnormal gene activation . . . Epigenetic modifications [can be] used therapeutically for medicinal . . . purposes."

Most recently, as reported in the *Journal of Nutritional Biochemistry* in 2018, there is a very potent role of mom's environment and nutrient intake for baby in utero, as well as in the first 2 years of feeding (collectively "the first 1,000 days") for early, lifelong, and multi-generational health. Beyond food, feeding, and critical nutrients (including folate from liver, as well as B12, choline, and iron from animal foods), epigenetic impacts are demonstrated by alcohol consumption and pesticide exposure, which can drastically rewire the epigenome, resulting in genetic changes, oxidative stress, cellular damage, reduced brain volume, impacts to dopamine processing, change in gut microbiome, and other risk factors for Alzheimer's disease and other 3Cs. It comes down to providing a nutrient-rich, toxic-reduced environment to ensure long-term health that will span generations for your family.

Often, we blame or credit genetics for healthy or unhealthy generations, as diseases often "run" in families. However, it is actually environmental influences on genes (epigenetics) traversing generations that explains why diseases are often in high concentration in certain families. In other words, as stated in the *Journal of Nutritional Biochemistry* in 2018, "It is now well recognized that the environmental effects experienced during the first 1,000 days of life, represented by the 9 months of pregnancy plus the first 2 years of life and as early as preconception, are transmissible to offspring and to subsequent generations." These multi-generational epigenetic impacts include "cardiovascular, . . . metabolic, and neurological diseases [which] may originate in utero and are associated with inheritance of epigenetic alterations to gene expression." In short, optimal nutrition, reduction of toxins, and low stress during pregnancy, infancy, and through toddlerhood are key not only to your child's immediate and long-term health, but also to the health of your grandchildren and their children.

It is time to feed our babies differently than our current standard. Instead of relying on the newfangled, overprocessed "Frankenfoods" of industrialization, we recommend going back to the more natural foods of pre-industrialized peoples that did a far better job of keeping the children of our ancestors healthy.

Cutting Edge but Traditionally Sound

Can food really protect your child? Hippocrates said, "Let food be thy medicine, and let thy medicine be food." Unfortunately, this ancient wisdom has been lost in the name of food companies' media storms, advertising blitzes, and continual tsunami of consumer data. Let's admit it: We've been relying on marketers to tell us what is healthy, to teach us how to feed our kids, and even to provide doctors with their "nutritional education" (which is lacking in conventional medical schools). But the truth is, those marketers and their advertisements aren't motivated to make healthy kids—they're driven to sell products and make profit.

To ensure the proper health of our children, we must resist being seduced by convenience-based processed foods. Too often parents focus on making sure their children get enough calories, rather than focusing on the nutrients their kids most need. And too often we say we're too busy for anything but fast food, or packaged food, or "junk" food. Yet, it is *whole* food that heals, *real* food that protects, and *traditional* food that nourishes.

We realize that what we present here is unconventional and . . . well, *different*. Yet a decade and a half of working with patients and finding considerable rates of success in improving health and quality of life for babies and young children—and ameliorating root-cause issues relating to the 3Cs—has incited us to spread the word. What we offer—*the fundamentals of Super Nutrition feeding for babies*—works differently than common baby feeding. It serves to safeguard health and normal development, as well as to restore quality of life in children with modern, chronic cognitive, emotional, and physical illnesses.

In addition to our own practical, personal, and professional application of Super Nutrition, we have extensively researched and studied the findings of world-renowned experts, who have also found remarkable success through such feeding principles. Though our approach to feeding babies is far from mainstream, it is both cutting edge and traditionally sound. Super Nutrition is a way of feeding your child that gives the best nutrition for optimal development, cognitively and physically, *and* is protective against illnesses and 3C conditions. Do this for your child and you'll be optimizing his/her health *now* and for years to come.

Implementing and practicing Super Nutrition is not easy—and we're saying this right from the get-go, just so there's no confusion. If you want easy and quick, stick with the Standard American Diet—its entire premise is convenience. If, however, you want optimal health for your baby, then you'll have to give up some conveniences. Our program is comprised of special foods and purposeful ways of preparing and making meals; therefore, special attention and time are required. We provide some tricks and guidance to make things easier, though, and the more you do it, the easier it will become.

And there's a bonus: Most of the parents we've worked with who start spending more time practicing Super Nutrition find a deep sense of satisfaction and fulfillment that they don't find anywhere else—it is one of knowing that they are truly nourishing their children, a gift no one else can give.

Although you might be excited to "get going" with Super Nutrition and flip to the age-appropriate chapter for your child, we hope you'll read this book in full. The chapters have been organized to follow the growth, age, and stages of development of your child, starting with nutritionally rich tips for the nursing mother (which are ideal for both preconception and pregnancy as well) and nutritious formula recipes and then stepping into his first food introduction, all coinciding with our program's foundational pillars of nutrition. Each age and stage described is accompanied by recipes that include foods appropriate for that age, but these recipes can be enjoyed from that point forward, and by the whole family, in many cases. We also describe food categories that will help you make nutritionally sound selections, and we'll discuss four fundamental pillars to leveraging protective nutrition.

Throughout each of the chapters, we've added tips, tricks, and ideas to help ease you into implementing our program—look for the boxes called "Mom to Mom." And we've provided additional information in the "Deep Dive" sections as we realize many parents appreciate and want the detailed science, research, and information behind our recommendations. Finally, we've included a thorough resources section that includes essential where-to-buy information on many of the ingredients we recommend, as well as countless books and websites to turn to for further information.

Super Nutrition for Babies will help you reap the benefits that traditional foods can provide. It will show you how to make better food choices for your baby and how to prepare those foods so that they can be most nourishing. Your baby deserves nothing but the *best*!

BABY FEEDING FUNDAMENTALS

Nutrition Is Necessary for Health

Other great healthy-baby feeding books will tell you to choose organic produce, alert you to choking hazards, urge you to make your own baby food, encourage breastfeeding, and provide you with some developmental expectations for your child. We'll tell you all of this too, but we're also going to provide you with much, much more.

Our recommendations are quite different from mainstream advice—this is because how we currently feed children isn't good enough. We'll tell you why and offer you much better options—what we call the Super Nutrition Baby Feeding Program.

These feeding guidelines will not just provide your baby with the ability to survive but will ensure she *thrives*. We recommend feeding your baby in a way that coincides with how her body works, considering her unique nutrient needs *as a growing baby*.

Our Super Nutrition program builds super-healthy babies. And today a healthy baby is not a certainty, as evidenced by the increasing numbers of children with chronic health issues. But diet and nutrition *can* make a tremendous difference.

A Tidal Wave of Disease

Chronic childhood illness has been on a steep rise over the last thirty to forty years. We call this scourge of *Contemporary Chronic Childhood* maladies "3C" conditions, and they include autism spectrum disorders; allergies, eczema, and asthma; attention deficit disorders and learning disabilities; emotional, mood, and behavioral disorders; recurrent pain disorders; metabolic

syndrome, obesity, and autoimmune diseases; digestive and gastrointestinal disorders; tooth decay; and cancer.

We consider the 3C conditions *contemporary* because they are relatively modern illnesses that were exceedingly rare in past generations and, in fact, nonexistent in pre-industrialized populations. They are *chronic* because they aren't an acute problem, like pneumonia, but instead chip away at health every day and are often considered incurable. They are designated as *childhood* conditions because they affect children or are increasing in prevalence in childhood. For instance, type 2, or non-insulin dependent diabetes (formerly known as adult-onset diabetes), metabolic syndrome, depression, dental problems, heart disease, and high rates of cancer are new to childhood, as previously they predominantly affected adults.

In fact, not only are the 3C conditions on the rise in children, but many, such as obesity, autism, and diabetes, are increasing quickly enough to be called epidemics. Current, common baby feeding practices have not safeguarded our children. Children born today face the following unfortunate statistical realities:

⊙ One in 2½ (40%) have allergies, compared to 30% of adults.

- One in 12 have food allergies; 1 in 6 of those have experienced anaphylaxis (life-threatening symptom of allergen exposure).

- One in 10 people in North America and Europe have one of 80 autoimmune conditions; that's nearly 25 million people, with a 2012 study by NIEHS (National Institute of Environmental Health Sciences) showing that more than 32 million have autoantibodies, the precursors to full-blown autoimmune disease.

- One in 8 have asthma.

- One in 3 have ADHD, allergies, asthma, or autism.

- Almost 1 in 10 show signs of depression.

- One in 59 were diagnosed with autistic spectrum disease (ASD) in 2014, per the CDC, up from 1 in 68 in 2012.

- One in 36 (2.76%) are, at some point in their lives, diagnosed as being on the autism spectrum.

- Developmental disability diagnosis went from 5.76% in 2014 to 6.99% in 2016, with an increase in diagnosis of "other developmental delays" from 3.75% in 2014 to 4.55% in 2016.

- One in 3 children in the United States are currently overweight or obese.

Assuming the diet and environment of children remain as they are now, the future for those born this century is bleak:

- Nearly 1 in 2 will become obese or overweight.

- One in 3 will eventually suffer with diabetes.

- By 2025, 50% of boys born in the United States will have some form of ASD.

What's worse is that these disease rates have been progressively increasing over the years. "If these trends continue," fears William Sears, M.D., pediatrician and author of more than forty books on children's health, "America's children face a future filled with sickness rather than health, of weakness rather than strength, of sadness rather than happiness."

Introducing Super Nutrition

With this book as your guide, we will empower you to put the odds in your favor for preventing your baby from developing such 3C conditions, despite the statistics. Our way to do that is with Super Nutrition. *Super Nutrition* is the term we've coined to describe a purposeful way of selecting, preparing, and combining foods; using specific supplements; and purposefully avoiding other foodstuffs in such a way as to be protective of health. Ideally, these choices will result in the *prevention* of chronic and degenerative disease in your child. This means that by feeding your baby following our Super Nutrition method, you can *protect* her from the very real, very scary, and very tragic 3C conditions.

How does the same feeding program protect against such a wide array of illnesses? It turns out there are significant commonalities in the underlying causes of many of the 3C conditions. So even though they seem different, the 3C conditions actually have two very important things in common: They are caused or made worse by nutrient deficiencies, and they are caused or made worse by toxic overload.

These contributing components are *environmental* factors of diet and lifestyle. Unfortunately, most people don't give much credit to the role environment plays in health. Perhaps you think that genetics or luck will determine the state of your baby's health. Previously, even experts hypothesized that health was equally determined by nurture (environment) and nature (genetics). But due to the findings of the Human Genome Project and the scientific field of epigenetics, we now know *there is a difference between our DNA* (with which we are born) *and what actually comes to be* (how the genes are expressed)— and that difference is often our *environment*.

Professor Jose M. Ordovas, Ph.D., director of the Nutrition and Genomics program at Tufts University and a recognized expert in the field of nutrigenomics, attests that *no more* than 25% of health is actually because of hard-coded genetics. This means *at least* 75% of health is up to environmental factors (and many experts think their influence is even greater!). Environment—because it influences genes—plays a far greater role in our health than does just "genetics." Restated another way: Your diet and lifestyle influence your health more than your genes.

This is great news! It means that *you* hold most of your baby's health in your hands because you have significant control over his environment. Even if he has "bad" genetics (or genetic susceptibility) that sets him up for autism, diabetes, obesity, learning disabilities, or emotional disorders, *it is most often* not *his genes, but rather his environment that will determine whether he actually ever develops any of these conditions.*

The impact of epigenetic changes, such as those caused by environmental changes on genes, can be passed down through generations. If a toxic exposure turns on genes that contribute to autism, those turned-on genes can be passed down to one's children. Additional contributing factors in subsequent generations, such as toxic exposure, stress, or poor nutritional status, might be enough to express these turned-on genes and thus explain the epidemic rise in autism. Unfortunately, unless these environmental

factors are corrected, the trend will continue and/or accelerate.

Dr. Philip Landrigan, pediatrician and researcher, reviewed biological, genetic, and environmental factors as contributing factors to autism in *Current Opinion in Pediatrics* (April 2010). A summary of his conclusions states, "Expanded research is needed into environmental causation of autism. Children today are surrounded by thousands of synthetic chemicals. Two hundred of them are neurotoxic in adult humans, and 1,000 more in laboratory models. Yet fewer than 20% of high-volume chemicals have been tested for neurodevelopmental toxicity."

We agree more research is necessary. However, research is not needed to know that reducing toxic exposure is important for reducing its epigenetic impact, and therefore 3C conditions.

We also know that nutrients combat toxins, either helping to clear them or reducing their ability to do harm. A diet that is nutrient rich, therefore, can directly protect your child from toxins in his environment. This is empowering information and is critical in the hands of concerned and caring parents. For more on how nutrients remove and deactivate toxins, see chapter 5.

IMPACT OF DIET AND LIFESTYLE ON HEALTH

For babies, diet is one of the most important environmental factors when it comes to influencing health. The foods selected, their source, their preparation, their timing of introduction, their quality, and their combination are all important in the protection of health ("good" gene expression) or the development of disease ("bad" gene expression). *Simply put: Good food keeps good genes turned* on *and keeps bad-disease genes turned* off.

Enemies and Allies in the War on Children's Health

Truth be told, we see modern food and conveniences as an attack, or veritable war, against children's health. In this war, we have identified "Allies" and "Enemies." Your Allies are the diet and lifestyle choices you make. They include not just what you choose to put into your baby's mouth but also what you include in her life to bolster her internal defenses, such as good bacteria, sunshine, clean water, fresh air, and loving embrace.

ANTI-INFLAMMATION. One of the fundamental problems seen in children with the 3Cs is underlying inflammation of various tissues and organs, most notably the brain. Calming this inflammation is a key factor in preventing disease. To tame the flames of inflammation, it is important to support intestinal health, minimize toxic overload, optimize nutrient balances, and bolster immune function—all of which are key to the Super Nutrition program.

PROPER DIGESTION AND DIGESTIVE AIDS. Children with the 3Cs often have digestive problems (including allergies). Therefore, it is critical to aim for complete protein digestion as well as adequate stomach acid to ensure proper nutrition is obtained from foods; it's also essential to prevent a variety of tummy troubles, from constipation to diarrhea.

HEALTHY GUT ECOSYSTEM AND INTESTINAL WALL. Proper nourishment will ensure that your baby's intestinal tissue is healthy and capable of protecting her from undigested proteins and pathogens that could otherwise gain access through a weak intestinal lining to the bloodstream and brain.

CLEAN WATER. Your baby's growing body is, in part, built based on the caliber of water you provide. Using filtered water, when your baby is ready, will help ensure that the water functions appropriately as a cleanser and source of alkalizing minerals, rather than a source of toxins.

VITAMINS AND MINERALS. Trace quantities of certain minerals enable the body to run complex biochemical processes. Vitamins and minerals are also called *coenzymes* and act as critical helpers in making most processes in the body function effectively and efficiently. In addition to ensuring the body "works" properly, nutrients are the building blocks for your baby's tissues, bones, and organs. Small nutrient deficiencies can cause *big* problems. Whole foods are your best source of nutrients.

DETOXIFICATION. Toxins are more likely to overwhelm a body that lacks nutrients; a well-nourished body fortunately can cope far better. By providing nutritious foods, you will support your baby's ability to detoxify and thus minimize the effects of these toxins.

HEALING ("SUPER POWER") FOODS. Certain foods provide optimal nutrition to support immunity, detoxification, and the formation and function of organs and of many systems in the body. These foods have been shown to protect and preserve pristine health. When abandoned in the diet, their absence has been associated with an increase in chronic disease, deformity, and degeneration. When replaced, these foods have the power to actually restore health. Thus, we have categorized these protective, nutrient-rich, healing foods as Super POWER foods.

REAL FOODS. Real foods—as we define them—are those that are as Nature designed them. They do not have refined elements or unnatural ingredients, such as additives, preservatives, colorings, flavorings, or texturizers. Real foods come from animals who naturally graze on pastures, enjoying fresh air and sunlight, and who are never given pharmaceutical drugs or synthetic hormones. They are grown in organic soil, free of pesticides, chemicals, and nitrates, where nutrients are replenished through natural sources such as manure and crop rotation rather than chemical fertilizer. While real foods are much more than just "organic," organic is a great place to start. Real foods are pure, are worthy of your baby's body, and support health, strength, character, and intelligence.

SUPPLEMENTS. Supplements are ideally just that: "supplemental" to a nourishing diet. Food provides nutrients in their most absorbable form, acting synergistically to provide the best support for the body. However, supplements are often beneficial to fill a nutrient void or to support a metabolic blockage.

ANTIOXIDANTS. Antioxidants are nutrients that protect your cells against free radicals, which cause damage to the body, resulting in inflammation and other problems. Antioxidants reduce the damage of today's free-radical onslaught from processed foods (predominantly from plant and seed oils) and our toxic environment.

PROBIOTICS. *Probiotics* is another term for beneficial bacteria, which serve untold health functions in the body. Maintaining healthy gut flora will protect against a damaged or "leaky" gut, thus minimizing the risk of allergies, mood alterations, nutrient deficiencies, digestive distress, and illness from infection.

STRONG IMMUNE SYSTEM. The immune system has several levels of protection that it invokes to maintain health, as well as prevent illness. Our baby-feeding regimen provides the best possible support for your baby's immune system troops. According to the National Institutes of Health, endorphins are being studied for their amazing immune-strengthening abilities, including "antibody synthesis, lymphocyte proliferation, and natural killer cytotoxicity." *Note:* Holding your baby releases endorphins, both comforting and immune boosting.

SUNSHINE, FRESH AIR, AND PHYSICAL ACTIVITY. It is a different world for the youth of today than even when we were children. By encouraging sun exposure, movement, and fresh air, you will improve immune function, detoxification, and your child's overall health.

The Enemies That Attack Your Child's Health

Supplying her body with Allies will help your baby be stronger, but there are Enemies lurking about that can overwhelm them rather effectively. What makes Enemies particularly powerful is that they are insidious—part of common diet and lifestyle for kids—and they're increasingly prevalent. It's impossible to avoid all Enemies, but becoming aware of them and reducing exposure to them will minimize their impact on your baby.

TOXINS. Toxins include pesticides, pollution, heavy metals, medications (including vaccines), industrial waste, chemicals (found in common items from cleaning and hygiene products to foods to tap water), dyes, artificial ingredients, preservatives, and even animal foods (such as arsenic and fluoride in poultry from chicken feed, mercury in meat from cattle's grain-based feed, and glyphosate in wheat and oats). Toxins accumulate in the body and disrupt normal metabolic activity, leading to multiple issues. Many children suffer from a reduced ability to eliminate toxic elements entering the body—due to digestive problems or insufficient nutrients to help enzymes do the job. Toxins then accumulate, crippling various organs and systems. At high enough doses, many of them are lethal, but even at lower doses, toxins cause trouble with normal function and development.

SUGAR AND REFINED GRAINS. Sugar and refined grains make up a (conservative) 50% of caloric intake! Both sugar and refined grains wreak havoc with health in myriad ways. We'll discuss sugar's detriments in chapter 7.

ANTIBIOTICS, VACCINES, AND OTHER DRUGS. The overuse of certain medicines— such as antibiotics and steroids, both in our children and in the animal foods they consume— can lead to imbalances in the endocrine system, the immune system, and in gut bacteria, all of which negatively affect the whole body. Keeping immunity strong will create less need for such drugs. Choosing higher-quality animal foods will also reduce exposure to such toxic drugs. Vaccines are injected into our systems with dangerous adjuvants that can cause systemic, and particularly brain, inflammation and a cascade of autoimmunity linked to many 3Cs, including autism.

PROCESSED FOODS. Processed foods are devitalized and fake, containing multiple harmful and damaging man-made ingredients, including growth hormones, excitotoxins, dyes, rancid fats, and genetically engineered components. These kinds of foods deplete the body of precious nutrient stores and give nothing back but calories and toxins. They are also difficult to digest, and can lead to gut problems, food allergies, and autoimmune conditions.

WRONG MACRONUTRIENT RATIOS AT MEALS. When babies and children are fed typical "kid-food" diets, often they become reliant on refined, processed carbohydrates and don't get adequate healthy fats and protein. The Standard American Diet (SAD) is at least two-thirds carbohydrate based. Even the new 2015–2020 USDA MyPlate portions are three-quarters fruits, veggies, and grains—all of which are carbohydrates. SADly, though, almost all of modern carbohydrate intake is sugar and refined grain, with very little nutrition to offer. Nutrient density of food is more important than is macronutrient ratio (the proportion of fat, protein, and carbohydrates), so long as sugar and refined flour are omitted and proteins and fats are from pastured sources. The false sense that sufficient calories alone will enable proper growth and development has excused the poor-quality food used to feed children for too long.

Super Nutrition Builds Super Health for Your Baby

With our Super Nutrition Baby Feeding Program, you will gain the skills to strengthen and protect your baby, maximizing both her mental and her physical health potential, and reduce her chances of developing 3C conditions. What you feed your baby now will impact both her immediate and her lifelong health.

In the foreword of the book *Healing Our Children*, Sally Fallon Morell, author, researcher, traditional-foods advocate, and founder and president of the Weston A. Price Foundation, compares fortifying your child's body to building a house. Well-built houses can withstand a storm of onslaughts, whereas weakly constructed houses built on subpar materials will crumble under little to moderate distress. "Most children growing up today live in the latter type of [weak] house.

Throughout life, in order to be healthy, such individuals will need to pay very careful attention to their diets at all times. Their houses will likely be constantly springing leaks—allergies, digestive problems, fatigue, behavior abnormalities, etc."

Super Nutrition ensures that you'll build the strongest "house" (body and mind) possible for your baby, optimizing the support of children's health Allies while minimizing exposure to Enemies.

The Pillars of Super Nutrition

We've built our Super Nutrition Baby Feeding Program on the foundation of protective nutrition. On this foundation stand four pillars, which are scientifically and clinically sound. We have incorporated medical research, experts' findings, scientific evidence, and our own clinical experience to focus on those factors that most influence children's health when it comes to 3C conditions. To prevent the 3Cs from taking hold, you must carefully select and prepare your baby's foods to be the most *digestible, pure, immune bolstering*, and *nutrient rich*.

PILLAR #1: DIGESTIBILITY. FACILITATE DIGESTION AND SUPPORT INTESTINAL HEALTH.

You can make digestion easier for your baby if you provide her with the right foods. Acknowledging that an infant's digestive system is different than that of an older child or adult is important in determining when you can introduce certain foods. How you prepare the food also makes a significant difference in digestibility. We will guide you in choosing and making easy-to-digest foods for your baby at each stage.

Natasha Campbell-McBride, M.D., focuses on the neurologic- and psychiatric-based 3Cs (autism, depression, ADD, etc.) in her book *Gut and Psychology Syndrome (GAPS)*. Dr. Campbell-McBride, a neurologist, nutrition expert, and autism specialist, suggests that because the digestive system impacts immunity, availability of nutrients, protection from toxins, and detoxification of toxins, it directly affects the health and functioning of the brain.

But there's more to it, as Dr. Campbell-McBride writes, "The gut-brain connection is something . . . many modern doctors do not understand." There's actually a "second brain" in the gut; though it doesn't "think" conscious thoughts, it *does* affect behavior. It is not only the master of digestion, but the gut also conveys massive quantities of information to the brain. In addition to impacting nutritional status and immunity, intestinal health also influences mood, behavior, mental health, and emotion.

Digestible foods are those that:

- Have had their digestive irritants neutralized (soaked, sprouted, or leavened)
- Are predigested (fermented or cultured)
- Contain enzymes (as in raw animal foods, tropical fruits, and fermented or cultured foods)

PILLAR #2: PURITY AND FRESHNESS. REDUCE TOXIC EXPOSURE AND IMPROVE DETOXIFICATION CAPABILITIES.

Our program will suggest foods that are least processed and least toxic. Avoiding even a few ingredients will go a long way in reducing the toxic burden your child carries. *Purity and freshness* are criteria we hope you'll begin to apply to feeding choices for your baby.

In light of the toxic reality babies face today (see chapter 5), detoxification is crucial. Luckily, your baby has built-in systems for detoxification—based on natural mechanisms that are designed to protect her. Unfortunately, this detoxification ability is often decreased due to nutrient deficiencies and toxins that can further block detoxification pathways. Consequently, optimizing nutrition and reducing toxin exposure are critical to detoxification and thus, good health and optimal development.

Ideally, pure foods meet the following criteria:

- No additives, synthetic nutrient "fortification," preservatives, or other chemicals

- No artificial sweeteners, colorings, or flavorings

- Organic—sustainably grown in nutrient-rich soils, without the use of chemical pesticides

- From animals that have eaten their natural diet and have lived a natural life (pasture fed and raised)

- No growth hormone, antibiotics, or other drugs given to farm animals

- In whole form—not refined, isolated, or concentrated

- Minimally processed with a short "shelf life"

- Not genetically modified

- Fresh, vine-ripened, recently and locally harvested

- Consumption occurs quickly after harvesting, picking, or gathering

- No chemical or high-heat treatments (pesticides, pasturization)

PILLAR #3: IMMUNE BOOSTING. STRENGTHEN AND SUPPORT NATURAL IMMUNITY.

You can foster a stronger immune system through nutrient-rich feeding, proper digestion, and purposeful microbial exposure (more in chapter 6). In particular, healthy bacterial exposure and colonization is critical to a healthy body and strong immune system.

Getting or being sick with viral or bacterial infections, while ultimately immune strengthening, still can cause more than just the uncomfortable symptoms. Infections—when they take root—excessively burden the body, cause inflammation, and use up priceless nutrients and enzymes, as the body works to regain a healthy balance. The proper functioning of your baby's immune system is important to the big picture of health because *staying healthy is easier on the body than getting health back* once infection sets in.

Surprisingly, the best way to prevent infection isn't to avoid microbes. It is actually to fortify the immune system from within. The vast majority of microbes are *good*—and those few that *could* make us sick don't always do so when we're exposed to them; it's the state of our body's health and immune capabilities that determine whether we will actually get sick.

Immune-boosting foods are those that:

- Support the immune system with critical nutrients

- Supply living immune cells (as in mom's milk and raw mammalian milk)

- Provide probiotics

- Supply enzymes

PILLAR #4: NUTRIENT RICH. PROVIDE OPTIMALLY NOURISHING FOODS.

Our program will educate you about what makes a food truly nourishing (see chapter 6). Part of this pillar also includes avoiding foods that rob your baby of nutrients or contain nutrient blockers (see chapter 5). *Nutrient worth* is an important way to judge foods—they should be "worthy" of supporting your baby's growth and development.

Focusing on nutrient-rich foods is worthwhile because they have been shown via extensive research to build healthy, robust babies. Revolutionary nutrition researcher and dentist Weston A. Price, D.D.S., studied health among cultures across the six inhabited continents of the globe during the 1920s and 1930s. He used saliva, food samples, observation, medical and dental examinations, interviews, skeletal remains, and photographic evidence to do his research. He reported his findings in his book *Nutrition and Physical Degeneration*, which has remained a seminal work on nutrition and health.

Dr. Price conducted his studies at a unique time in history, when many primitive stocks of people had yet to be touched by modern industry. He specifically chose peoples who were living and eating off their land as they had for thousands of years. At this time, he was also witness to the building of roads, the coming of boats, and the arrival of missionaries who brought "industrialized" foods such as jellies, jams, canned meats, and white flour. In his studies that spanned two decades, he saw that the generation eating "modern" foods got sick far more than the same genetic stock not eating modern foods and also gave birth to unhealthy babies! He later documented that a return to the traditional-foods diet would restore their health.

Dr. Price found that lack of proper nutrition was *causal* in physical degeneration and most chronic diseases. He concluded that optimal nutrition was key to both physical *re*generation and the prevention of degenerative disease.

Foods with high nutrient worth are those that:

- Are nutrient dense, containing rich amounts of nutrients per calorie

- Do not contain antinutrients (chemicals that block mineral absorption)

- Do not contain sugars or refined salt that strip the body of pre-existing nutritional stores

These four pillars of Super Nutrition guide each and every recommendation in this book. By focusing on them, you can expect your baby to have the best overall health on many levels—including but not limited to strong immune system functioning, emotional control, focus, dental health and orthodontic positioning, metabolic functioning, and countless other facets of well-being. With Super Nutrition, you will be helping your baby become the smartest, happiest, and healthiest he can possibly be.

In our recommendations, you may question foods such as organ meats, including liver or raw (fresh, unpasteurized) milk. We include such foods and, in fact, make all of our recommendations to use them because of their impressive ability to nourish, protect, and grow optimally healthy children. For more, see Deep Dive into Raw Dairy on page 24.

DEEP DIVE INTO RAW DAIRY:
GOT RAW? WHEN IT COMES TO MILK, FRESH IS BEST!

Raw milk is not pasteurized. Fresh, intact, and unadulterated, it is a healing food meant to sustain life and nourish those who consume it. Fresh milk confers nutritional, neurological, digestive, and immune benefits. Fresh, raw dairy from cows is remarkably similar to fresh, raw milk from humans. Pasteurized milk is a processed food, whereas raw milk is simply "milk" as Nature intended.

Raw, fresh milk from a trusted, clean dairy comes from cows, goats, sheep, or camels that graze on green pastures in sunlight and fresh air. Raw, fresh milk cows are also *not* given drugs, growth hormone, or antibiotics, so raw milk does not contain these toxins. Furthermore, raw milk's transit time from cow to consumer is very short, making the milk very fresh when consumed.

Milk in this pure state upholds all four pillars of Super Nutrition. Organic, grass-fed, raw milk is worth getting from the farm for four main reasons:

1. With a complete suite of enzymes, fresh milk aids digestion and even digests itself.

2. Pure raw milk is absent of toxins such as drugs, vaccinations, synthetic nutrients, and pesticides.

3. Raw milk is an immune booster and protector against pathogens.

4. Raw milk is a healing, Super POWER food rich in vitamins and very rich in absorbable minerals and probiotics.

So, why do we pasteurize? Pasteurization is processing of milk with high heat to kill pathogens that might have contaminated the milk. These bacteria don't naturally occur in the milk, but rather can contaminate it during collection, processing, and storage. Back in the early 1900s, when cleanliness wasn't a priority, city-milk cows (not on pasture) were kept in filth and fed poorly, and milk containers were reused and not washed. These sick cows and deplorable conditions led to rampant contamination of milk, which made many people sick. Pasteurization was developed to sterilize *this* kind of milk.

Today's conventional dairies of aren't much better. Cows are fed unnatural diets and kept in dirty, cramped conditions, which makes pasteurization necessary. Unfortunately, pasteurization doesn't ensure safe milk. *Pasteurized milk can easily be contaminated after sterilization, just like your hands can get dirty after you've washed them.*

Raw-milk farms, on the other hand, resemble the ideal farm from days of old. Grazing cows have healthier guts and healthy bacteria growing within. Before milking, the cows' teats are cleaned with iodine to kill potential bacteria, and the milk is collected into a sterile container and immediately refrigerated. Typically, from milking to consumers' refrigerator takes only 24 to 48 hours. With such minimal storage, no processing, and limited transportation, there is very little chance for raw milk to be exposed to contaminants. But even if it were somehow contaminated, raw milk keeps itself healthy. Its living immune factors and enzyme-based pathogen killers can stop the bad bugs just like mom's milk does. It's these amazing and unique living components in milk—hormones, enzymes, heat-sensitive nutrients, and probiotics—that are damaged, denatured, or rendered inactive after pasteurization and homogenization. This processing renders a super health food into one that is tragically allergenic and irritating to the immune system.

Raw milk is protective to the immune system. Reuters stated that according to a large study, "Children who drink raw milk are less likely to develop asthma and allergies than those who stick to the . . . pasteurized version." In fact, raw-milk drinkers had a 41% reduction in their risk of developing asthma and a 50% reduction in their risk of hay fever as compared to store-bought or boiled-milk drinkers. This corroborates earlier studies showing that "farm milk" is protective against such 3C conditions and their symptoms, as published in journals such as *Lancet*, *Experimental Allergy*, *European Respiratory Journal*, and *Nature Reviews Immunology*. Whether due to the unadulterated whey proteins in raw milk or its immune-boosting components, helpful hormones, enzymes, or wholesome suite of vitamins and absorbable minerals—we aren't quite sure. What is important is that raw-milk consumption can reduce the epidemic of asthma and allergies in our children!

Quite clearly—and scientifically shown—raw milk (*not pasteurized*) has potent protective benefits for children against 3C conditions! Raw milk from a clean, trusted dairy is not only safe, it is one of the *best* elements in your child's diet (or yours if you're a nursing mom). According to the Weston A. Price Foundation, consumption of raw milk is increasing by 25% every year, due to its health benefits, safety, and deliciousness. Visit www.realmilk.com to find fresh-milk dairies near you. In some states, raw milk is available for purchase in grocery stores. In many, though, you're required to join a "cow-share" program directly with the farm. Basically, this means you pay for the care and feeding of your cow, and you're entitled to the dairy products of that cow.

A FURTHER Q&A ON RAW MILK

Q: Isn't there bacteria in raw, unpasteurized milk?
A: Mammals' milk is designed to nourish infants who have immature immune systems, and is not dangerous or inherently contain pathogenic bacteria. It can become contaminated with bacteria if cleanliness measures are not taken or if the cows providing the milk are not healthy. Thus it is critical to obtain raw milk from the highest-quality farm with the healthiest of animals.

Q: Isn't pasteurized milk safer to buy than raw milk?
A: Raw milk is a surprisingly safe food compared not only to pasteurized milk, but also to all foods. After statistical analysis relating to the four most common pathogens and food-borne illness they cause, Ted Beals, M.S, M.D., reports that less than 42 cases of the annual 1,937,561 cases of food-borne illnesses are attributable to raw-milk consumption. That means that 1,937,519 cases are caused by foods *other* than raw milk. Relatively speaking, you're very safe drinking raw milk! *Pasteurization offers a false sense of security.* Pasteurized milk can and does get contaminated and can and does cause food-borne illness. According to William Campbell Douglass II, M.D., author of *The Raw Truth about Milk*, "Over the past few decades, outbreaks due to pasteurized milk have led to well over 200,000 cases of food poisoning and over 600 deaths." *Pasteurization does absolutely nothing to protect the milk from becoming contaminated after it is pasteurized.* At one of the largest raw-milk farms in California, a 10-year study showed *no cases* of their raw milk causing illness.

Q: Why not go "dairy free"?
A: Don't throw the baby out with the bathwater. First, we advocate long-term nursing. Babies and young children benefit from consuming their mom's milk—the best raw milk there is! Real milk is the richest source of minerals and several other nutrients available to us in our modern, nutrient-depleted diet. With its immune-supporting factors, enzymes, vitamins, and probiotics, it might well be the healthiest element of your (or your child's) diet. Raw milk is the easiest way to get amazing nutrition into your child. If you do nothing else except provide raw dairy, you'll be doing a great favor to your children.

Q: What if raw milk were to get contaminated? Wouldn't it make me sick?
A: As with any food—from peanut butter to spinach—contamination with bacteria can make people sick. However, studies show that raw milk can be exposed to *Salmonella, Listeria, and E. coli* and due to its enzymes and living immune cells, can completely destroy or stop the pathogens from growing! The same bugs dropped in pasteurized milk, which is devoid of immune protectors, would have nothing to stop them from proliferating and completely contaminating the milk. Government figures show that people are 35,000 times more like to contract food-borne illness from other foods than they are from raw milk. For more information visit: http://westonaprice.org/press/government-data-proves-raw-milk-safe.

Super Nutrition Food Categories

These Super Nutrition food categories illustrate which foods are most important to avoid and which are most critical in your baby's diet. We've grouped them in accordance with the four pillars and categorized them as CRAP, OKAY, PURE, or Super POWER foods. We'll refer to these categories throughout the remaining chapters as a helpful tool for you in meal planning, purchasing, and preparation. The handy acronyms will help you understand why each of the foods belongs in its category. Eventually you'll come to recognize whether a certain food incorporates elements of Super Nutrition.

CRAP FOODS

Stated purposefully in such a vulgar way, CRAP foods contribute to the toxic burden your baby must carry. They do not provide proper nutrition and detract from the nutrients your baby needs for growth, development, detoxification, and immunity. Refer to the acronym CRAP to help you remember why you want to eliminate, or at least minimize, these foods in your baby's diet.

CRAP

Chemical
Removes body's nutrients
Addictive
Processed

Foods that are in the CRAP category do not meet any of the criteria within the pillars of Super Nutrition: They are not digestible, they are not pure or fresh, they are not immune boosting, and they are not nutrient worthy. Most processed foods fall into this category.

Counter to being protective, CRAP foods are most often harmful. When you feed them to your child, not only are you *not* supporting proper health, growth, or development—you are likely hindering these processes, adding to your baby's toxic burden and reducing nutrient abilities. We realize that all children will have some CRAP foods, but we also want to be sure you understand how important it is to reduce them as much as possible. CRAP foods include the following:

- Fast food and prepackaged meals (especially microwavable)
- Foods made with white flour (crackers, pretzels, bagels, and bread)
- Most food served through school lunch programs
- Margarine/any kind of oil-based spreads
- Vegetable, plant, and seed oils refined and high in polyunsaturated fats (cottonseed, corn, soy, and canola)
- All boxed breakfast cereal
- Candy and other white-sugar-containing foods
- Cookies, snack bars, cereal bars, and protein bars
- Nonorganic lunch meat
- Soda pop or any sweetened carbonated beverages and store-bought juice
- Most soy products, including soy formula
- Nonorganic, low-fat, rBGH-containing, pasteurized dairy
- Organic ultrapasteurized dairy
- Genetically modified organisms/foods (GMOs) (soy, corn, canola, beet sugar, high fructose corn syrup, and cottonseed)
- Refined white salt, refined sugar, and other sweeteners

OKAY FOODS

Although these foods aren't the very best available, they are often part of the Standard American Diet. They are convenient, easy to come by, inexpensive, and found in most grocery stores. Truthfully, it is hard to have a diet that doesn't include OKAY foods. A diet of only OKAY foods won't be adequate to provide Super Nutrition, but they can be okay as *part* of a healthier diet. If your baby's diet is made up of some OKAY foods, some PURE foods, and some Super POWER foods, you will be doing very well by her.

OKAY

Ordinary
Knockoffs of real food
Adequate, not optimal
Yield subpar health if fed exclusively

OKAY foods include the following:

- Whole grains (unsoaked, unleavened, unfermented, or unsprouted)
- Nuts and seeds (unsoaked, unleavened, unfermented, or unsprouted), including hemp, chia, and pumpkin seeds
- Dried fruits (sugar and sulfite free)
- Grocery-store eggs
- All-natural and organic grain-fed meat
- Farmed fish
- Pasteurized (not ultrapasteurized), organic, full-fat dairy products
- Fresh-squeezed juice
- Nonorganic vegetables and fruit
- Low-polyunsaturated oils (high-oleic safflower oil and olive oil)
- Nut butters

- Non-cold-pressed, nonorganic, non-virgin, refined plant and seed oils, such as olive oil, walnut oil, avocado oil, and coconut oil
- Organic, nitrite-free lunch meat
- Legumes (including edamame, peanut butter, hummus, and beans)
- Fermented non-GMO soy (miso, natto, tempeh)
- Whole-foods sweeteners (raw honey, rapadura, maple syrup)

PURE FOODS

These foods are clean, digestible, and offer improved nutrient richness. They are important to incorporate into your child's diet as much as possible, as they support the serious nutrient needs of the body, aiding in cognitive, neurological, immune, and physical development.

PURE

Pasture based
Unadulterated
Rich in nutrients
Enzyme containing

In a perfect world, the ideal diet for your child would consist of only PURE and Super POWER foods. Yet more realistically, if we consume some OKAY foods but we are sure to also include Super POWER foods and rely mostly on PURE foods for our baby's nutrition, we'll improve the 3C disease statistics that come with average baby feeding. PURE foods include organic versions of the following:

- Soaked or sprouted whole grains and legumes
- Soaked or sprouted nuts and seeds (and nut butters of such preparation)
- Organic, local, seasonal, fruits and vegetables

- Organic tropical fruits
- Eggs from free-range chickens eating an omega-3-enriched diet
- Pastured/grass-fed meats, poultry, and pork
- Wild-caught fish and seafood
- Sea vegetables (kelp, nori)
- Unrefined, animal fats such as duck fat, lard, tallow, and ghee
- Unrefined, cold-pressed oils (olive oil, avocado oil) and tropical fats (coconut and palm)
- Low-temperature (VAT) pasteurized, organic, grass-fed, non-homogenized dairy products
- Unpasteurized, commercial fermented condiments and beverages (for example: trace-alcohol-containing kombucha [fermented tea], Bubbies brand pickles and sauerkraut, kimchi, Gut Shot brand sauerkraut and pickle juice, raw apple cider vinegar)

SUPER POWER FOODS

These foods are digestible, pure, fresh, immune boosting, and nutrient rich—and as a result, they can protect and even regenerate and restore health. They are absolutely the "superheroes" of the diet, found by researchers, nutritionists, historians, and anthropologists to be traditionally honored as "sacred" foods.

POWER
Protective
Optimal nutrition
Wisdom of the ancients
Enriching
Regenerating

Super POWER foods have qualities most other foods don't:

- Complete, whole, real, natural foods
- Nutrient dense and uniquely able to heal
- Part of traditional wisdom and used by ancient cultures for healing
- Free of toxins
- Packed with a wide array of antioxidants, vitamins, and minerals
- Supply inflammation fighters
- Often a source of the all-important, fat-soluble mineral activators
- Many also contain probiotics and enzymes

What can Super POWER foods do that other foods can't? They are heavy-hitting, healing foods. They are the "strongest" against pre-existing problems and act as preventive measures in the diet. Due to their super nutrition, they are the best to support the body, build the brain, bolster gut integrity, heal tooth decay, grow optimally healthy babies during pregnancy and after, and fortify mom's milk. Few foods have this kind of résumé.

We give much credit to researchers and nutrition pioneers who've studied pre-industrialized peoples to understand their natural and traditional eating habits. It is from such research, like that of Dr. Price and Dr. Pottenger (whose studies demonstrated that fresh foods, likely due to enzyme content, are potent health protectors), that we've learned what should be held sacred in our diets. Science has corroborated that these sacred foods are the most nutrient dense available and therefore confer the most health benefits.

Dr. Price's research particularly highlights the importance of fat-soluble activators, which allow minerals to be used in the body. Fat-soluble activators are the mortar, and minerals are the bricks, of the healthy house you're building for your baby; they need each other to work effectively. Many of our Super POWER foods are classified as such because they contain these mineral-activating vitamins (A, D3, and K2). Minerals are critical to health, and as Dr. Price warned, "It is possible to *starve for minerals* that are abundant in the foods eaten *because they cannot be utilized without an adequate quantity of the fat-soluble activators.*" Super POWER foods include the following:

- Mom's milk
- Liver and other offal (organ meats) from pastured, organically raised animals
- Cod liver oil
- High-vitamin butter oil, grass-fed and/or organic butter, and ghee
- Raw, grass-fed, organic dairy and cultured dairy products, including yogurt, kefir, cheese, and milk
- Pasture-raised animal fats
- Bone marrow
- Mineral-rich, bone-based soup stock
- Eggs from organic, pasture-raised poultry
- Oily, whole seafood (e.g., sardines) and shellfish from clean sources
- Fish roe
- Probiotic-rich and unpasturized condiments (chutney, salsa, sauerkraut, natto, kimchi)
- Lacto-fermented and homemade, fermented foods and beverages (yogurt, ginger ale, kombucha, kefir)
- Unrefined salt, such as Celtic sea salt and Himalayan sea salt

At first you might think your child won't like these foods. Yet parents whom we've seen in our practice are often surprised to find that their babies *love* them.

Putting It All Together

Some of the foods we recommend may seem strange to modern tastes and habits. But they are the most nutrient-dense foods on Earth; for almost all of human history, they've been the source of nourishment for adults and children alike and they improve your child's health outlook in an era of ever-increasing health risks for children.

Though you might be motivated to provide a 100% Super POWER diet, realistically we expect that your child will be fed a diet made up of a mixture of CRAP, OKAY, PURE, and some Super POWER foods. But even simply recognizing and reducing CRAP foods, increasing PURE foods, and offering some Super POWER foods when you can will significantly contribute to your child's health.

DEEP DIVE INTO TERRAIN VS. GERM THEORY

Getting or being sick with viral or bacterial infections can cause more than just uncomfortable symptoms. Infections, when they take root, excessively burden the body, cause inflammation, and use up priceless nutrients and enzymes, as the body has to work to regain a healthy balance. The proper functioning of children's immune system is very important to the big picture of health, because staying healthy is easier on the body than getting health back to baseline once infection sets in.

Dr. Amy Yasko, Ph.D., N.D., N.H.D., A.M.D., H.H.P., F.A.A.I.M., and Dr. Gary Gordon, M.D., D.O., M.D.(H), have had remarkable success in treating various 3C conditions, particularly the most challenging and severe cases of autism. In their book *The Puzzle of Autism: Putting It All Together*, they tell us that part of the problem with our sick kids today is that they are battling multiple chronic viral and bacterial infections, because their immune systems are battered and weak.

Surprisingly, the best way to prevent infection isn't to avoid microbes. It is actually to fortify the immune system from within. The father of modern-day germ theory, Louis Pasteur (1822–1895), taught that we become ill from the simple exposure to bacteria—because the bacteria itself makes us sick. That's why his "pasteurization" model is based on killing all microbes—to keep us from ever being exposed. Others, such as Robert Koch and Joseph Lister, were also early germ theorists. However, this science from almost 200 years ago is sadly outdated.

We now know that we can be exposed—and are exposed—to countless bacteria (and viruses) every day without getting sick. In Pasteur's limited understanding, he thought all bacteria were bad, and that they were static when they are, in fact, pleomorphic: able to adapt to their environment or terrain, as demonstrated clearly by antibiotic-resistant bugs. However, we've learned that the vast majority of microbes are good and those few that could make us sick don't always do so when we're exposed to them. In Pasteur's time, as stated in *Current Opinion in Pulmonary Medicine* in 2011, Claude Bernard (1813–1878) openly spoke out against germ theory, saying that the "internal milieu," or terrain, was the key determinant in infection. At the end of his career and life's work, Pasteur stated, "Claude Bernard is right, the microbe is nothing, the terrain is everything."

So, it isn't the bacterium itself, but rather whether or not the microbe can take root, grow, reproduce, and proliferate in our body ("terrain") that is making us sick. If bad bacteria *is* able to take hold, it, in large part, is because our immune system is weakened. Our terrain—or the state of our body's health and immune capabilities (including blood pH, nutritional status, microbiome health, and toxic burden)—is the key to determining if we will actually get sick or not. This is called the Germ-Terrain duality theory, which states, according to the *JOJ Nurse Healthcare* in 2017, "The etiology of certain diseases/diseased states is better explained as a complex interplay between germs and the inherent anatomical/physiological integrity of the body cell."

Your Baby's Health Is in Your Hands

Literally, as it's in this book! We agree with the January 2018 American Academy of Pediatrics (AAP) publication stating that nutrition, particularly in the first 1,000 days, is critical to proper optimal brain development. Indeed, the first 2 years of feeding your baby are substantial in setting his or her health trajectory. The AAP states, "Child and adult health risks, including obesity, hypertension, and diabetes, may be programmed by nutritional status during this period."

They go on to state that particular nutrients, specifically protein, zinc, iron, folate, iodine, retinol (vitamin A), and vitamins D, B6, and B12, along with long-chain polyunsaturated fatty acids (for example, DHA), are vital for neurodevelopment. "Lifelong deficits in brain function," they state, are a consequence of failing to provide such key nutrients, even if such nutrients become plentiful after 2 years of age.

The AAP goes on to clarify, "Although neurodevelopment continues throughout the life of a healthy person, by age 2 years the brain has undergone tremendous restructuring. Many of the developmental changes expected to occur during this period will not be able to occur in later life."

Relative to these recommendations, our program ensures all critical nutrients required (for not only avoiding lifelong neurological and neurobehavioral problems but also for optimal development) are sufficient, digestible, and bioavailable.

Even if you follow just some of our recommendations, you will improve your child's odds for achieving and maintaining optimal wellness. We realize our suggestions are often off the beaten path and take significantly more effort than just opening a jar or reheating in the microwave. We know what we're asking of you is significant—in terms of time and effort; we know this firsthand because we've been there as mothers as well as practitioners and have guided countless patients through this process.

Put Super Nutrition in place by following our guidelines and recommendations. You will create the strongest foundation for your baby, maximizing her current and long-term health. We know that as a parent, you wouldn't want it any other way.

In the following chapters, we'll walk you through the ages and stages you'll cherish as your baby grows. Along the way, we'll guide you and educate you about development, nutritional needs, and the best way to nourish your baby, supplying "Allied" reinforcements to keep her safe from "Enemies" in her diet and environment. We are so happy that this book has reached you—so that you can follow these guidelines toward optimal health for your darling baby.

MOM'S DIET DOES MATTER

Critical Feeding Information for Pregnant and Nursing Mothers and Babies

(0 TO 6 MONTHS)

If you've gotten this book into your hands prior to conceiving or during pregnancy, that's great! Your pre-pregnancy and pregnancy diet is crucial to giving your future baby the best shot at health and is the greatest way to boost your fertility and available nutrients to build your baby. This chapter focuses on your diet as a nursing mom, but the same recommendations apply to women who are pregnant or trying to conceive.

Mom's Diet Matters

The most common advice given to pregnant and nursing moms about nutrition is this: "Don't drink, smoke, or do drugs. Keep taking your prenatal vitamin, and all will be fine." If more is said on the matter, it is usually only this: "Try to maintain a healthy diet, but if you can't, your body will give your baby what is needed."

But your diet is actually extremely important. What you eat and what you avoid both impact your baby's health. As Robert Sears, M.D., says in *Happy Baby: Organic Guide to the First 24 Months*, "when you're feeding Baby your breast milk, she *is* what *you* eat."

WHAT'S OKAY

While nursing, you *can* eat many of the foods that are conventionally prohibited during pregnancy: soft and raw (unpasteurized) cheeses, pâté, and raw eggs, as long as they are fresh from pasture-raised chickens. There is no reason to avoid seasonings, especially as your milk will change flavor, enriching your baby's palate. Raw honey, too, is fine for nursing moms (just not babies under 1 year old).

Teas (white, green, black, and oolong) contain tannins, which are digestive irritants and can block protein digestion and mineral absorption (particularly iron), so should be used sparingly. Though herbal teas do not necessarily contain actual tea, but rather herbal infusions, we recommend talking to an herbalist to learn more about herbs while nursing.

WHAT'S NOT OKAY

Smoking, drugs, and drinking too much alcohol while nursing are obviously not okay. You'll also want to avoid highly polluted fish (like swordfish, king mackerel, tilefish, and shark), hydrogenated

---

HUMAN MILK— "BREAST" MILK OR "MOM'S" MILK?

Though it is common to call human milk "breast" milk, we feel this unduly objectifies the breast and incorrectly separates the milk from the mother. (We don't call bovine dairy "udder milk," do we?) It is the *whole* mom (not just her breast) who is making milk for her baby—her nutrient stores, her diet, her energy, her hormones, her enzymes, and her time, effort, and enjoyment to nurse—so we refer to human milk as *mom's milk*.

or partially hydrogenated oils (trans fats), and all artificial sweeteners. Soy, sugar, GMOs, and nonorganic food are additional important ingredients to limit while nursing.

SOY. Soy contains plant-based estrogens that cause hormonal disruptions in both mom and baby. Further, most soy is GMO and overdosed with pesticides. Additionally, goitrogens (thyroid-blocking factors) in soy can lead to metabolic problems (including thyroid issues), leaving you exhausted, chilled, and unable to lose weight. Children born to mothers with underactive thyroids have been found to have IQs 10 to 15 points below average. (Learn more in chapter 3.)

SUGARS. One of the many problems with sugar is its influence on yeast. When you eat sugar (table sugar, high fructose corn syrup, juice, white flour, etc.), you feed harmful yeasts (like *Candida albicans*) in your body, allowing them to overgrow and potentially cause vaginal yeast infections, sugar cravings, and mastitis. Yeast overgrowth can also contribute to brain fog, anxiety, depression, ADHD, and digestive issues. If a mother has yeast overgrowth, the yeast will likely pass to her baby and can result in thrush, diaper rash, food intolerances/food allergies, and nutrient deficiencies. When yeast eats sugar, it puts out toxic by-products that pass to your milk. In your baby's stomach, these by-products reduce stomach acid. Because sufficient stomach acid is required to ward off acid reflux, food allergies, and even infection, it is wise to avoid eating sugar as a nursing mom, especially if your child has reflux or colic.

Further, your baby's initial good bacteria come from you and teach your baby's body what is good and what is bad. If your baby acquires unhealthy yeast early in life, her body is more likely to perceive it as normal, thus potentially setting her up for a lifelong struggle with yeast-related issues such as sugar cravings, obesity, diabetes, mood/emotional disorders, asthma, allergies, alcoholism, digestive distress, and even heart disease. Limiting sugar as much as possible, especially during your final month of pregnancy, will ultimately help optimize your baby's long-term gut flora.

MOM'S DRINKS

If you're a nursing mom, stay hydrated to provide enough fluid to produce milk. In addition to how much you drink, *what* you drink is also important for both you and your baby.

CAFFEINATED BEVERAGES. Caffeine can make you more prone to inadequate hydration. Also, it does get into breast milk, so watch for signs of caffeine sensitivity in your baby: wakefulness, hyperactivity, colicky behavior, and shorter duration of feedings.

In addition to being caffeinated, soda contains a metabolic nightmare of ingredients: high fructose corn syrup, phosphates that block calcium, and artificial flavorings and colorings. The artificial sweeteners in diet soda are unhealthy for anyone, particularly your baby.

ALCOHOL. You wouldn't feed your baby a martini in her bottle, so limit (or preferably cease) alcohol consumption while nursing. Alcohol enters breast milk 30 to 60 minutes after consumption. Feeling the effects of alcohol means alcohol is in your milk. Wait at least 2 hours after any drink to nurse. If you have any more than one alcoholic drink, we advise you to "pump and dump."

Super Nutrition for Nursing Moms

The Weston A. Price Foundation (WAPF) is a national nonprofit nutrition organization and traditional-foods advocacy group. Founded in 1999, it has extensively studied the work of several researchers, who surmised from traditional, pre-industrialized people that optimal health is entirely possible with the right form of foods and nutrient density. WAPF has compiled and recommends a diet for pregnant and nursing mothers, as follows (reprinted with permission, https://www.westonaprice.org/health-topics/diet-for-pregnant-and-nursing-mothers)

- Cod liver oil (for omega 3s, vitamin A and vitamin D) to supply* (no more than) 20,000 IU vitamin A and 2,000 IU vitamin D per day (we recommend 2–4 teaspoons per day)

- 1 quart (or 32 ounces [950 ml]) whole milk daily*, preferably raw and from pasture-fed cows (Learn more about raw milk on page 24.)

- 4 tablespoons (55 g) butter* daily, preferably from pasture-fed cows

- 2 or more eggs daily, preferably from pastured chickens

- Additional egg yolks daily, added to smoothies, salad dressings, scrambled eggs, etc.

- 3 to 4 ounces (85 to 115 g) fresh liver, once or twice per week

- Fresh seafood*, two to four times per week, particularly wild salmon, shellfish, and fish eggs

- Fresh beef or lamb daily, always consumed with the fat

- Oily (small) fish* or lard daily, for vitamin D (with sunshine or supplemental D, if low)

- 2 tablespoons (28 g) coconut oil daily, used in cooking or smoothies, etc.

- Lacto-fermented condiments and beverages (see page 182)

- Bone broths used in soups, stews, and sauces

- Soaked (or sprouted) whole grains and soaked or sprouted nuts and seeds (see page 196)

- Fresh vegetables and fruits

These recommendations are scientifically geared to nourish a nursing mother with all the minerals, enzymes, immune factors, vitamins, antioxidants, and fat-soluble activators she needs for herself and her baby. Many items should be consumed daily, but some should be a weekly goal. Below, we offer clarification on the guidelines noted with (*), as well as important information for best adapting them to your diet.

VITAMIN A AND COD LIVER OIL. Taking cod liver oil (CLO) provides benefits to both you and your baby. It is an excellent source of vitamins A and D, as well as the anti-inflammatory and brain development–promoting essential fatty acids DHA and EPA. The nutrients in CLO are in their most natural and "body-ready" form, making it extremely powerful in terms of health benefits. As for vitamin A, you'll get it predominantly from liver or cod liver oil, as well as *some* from eggs and butter. Though it is important to get enough vitamin A, you don't want to exceed 20,000 IU per day. As a rule of thumb, on days you eat liver, you can skip cod liver oil, though you might want to add fish to your menu those days, as it will provide some DHA.

ALL THAT MILK! Thirty-two ounces (950 ml) of milk is equal to *4 big glasses.* If the milk you're drinking is fresh, raw, and grass-fed, your hard-working, nursing body will likely love it. If you don't have access to a clean, raw dairy, hold off on drinking that much, as pasteurized milk is often irritating and inflammatory. To minimize inflammation and maximize nutrition, choose milk that is organic, grass-fed, non-homogenized, and vat pasteurized (lower heat). Or instead, combine some high-quality whole-milk plain yogurt (8 to 16 ounces, or 225 to 455 g) and cheese (about 4 ounces, or 115 g) daily, and make sure you get Souper Stock (page 45) several times per week, if not daily, as well.

If you suspect your baby is irritated by pasteurized dairy, procure a trusted source of raw dairy. (See page 260.) But if raw dairy is truly inaccessible, we suggest Souper Stock *with each meal,* daily, to attempt to provide the absorbable minerals that would've been found in dairy in your diet. Additionally, probiotics and cod liver oil are a must in the absence of high-quality dairy. Usually, butter is tolerable (and desirable!), even if pasteurized milk is not; but if not, we recommend ghee.

Does it have to be whole milk? Yes, whole milk is a whole food. Stripping away the fat does far more than just reduce the calories. Important nutrients, including vitamins A and D, are housed in the fat. These vitamins need to be consumed with fat to be used by the body, and without them, you can't use the minerals in the foods you eat either. Whole (or unchanged) milk provides fat, fat-soluble vitamins, and minerals—all of which work together. (Remember, nursing burns calories, and fat is satisfying—so you eat less—so don't worry that you'll "overindulge"!)

BUTTER—BETTER THAN YOU THOUGHT! Butter from grass-fed cows is an amazing healing food. Grass-fed, raw butter contains fat-soluble vitamin A (retinol), fat-soluble beta-carotene, conjugated linoleic acid (a potent cancer-fighting fat found almost exclusively in grass-fed dairy and animal fat), omega-3 fatty acids (like brain-building DHA), and fat-soluble vitamin E. Several additional fatty acids in butter support the immune, digestive, and nervous systems. High-quality butter is a Super POWER food because it provides such excellent nutrients, along with the fat to make sure your body can use them! No longer should you view butter as a stick of fat, but as a great source of nourishment that also makes foods taste great! It is undeniably a heart- and health-*helpful* food.

SEAFOOD SAFETY. We recommend *wild-caught* seafood, but high-quality farm-raised is acceptable if no antibiotics, vaccines, or GMO feed are used. While Weston A. Price recommends 2 to 4 servings of fish per week, these recommendations were initially made at a time when oceans were much cleaner. Today, while the benefits of fish are great, the toxins, including radiation, are worse, and so we recommend less and smaller fish, only one or two times per week. To minimize heavy metal and pollutant risk, we strongly recommend that at least half fish servings come from small, oily fish (such as sardines or anchovies) or fish roe (caviar), which are the least contaminated. Seafood is a panacea of health benefits, but must now be weighed with the risks of toxins. Cilantro, and other detoxifying foods (see chapter 5), can be consumed with fish.

ANIMAL AND SEA FOODS

We urge you to consume plenty of animal foods, as well as some seafood. The source of the animal foods you eat, though, and what *they* ate, are very important. Pastured, grass-fed animals and wild-caught seafood are the very best. Next best is organic. Less nutritious is "all natural." Finally, you've got conventional animal foods and seafood.

THE RIGHT FATS

By design, mom's milk is made of high quantities of saturated fat and cholesterol, which are essential to your baby's development, most importantly her brain development. Your milk is naturally made of close to 60% fat and cholesterol, almost identical to the fat content of babies' brains. Without enough fat and cholesterol in your diet, your body will be taxed with making them for your milk.

PROPER PROPORTION OF FATS. Most of your fats should come from butter, eggs, cheese, and meat from pasture-raised animals. Coconut fats (oil and milk) should contribute significantly to your fat intake, due to their special medium-chain triglycerides (that feed probiotics, spur metabolism, and support healthy thyroid function). Fish, oily fish, nuts, and cod liver oil round out essential fatty acid needs.

HEATING AND PROPER USAGE. Heat, light, time, pressure, and chemicals damage fats, but some are more vulnerable to rancidity than others. Rancid fats are dangerous, contribute to oxidative stress, use nutrient and antioxidant stores, and are a significant source of disease-causing free radicals. Polyunsaturated fats are most vulnerable, whereas saturated fats are the least susceptible. All oils should be cold-pressed and unrefined, if possible. Below describes various kinds of fats and their best cooking applications (despite what their label might say) and heat tolerances.

- **Saturated fats:** Coconut oil, butter, ghee (butter oil), red palm oil, or palm kernel oil; use for sautéing at high heat. Such fats are solid at room temperature and are molecularly stable enough to withstand damage from high heat. Best baking fats include butter, ghee, and coconut oil.

- **Combination saturated/monounsaturated fats:** Fats that are saturated, monounsaturated, and polyunsaturated, such as suet and beef tallow, lard, duck fat, and schmaltz, are best used at medium-high heat.

- **Predominantly monounsaturated fats:** Olive oil, avocado oil, hazelnut oil, macadamia nut oil, high-oleic safflower oil, and almond oil; these can handle moderate heat, so use in medium- to low-heat cooking and in dressings.

- **Combination monounsaturated and polyunsaturated fats:** Peanut oil and pumpkin seed oil; these can be used in medium-low-heat cooking, like light sautéing. Sesame oil is both a mono- and a polyunsaturated fat but has antioxidant factors (sesamin) that make it better able to handle moderate heat.

DEEP DIVE INTO FABULOUS FATS

All fats—saturated and unsaturated—are 9 calories per gram. Vegetable fats are not "lower fat" than fats in steak, and fats in bacon are no "fattier" than fats from corn, soybeans, or cottonseed. If anything, vegetable oils may be more likely to contribute to fat storage. According to Alan Greene, M.D., in *Feeding Baby Green*, vegetable fats are inflammatory and consequently slow down the body's fat-burning capabilities, contributing to fat storage and thus, weight gain. Following are some of the myriad benefits of animal fats.

BUTTER helps with cholesterol metabolism, growth, and glucose tolerance; promotes healthy bones and teeth; aids metabolic and biochemical pathways; builds the brain; and fights free radicals, toxins, cancer, infection, and inflammation. If it is raw and grass-fed, it helps prevent arthritis and calcification of the arteries. Farm-fresh is best, organic is great, and "regular" butter is better than any "spreads."

GHEE is clarified butter and is typically safe for those who react to the milk protein casein. Ghee still has all the vitamins of butter. Although some factors found in raw butter are lost, it is very similar to Weston Price's High Vitamin Butter Oil if organic and grass-fed (such as Pure Indian Foods); as pointed out in the *Vitamin K Paradox*, by Kate Rheaume-Bleue.

LARD is mostly a monounsaturated fat, like olive oil. If from pastured pigs, it is an excellent source of vitamin D. See page 40.

RENDERED CHICKEN FAT (SCHMALTZ) can be used for sautéing (see page 37). It contains palmitoleic fatty acid—an antimicrobial (immune-supporting) fat.

DUCK FAT contains about 62% unsaturated fat and about 33% saturated fat. It is high in oleic acid, which aids mineral absorption and is associated with lowered risk of heart disease, cancer, and other diseases of aging. Duck fat also contains linoleic acid, which is used by the body to maintain the health of cells.

BEEF SUET AND TALLOW. Suet (fat from the cavity of the animal) is predominantly saturated fat, so it's a great fat for high heat. Tallow, the rendered fat, is just over half saturated fat and about 40% monounsaturated. Both can be used for frying and have antimicrobial (immune-boosting) fatty acids. Often suet and tallow can be found at local farms.

BONE MARROW is an organ mostly made of fat within the hollow core of bone. It contains nutrients not found in muscle meat and has iron, vitamin A, phosphorus, and unique AKGs (alkylglycerols)— special fats that boost the immune system.

COCONUT OIL is an excellent source of virus-fighting lauric acid. It is also remarkably rich in special fatty acids that help support gut health and are much less likely to turn into body fat. Coconut oil provides great support for the thyroid gland—the master of metabolism.

RED PALM OIL is a very stable fat, great for high-heat cooking. Extremely rich in antioxidants, it provides all eight kinds of vitamin E and four kinds of carotenes, as well as more lycopene and lutein than tomatoes and carrots combined. It is great for frying.

EMU OIL contains a mix of bioavailable omega-3s, -6s, and -9s, and contains conjugated linoleic acid (CLA, a cancer-fighter, also found in grass-fed butter) and fat-soluble, mineral-activating vitamins D3 and K2 (as MK-4), as well as E. This oil should not be heated and is wonderful when applied to the skin. (Walkabout is one brand that offers emu oil capsules, as well as a liquid oil that can be topically applied, and is touted to help eczema.)

- **Polyunsaturated fats:** Walnut oil, flaxseed oil, perilla seed oil, and borage oil; these are great for cold applications of oils, like salad dressings, and need protection (from heat, light, and time). They should be kept in dark bottles, stored in the refrigerator. Polyunsaturated fats should make up the lowest portion of your fat intake, including cod liver oil (taken in small quantities).

WISE CARBS

As for carbohydrates, eat a variety of greens, vegetables, fruits, properly prepared nuts and seeds (grains), and smart starches. We call these "wise" carbs because they pack a ton of nutrition and fiber—and don't spike your blood sugar as much as the more commonly consumed carbs, such as refined grains, beans/legumes, and tubers. Grains and beans need special preparation to make them safe to ingest and most nutritious. (See chapter 8.) Smart starches include water-soluble fiber (pectin, gums, and mucilage), cellulose (found in some fruits and vegetables), and resistant starches (specifically when cooked, cooled, and then reheated before consumption, such as sweet potatoes, plantains, yucca, and taro). All these are a healthy source of fiber. Resistant starches "resist" being digested by our digestive enzymes, but they feed our gut bacteria, resulting in important short-chain fatty acids, which improve blood sugar control, boost immunity, and could reduce certain cancers.

Though you may be in a hurry to lose "baby weight," we remind you that nursing will help you return to your pre-pregnancy weight, and caution you at this time to be first concerned with the nutrient value of the food you consume. Nursing burns calories and you will naturally lose weight on our healthy recommended diet. Provide optimal nutrition, which will also protect your baby from any toxins being released during weight loss.

Supplements for Mom and Baby

Before you brought your baby home from the hospital or birthing center, you were likely advised to continue taking your prenatal vitamins if breastfeeding. And that's a good idea, but supplements are never enough to provide you with what you need to maintain your own health, let alone that of your baby, so your diet remains of utmost importance.

RECOMMENDED SUPPLEMENTS FOR YOU

The dietary recommendations we've given, as well as the guidelines from the Weston A. Price Foundation, are an ideal *goal*. As we realize that you may not consume all these foods on a regular basis, we recommend supplements to fill in the blanks. We recommend nursing moms take the following *daily*:

MULTIVITAMIN. If your diet is close to our dietary recommendations for nursing moms, you won't need a multivitamin. However, if you are still working toward such a diet, you might be wise to take a multivitamin or prenatal vitamin. We advise either a 100% food-based vitamin and mineral supplement (such as Megafood's Baby and Me) or a high-quality synthetic supplement containing activated vitamins like 5-MTHF, such as Seeking Health or Vital Nutrients Prenatal.

COD LIVER OIL. Carlsons, Rosita, and Nordic Naturals are good brands, tested for purity and freshness. Combining this rich source of vitamins A and D with sources of K2 (see below), provides a trifecta of health power.

VITAMIN K2. Consuming high-vitamin butter oil (from Green Pasture, or as in Pure Indian Foods grass-fed organic ghee) and emu oil offer the MK-4 type of vitamin K2, supplementation (MK-7 form), or directly consuming natto are all predominant sources.

LIVER. If you don't eat liver, we recommend taking desiccated liver: six pills is equivalent to 1 ounce (28 g) of liver.

PROBIOTICS. For most, a capsule or two per night is appropriate, but some will need more. Each person's bacterial makeup is individual and there is no perfect probiotic for everyone. Multistrains are often best. Rotating probiotics helps to get more diversity, as does consuming probiotic-rich foods.

VITAMIN D3. Nursing mothers and babies benefit from vitamin D3 doses higher than the 1,000 IU per day recommended by most OB/GYNs, except moms who get plenty of midday sunlight or frequently eat fish roe. Studies show moms taking 6,400 IU vitamin D3 per day provide breast milk levels of 873 IU/L. Thus, a daily dose of 5,000 to 6,000 IU of vitamin D3 with 1 teaspoon of cod liver oil (containing 400 IU of vitamin D) is ideal, with no additional vitamin supplementation necessary for your baby. There can be significant variability between people with regard to ideal vitamin D dosing. Because vitamin D is a fat-soluble vitamin, it can accumulate, so it is best to check your blood vitamin D level (ask your doctor for the 25-OHD3 test) after 3 months on high-dose vitamin D with a target goal between 60 and 80. Once reached, reduce your vitamin D intake by half. *Note:* More vitamin D is usually needed in winter months, when less sun exposure is available. Sunscreen blocks 95% of vitamin D from the sun.

DEEP DIVE INTO VITAMIN D3, ESSENTIAL FOR HEALTH

Vitamin D3 is critical for everyone, from fetuses to the elderly. Inadequate vitamin D3 levels are found to increase the risk of everything from both types of diabetes, asthma, and multiple sclerosis to heart disease and cancer. By supplementing vitamin D3, the risk of overall illness decreases, and even small increases in vitamin D levels have been shown to make a positive impact. Research shows that when moms have enough vitamin D3, babies have better birth weights, larger head circumferences, better tooth enamel, and less asthma and allergies. If newborns have good vitamin D3 levels, they'll have increased bone mass and better bone mineralization for at least 9 years, which safeguards against bowed legs, rickets, osteopenia (low bone mineral density), and fractures. *Note:* D3 (cholecalciferol) is the animal form of this critical nutrient, and is vastly more beneficial than other forms of vitamin D. Vitamin D2 (ergocalciferol), is the synthetic form and should be avoided.

FOLATE is vitamin B9, as it is found in food, whereas folic acid is the man-made synthetic form of this critical nutrient. Folate is vital to the function of our biochemical pathways and detoxification. Experts like Dr. Amy Yasko are finding that the majority of people with illness have difficulty with efficiently processing folate, derived either from food or from supplementation, and therefore have impaired detoxification (methylation) abilities. In our world full of toxins, detoxification is critical to maintaining good health. Thus, we recommend moms get tested for the methyltetrahydrofolate reductase mutation, which is fairly common, and take 1 mg daily of a special form of folate, called

5-methyltetrahydrofolate ("5-MTHF" for short). As B12 assists this pathway, we encourage getting plenty of B12 from animal foods (liver, meat, fish, eggs, and dairy).

RECOMMENDED SUPPLEMENTS FOR YOUR BABY

With your stellar diet and additional supplements, it is unlikely that your baby needs supplementation during these first 6 months. There are, however, some circumstances that call for them.

PROBIOTICS. Give supplemental probiotics to your baby if:

- Your baby was born by C-section
- Antibiotics were given during pregnancy, delivery, while nursing, or to your baby
- The mom has a history of yeast infections or yeast infection before or during pregnancy
- Your baby has thrush or a yeast diaper rash
- There is a family history of alcoholism, sugar addiction/carb cravings, diabetes, metabolic syndrome, or other sugar-related illnesses

Powdered-probiotics baby dosing is about 3 billion CFU/day, but more importantly, pay attention to the strains, specifically *Lactobacillus acidophilus* and *Bifidobacterium infantis* (aka *Bifidobacterium animalis*), and choose the highest quality brand you can. Probiotics can be given by simply putting ¼ teaspoon on your wet finger and letting your baby suck it off or by putting it on your nipple during nursing once or twice a day. Probiotics can also be added to the contents of a bottle.

COD LIVER OIL. In most cases, the cod liver oil you are taking will provide for the most nutritious milk for your baby. In certain circumstances, including sibling or parental history of

a 3C condition, it might be wise to provide CLO directly. For dosing and administration information for your baby, see page 103.

VITAMIN D3. A nursing baby will only need additional vitamin D if you are taking less than 5,000 IU per day, which then should be supplemented with 400 IU per day.

The Magic of Mom's Milk

In the early 1900s, 95% of mothers nursed their babies. Today, according to the CDC, more moms (81%) are trying to breastfeed than 5 years ago (75%), but only about 35% of babies are exclusively breastfed for the first 3 months, and only 20% are still being exclusively nursed at 6 months. By 1 year, 21% are still getting some milk from mom. Countless international and national health authorities (including The American Academy of Pediatrics [AAP]) stress "mom's" milk is the best source of nutrition for an infant for *at least* the first year of life and thus recommend breastfeeding *exclusively* (no water, juice, nonhuman milk, or foods) for the first 6 months.

Various studies tout the health benefits of breastfeeding for your baby, many of which you've likely already heard. They include: improved speech and vision development, superior fine-motor coordination, fewer behavioral problems, better bonding between mother and baby, healthier weight, less digestive distress, fewer food allergies, fewer infections, higher IQ, and better intellectual, cognitive, and neurological development.

Some of these benefits are due to the nutritional elements in the mother's milk, while others can be associated with the infant's sensory stimulation, which contributes significantly to the infant's neurodevelopment. Studies in hormonal physiology suggest that skin-to-skin contact reduces newborn stress and stress

DEEP DIVE INTO MOM'S MILK: NUTRIENT PROFILE

The composition and ratio of lactose, fats, oligo-saccharides, and protein make mom's milk the perfect diet for your baby. Because of infants' relatively large brains (compared to their bodies) and brain growth rate, they need more specific brain-building carbohydrates and more short-chain and medium-chain fatty acids in their diet than do adults. By consuming appropriate and sufficient nutrients, your body will be able to best support your baby's needs.

In addition to critical cholesterol, fats, and protein, very specific saccharrides exist, particularly galactose and sialic acid. Galactose, which, along with glucose, makes up lactose, milk's main sugar, is used to build glycolipids that ultimately provide immune- and intelligence-boosting capabilities. Sialic acid (a monosaccharide found in highest concentrations in the brain and mom's milk) is believed to be conditionally essential in infancy: mom's milk to the rescue!

According to the *American Journal of Clinical Nutrition*, sialic acid in the diet during early development enhances learning and even influences genes positively associated with learning. And, according to the *European Journal of Clinical Nutrition*, levels of sialic acid correlate with the amount of DHA (both found to be significantly higher in breastfed babies); these two brain boosters work together to make neurons function more fluidly.

hormones. Nursing also has great benefits for mom: it releases oxytocin, prolactin, and beta-endorphins, which reduce stress and contract the uterus, speeding mom's recovery.

Something you might *not* be aware of, however, is the awesome protective power of mom's milk. There is a 36% lower infant death rate in babies who were ever breastfed. These babies are also offered protection from chronic childhood diseases such as multiple sclerosis, inflammatory bowel disease (like Crohn's and ulcerative colitis), arthritis, celiac disease, hypertension, high cholesterol, heart disease, type 1 diabetes, and obesity.

Nursing and Feeding Advice

During the first 3 months after birth, your baby isn't familiar with stillness, quiet, or fabric surroundings. Comfort is found in you—your voice, breathing, gait, smell, and the rhythm of your heartbeat. Talk softly to her, try skin-to-skin contact or swaddle her tightly (especially if fussy), and gently rock or carry her. Your baby is used to a nearly constant source of nutrition; to mimic that as much as possible, allow her to eat any time she is hungry (breastfed babies *need* to eat frequently).

GET IN SYNC WITH YOUR BABY. Your body's goal is to make exactly the amount of milk your baby needs, and it is your baby's act of sucking that provides this information. Nurse too infrequently and your body makes less milk; nurse too frequently (like by pumping in between feedings) and your body overproduces. By letting your baby be the sole guide for your body for the first 2 weeks, you'll get in perfect synchronization.

FEED ON CUE. Rather than clock-watching, tune in to your baby. When she signals, with simple alertness, rooting, mouthing, physical activity, or any other message to you, let her nurse. The AAP states, "During the early weeks of breastfeeding, mothers should be encouraged to . . . [offer] the breast *whenever* the infant shows *early* signs of hunger" Crying, the AAP says, "is a *late* indicator of hunger" [emphases added].

Rather than calling this "on demand," we prefer to call it "on cue." "Demand" implies that your baby is bossing you around. "Cues," on the other hand, signify the special nonverbal communication that occurs between mother and child, best communicated when your baby is very near you.

WHEN FORMULA IS NOT NECESSARILY NECESSARY. In the first few days, parents often have concerns that their baby isn't getting enough milk. Be assured that frequent nursing (which stimulates your milk to come in) and weight loss are both to be expected. In most cases, formula feeding is counterproductive to nursing and can further decrease milk supply. Though your milk hasn't yet come in, colostrum, the early yellowish, thick liquid that is present before "mature" milk comes in, is the ultimate protective nutrition—your baby needs nothing more. Colostrum is rich in nutrients, probiotics, and immune factors. The human baby is designed to feed first on it for several days before having *anything* else; it prepares your baby's gut to digest the coming milk. Her stomach has never had any significant volume of liquid, and she isn't expecting or ready for that much in her early days. Feeding formula will expand her stomach unnaturally and that confuses the natural progression of development, particularly of her digestive tract.

We recommend relaxing standards on housecleaning, socializing, working, and exercising. Focus your attention and time on nourishing and comforting your growing baby. If you try to do

MORE SERIOUS CONCERNS

If your baby isn't growing in length or head circumference, is losing weight, or is not nursing enough, these are real concerns. If your instincts tell you something is wrong, follow them, regardless of what your pediatrician says. Lack of increasing head circumference specifically can be related to B12 deficiency if mom is not getting adequate animal foods. B12 supplementation might be necessary for mom and baby, especially when mom has been a vegan or vegetarian. A urine methylmalonic acid test is the best test to determine B12 deficiency. For more information, see Sally Pacholok's book *Could It Be B12?*

everything, your ability to respond to her cues will be diminished and the strain and stress will have an impact on both of you.

SPECIAL FEEDING CONCERNS

Stress and anxiety can interfere with digestion because they shift nutrients and blood away from digestive functions. Studies show that when your baby is being held, pain-relieving endorphins are released by her brain. If your baby is experiencing tummy trouble, fear, chill, loneliness, anxiety, or other distress, holding her dulls or takes away her pain and discomfort. Minimize your baby's stress by holding her continuously and making eye contact, particularly as you nurse her.

TUMMY TROUBLE (GAS). Foods that cause gas in you can cause gas in your baby. That includes raw, fibrous greens and veggies; some fruits; and onions, grains, and beans. If your baby is gassy, cook all fruits and vegetables you eat and prepare grains and beans as described in chapter 8. It is also helpful to consume enzyme- and probiotic-rich foods such as any of the lacto-fermented foods or beverages found in this chapter and others.

COLIC FROM ACID REFLUX. Colic, or excessive and unreasonable crying, occurs in one out of every four infants. Though the exact cause is unknown, colic is often due to reflux or some other cause of pain. When acid reflux is the cause, giving your baby ½ teaspoon of sauerkraut juice or ¼ teaspoon of raw apple cider vinegar should help provide some relief. These increase the acid in the stomach, keeping the sphincter at the top of the stomach closed. Zinc deficiency is another frequent cause of low stomach acid, contributing to colic. Liver is a great source of zinc. Avoiding sugar and refined grains helps to minimize unhealthy microbes in your gut (and their toxic by-products) that can lead to digestive distress in your baby. Eat lactic acid–rich foods, like unpasteurized pickles or sauerkraut (or other lacto-fermented foods or cultured

dairy—see page 107). It may also be beneficial to directly supplement yourself and your baby with probiotics (see page 19). Finally, nursing moms can consume oysters and mussels for an infusion of zinc and iodine or to help baby with acid reflux or related colic.

Colic often stems from too much sugar, and not enough fat. The duration of a feeding will influence the quality of nutrition and fat content your baby receives. If she is getting too much lactose (in foremilk, the milk in the early part of a feeding) without adequate fat (from hindmilk, which comes later), the milk sugar will ferment in her gut, creating gas. This leads to fussiness and colic symptoms. Allow your baby to nurse for as long as she desires on one breast *before* switching to the other. This should ensure the right balance of foremilk to hindmilk.

RECIPES FOR NURSING (AND NON-NURSING) MOMS AND THEIR FAMILIES

The ultimate resource for the most nutritious and most digestible foods is *Nourishing Traditions* by Sally Fallon, author, researcher, traditional-foods advocate, and founder and president of the Weston A. Price Foundation. We've adapted several of her recipes throughout this book, with permission. Though these recipes are ideal for nursing moms and babies, they are extremely beneficial to the health of your entire family.

Use the highest quality animal products available to you, most importantly grass-fed, pasture-raised, and organic.

Note: Though we have the recipe for Souper Stock here in mom's chapter, it is important to note that we also include Souper Stock as an early food for your baby. Using Souper Stock as a base for soups, stews, chilis, roux, and other cooking concoctions is recommended.

SOUPER STOCK

Real soup, made from bones, is excellent for the digestive system because it contains gelatin, which is uniquely able to stimulate and support digestion, making whatever you eat with it easier to digest. Decades of research on gelatin has been summarized by Nathan Gotthoffer in his book *Gelatin in Nutrition and Medicine*. The collagen and cartilage (gristle) in bone broth are even more important to building strong bones than calcium. The minerals obtained from soup stock made with bones are extremely nutritious and in highly absorbable form, resulting in an electrolyte (mineral) solution far superior to any commercially produced, additive-laden, dyed, sugar-spiked beverages such as Pedialyte or Gatorade. Sally Fallon's book *Nourishing Broth* is a wonderful resource. Known for generations, across geographies, religions, and ethnicities, broth has the ability to improve and protect digestive, skeletal and joint health.

1 to 2 pounds (455 to 910 g) soup bones from organic, grass-fed animals (such as beef, lamb, or poultry)

2 tablespoons (28 ml) raw apple cider vinegar

2 chicken feet for extra gelatin

Celtic or Himalayan salt, to taste

For beef or lamb bones, soak for 1 hour in enough water to cover the bones. Then add the vinegar to help pull the minerals from the bones into the consumable liquid. Add the chicken feet.

Add enough water to fill the pot and simmer on low for 12 to 24 hours for poultry or 24 to 72 hours for beef or lamb (the longer the bones simmer, the more minerals and gelatin will be present in your stock).

Let cool. Add sea salt to taste and to provide trace minerals (see discussion of salt in chapter 6).

Serve warm, not hot, to your baby.

Allow to cool in the refrigerator and then skim off the fat that rises and firms as a top layer. (This fat can be saved and later used for cooking.)

YIELD: 3 quarts (2.8 L)

⤴ The acidity in the water helps to pull minerals from the bones, but too much vinegar will alter the taste of the broth; typically 1 to 2 tablespoons (15 to 30 ml) to ½ cup (120 ml) of vinegar is used, depending on the amount of water.

STORAGE

⊙ Pour through a mesh strainer into either Mason jars or stainless steel ice cube trays as an option for freezing individual serving sizes. (If you use plastic ice cube trays, ensure broth is at room temperature or cooler before pouring into the tray.)

⊙ For use within a week or two, place in refrigerator; otherwise, freeze. Once defrosted, use within 3 to 4 days.

⊙ When refrigerated, Souper Stock should become gelatinous (jiggly like Jell-O).

MOM-TO-MOM

Make Souper Stock every other weekend and use frozen in between. If you run out, you can use Great Lakes, Vital Amines, or Bernard Jensen's unbleached gelatin (check out www.radiantlifecatalog.com) sprinkled into filtered water to eat with small amounts of puréed meat. Digestion will still be aided, though the important minerals will be absent.

CHOPPED NUT AND FLAX MIX

This nut mixture tastes good in a variety of recipes. Keep a bowl made up so it is available for quick snacks, breakfasts, and desserts. Nuts contain important fats (monounsaturated) and arginine (an amino acid), which can improve heart health. According to Jonny Bowden, Ph.D., C.N.S., in the book *The 150 Healthiest Foods on Earth*, people who regularly eat nuts have a lowered risk of heart disease. Do not heat or cook flaxseed, as it contains delicate polyunsaturated fats that are easily damaged, rancidified, and rendered toxic. We recommend limited use of flaxseed.

1 cup (145 g) soaked and dried almonds, chopped (for proper nut preparation, see page 196)

1 cup (100 g) soaked and dried walnuts, chopped

1 cup (100 g) soaked and dried pecans, chopped

1 to 2 tablespoons (15 to 30 g) sea salt

2 teaspoons ground cinnamon

1 cup (112 g) flaxseed, freshly ground

One to 2 days prior, soak the nuts fully submerged in water and 1 to 2 tablespoons (15 to 30 g) of sea salt. After 24 hours, drain the water and dehydrate in a dehydrator for 4 to 8 hours or in your oven on baking sheets at the lowest possible temperature setting for 6 to 8 hours.

Mix all the ingredients together.

Mix with raw, plain yogurt and fruit for a great breakfast. Mix with fruit and cream for a great dessert. Sprinkle on your salad to add a nice crunch. Mix into a crepe or pancake batter for a great addition of texture and taste. Use this mix as a substitute for the sprouted seeds or nuts in the Nut 'n' Honey Balls recipe (page 48).

You can store this mixture in the refrigerator for 3 to 4 weeks.

NOTE

⊙ For maximum health benefits, flaxseed should stay intact and be refrigerated until ready to consume. Use a coffee grinder or Vitamix to grind what you need when you are ready to use it.

YIELD:
3½ cups (345 g)

NUT 'N' HONEY BALLS

Honey—if unfiltered, unheated, and raw—is a solid choice for a natural sweetener. It contains amylase, so it aids carbohydrate digestion, and ideally will contain some of the comb, propolis, and royal jelly. The honey will help with digesting starches if you allow it to work on the foods it is mixed with for 15 minutes or so before eating it (as with oatmeal). A good snack for you, this can be a terrific special occasion treat for your baby over 1 year, at which time very sparing amounts of honey might be used.

1 cup (260 g) soaked nut butter (page 198)

1 cup (104 g) Sprouted Seeds or Nuts (page 197), ground or chopped

½ cup (170 g) raw, unheated, unfiltered honey or other whole-foods-based, nutrient-containing sweetener

1 teaspoon vanilla extract

1 teaspoon ground cinnamon

1 teaspoon almond extract, *optional*

½ cup (43 g) unsweetened, unsulfured, shredded coconut

Stir together the nut butter, seeds, nuts, honey, vanilla extract, cinnamon, and almond extract, if using. Mix well.

Roll the mixture into 1-inch (2.5 cm) balls. Roll the balls in the coconut.

NOTES

⊙ You can add blueberries—fresh or frozen—for a fun flavor and antioxidant boost.

⊙ The Nut 'n' Honey Balls keep well in the freezer so can easily be tossed in a lunch or for an on-the-go snack. For a variation, these can be formed into 2 × 1-inch (2.5 × 5 cm) bars. Wrap them up in parchment paper and toddlers over 18 months will love these healthy "candy bars." Use a cup of the Chopped Nut and Flax Mix (page 47) in place of the sprouted seeds or nuts and it makes these quick to prepare and extra yummy with the cinnamon and extra healthy with ground flaxseed.

YIELD: 10 to 12 balls

AMAZING EVERYDAY PALEO SALAD

Amounts in this recipe are left out so they can be changed based on your needs and tastes. The amounts of the ingredients in the salad dressing are included because these ratios work optimally, though you can use them simply as a guide. For mothers with autoimmune conditions who are on the Autoimmune Protocol (AIP) diet, there are ingredients that can be omitted.

SALAD

Lettuce—romaine, butter leaf, and baby greens mixture

Green onions, chopped

Organic, pasture-raised bacon, cooked and chopped (the more, the better)

Cilantro, chopped

Cucumber, thinly sliced or chopped

Red onion, chopped

Tomatoes (nightshade, do not use if doing AIP diet), chopped

Red pepper (nightshade, do not use if doing AIP diet), chopped

Green pepper (nightshade, do not use if doing AIP diet), chopped

Sprouts, *optional*

MOM-TO-MOM

HYPOTHYROIDISM (abnormally low thyroid function) is a common condition that essentially puts your body into a hibernation state, resulting in a lower-than average body temperature, inability to feel warm, lack of ambition, infrequent stooling, unexplained weight gain, inability to lose weight, exhaustion and fatigue, depression, hair loss, and eyebrow thinning. It is one of the most common causes of infertility, and pregnancy can trigger or uncover it.

As lactation requires thyroid hormones, hypothyroidism has been linked to lower milk production. If you are having trouble with milk production, check your thyroid hormone level. If you find that you have hypothyroidism, supplementing with iodine (unbound, such as Wellness Resources) might be preferred or more tolerable than potassium iodide (such as Iodoral). Selenium, trace minerals, and natural desiccated thyroid hormone should also help. Suzy Cohen, Izabella Wentz, and Janie Bowthorpe are excellent, thyroid-specific resources. The Autoimmune Protocol (AIP) diet can reduce antibodies in those with Hashimoto's disease (an autoimmune thyroid disorder).

KELLY'S SALAD DRESSING

⅓ cup (80 ml) raw apple cider vinegar

⅔ cup (160 ml) oil of choice (see Notes)

1 teaspoon minced garlic

2 teaspoons granulated onion

1 teaspoon turmeric

2 teaspoons dill, fresh or dried

2 dashes green stevia powder, *optional*

1 teaspoon Celtic sea salt,
or more to taste

1 teaspoon poppy seeds, *optional*

KATHY'S SALAD DRESSING

⅓ cup (80 ml) lemon juice

⅔ cup (160 ml) extra-virgin olive oil

1 to 2 teaspoons Dijon mustard

1 teaspoon Celtic sea salt

1 dash organic Worchestershire sauce

1 dash pepper (omit if doing AIP diet)

1 dash cayenne pepper

Salad dressing can be stored in a glass container
in the refrigerator for 2 to 3 months or on the
countertop for 3 to 4 weeks.

YIELD: 1 cup (235 ml)

NOTES

- High-oleic safflower oil can be used sparingly, as
  it is not GMO, but does go through heavy chemical
  treatments.
- Chosen Foods oil blend is a combination of coconut oil,
  avocado oil, and high-oleic safflower oil.
- Oils of choice include warmed coconut oil (to a liquid),
  extra-virgin olive oil, and unrefined avocado oil.

GRANDMA'S SQUAGHETTI

Spaghetti squash is high in fiber and water content, so it is good for digestion. It also contains B vitamins, folate, potassium, and vitamins A and C. It is good for your immune system and helps reduce your chance of heart disease and cancer. Squash also contains lutein and zeaxanthin, which are antioxidants that protect your eyes. Lutein requires additional fat to be best absorbed; therefore, we urge you to use some of the drippings from your meat in your rich *squaghetti*! Further, combining these great nutrients with tomato sauce provides a rich source of the red pigment lycopene, an antioxidant that is associated with lower risks of cancer and heart attacks.

SQUAGHETTI

1 large or 2 small spaghetti squash

SQUAGHETTI SAUCE

1 pound (455 g) ground beef from grass-fed pastured cows (with ground heart for extra nutrition), and drippings to taste

½ cup (80 g) chopped onion

½ cup (75 g) chopped green or red bell peppers

4 to 6 cups (946 to 1,420 ml) Souper Stock (see pg 45)

4 medium, or 2 large, fresh tomatoes (or 1 non-BPA can or glass jar [15 ounces, or 425 g] organic tomatoes)

1 teaspoon oregano

1 to 2 cloves garlic, minced

1 teaspoon dried basil

½ teaspoon Celtic sea salt, or to taste

Preheat the oven to 375°F (190°C, or gas mark 5).

For the Squaghetti: Cut the squash in half the long way and remove the seeds.

Sprinkle several tablespoons (90 ml) of water on a baking dish and place the squash cut-side down on the pan.

Bake the squash for 30 minutes.

Allow it to cool and, using a fork, scrape the "noodles" out into a dish.

For the Squaghetti Sauce: Brown the ground beef with the onions and peppers in a skillet over medium heat. Remove excess fat and liquid if desired. We find this step is not necessary if using lean ground beef, and keeping the fat will add flavor and nutrition.

Add the remaining ingredients and bring to a slow simmer. Allow to cook, stirring occasionally, for at least 30 minutes. Add sea salt to taste.

Pour the sauce over the cooked spaghetti squash noodles and serve.

YIELD: 8 servings

NOTES

- *Optional:* Add cooked broccoli, fresh spinach, or other vegetables to the sauce for the last 5 minutes.

- Spiralized zucchini and summer squash can be used for the "noodles."

- No time to make the Squaghetti Sauce? Another way to enjoy this great squash is to sprinkle the cooked "noodles" with a bit of lemon juice, your favorite spices (basil, dill, or black pepper), or top it with sea salt and coconut oil, or raw organic butter or ghee and cinnamon.

MOM-TO-MOM

SKIN-TO-SKIN CONTACT. Infants who are held more cry less and sleep better. Skin-to-skin contact has also been shown to promote newborn emotional connection, energy consumption, glucose levels, respiration, and brain development.

LARD

Lard has been maligned and is generally regarded as a highly saturated fat. Due to the false fears of saturated fats for the last several decades, lard has been used less and less in kitchens of late. However, the makeup of lard's fatty acid content is rather closer to olive oil in that it is nearly half monounsaturated fat.

LARD

1 pound (455 g) unrendered leaf lard (the fat from around the kidneys), procured from a local farm from pastured, organic pigs

Cut the lard into 1-inch (2.5 cm) pieces.

Put the lard in a pot, pan, or slow cooker (do not add water) on low. Once every half an hour, flip it with tongs and pierce the white sections, which should liquefy in the warmth.

Not everything will turn to liquid; you'll be left with pieces of brown "cracklin" (which is a tasty and crunchy treat when drained on a paper towel and sprinkled with sea salt). When no or few white parts remain, it is done.

Strain into a glass container to cool on your counter. The rendered lard will turn white as it cools. You can leave some out and store the rest in the refrigerator.

Store up to 6 months in the refrigerator or up to 1 year in the freezer.

HERE ARE A FEW GREAT USES FOR LARD:

- Used with sea salt, it's great for potatoes. According to Sally Fallon in *Nourishing Traditions*, "Potatoes deep fried in lard may be cooked in less time at a higher temperature, leaving less total fat embedded in the finished, more thoroughly cooked, less soggy, less rancid food product."
- Pemmican made with lard harkens back to traditional foods of the Native Americans. It is a concentrated blend of fat and protein from lean, dried meat. Pemmican is a great snack, as it is filling and can supply energy for hours.

YIELD: 2 cups (475 ml)

PEMMICAN

1 cup (weight will vary) dried/dehydrated meat

1 to 2 cups (weight will vary) dehydrated or unsulfured, unsweetened dried fruit (such as raisins, apricots, mulberries, goji berries, or cherries)

⅓ cup (75 g) coconut butter/manna

⅔ cup (150 g) rendered animal fat, such as lard, tallow, or duck fat

1 cup (225 g) chopped bacon

1 to 2 teaspoons Celtic sea salt

¼ cup (32 g) arrowroot starch

½ cup (weight varies) chopped nuts, presoaked, *optional*

INGREDIENT SPOTLIGHT: FATS

In the age of fearing fats, particularly saturated fats, polyunsaturated fats were all the rage. However, when studying the science of traditional diets (coveted for their protective health properties), polyunsaturated fats make up very little of the total fat content, around 4%. And, of that small percentage, the ratio of omega-3s and omega-6s (both polyunsaturates) should be around 3:1. Diets today contain much more polyunsaturated fat than a mere 4%, and a ratio of 20 to 50:1 omega-6 to omega-3, which yields a disease state, spurred on by the inflammatory properties of omega-6 consumption unchecked by a balanced amount of omega-3 intake.

The ideal fat intake ratio should be approximately 50% monounsaturated fat, 45% saturated fat, and <5% polyunsaturated fat (with equal amounts of omega-3 and omega-6). Lard is a great fat when provided from pasture-raised, organic animals, as it is typically about 48% monounsaturated fat and 40% saturated fat.

There are three ways you can make dehydrated fruit and meat: in a food dehydrator, using sunlight, or in the oven.

For meat, first remove all of the fat, cut the meat into strips, and rub with sea salt (or soak in a marinade, then drain; see page 194 for marinades). For fruit, slice it thin (removing pits/seeds).

To dry in a food dehydrator, lay either the meat or the fruit evenly on the dehydrator tray and process according to the manufacturer's directions (it usually takes 18 to 24 hours).

To use direct sunlight, lay the food to be dehydrated evenly on a stainless steel cookie sheet and cover with cheesecloth. Place the tray in the full sun in a well-ventilated area. Stir occasionally and dry until it is hard.

To use the oven, spread the meat or fruit onto a tray and place into an oven preheated to 140°F (60°C), or with the door ajar at 170°F (77°C), for 6 hours, or until hard.

Once dry, grind the fruit or meat in a food processor until it is powdered. Mix the fruit and meat with the nuts in a large bowl, leaving room for the fat.

Heat the coconut butter and fat until liquified and slowly pour it into the meat mixture and stir well. Add sea salt to taste. If the mixture seems too wet to form bars, you can add more nuts or starch.

Form the pemmican by spreading the mixture into a casserole dish. Let it cool in the refrigerator before cutting it into squares or bars.

YIELD: 15 to 20 bars

JANET'S CHILI ZUCCHINI BAKE

Red meat is important, especially while you are nursing. This recipe uses ground beef combined with ground beef heart or ground or chopped liver. The optimal diet for nursing moms (see page 33) recommends 3 to 4 ounces (85 to 115 g) of liver every week; here is a way to include it in a flavorful sauce.

CHILI ZUCCHINI

1 pound (455 g) ground beef with beef heart or liver

1 large onion, chopped

2 cloves garlic, minced

2 teaspoons curry powder

2 teaspoons chili powder

1½ cups (368 g) Tomato Sauce, divided (recipe follows)

Celtic sea salt to taste

4 to 6 large zucchini, thinly sliced

2 cups (about 230 g) shredded raw cheese

Preheat the oven to 350°F (180°C, or gas mark 4).

In a large skillet over medium heat, brown the ground beef with the onion and garlic. Add the curry and chili powder, and stir until combined. Add 1 cup (245 g) of the tomato sauce and stir. Add sea salt to taste.

Lay the zucchini in the bottom of a 9 × 13-inch (23 × 33 cm) baking dish. Spoon the ground beef mixture on top of the zucchini layer and cover with half of the shredded cheese. Repeat with the remaining zucchini, ground beef mixture, and cheese. Top with the remaining ½ cup (123 g) tomato sauce.

Bake for 20 minutes, until the cheese is melted.

YIELD: 6 to 8 servings

INGREDIENT SPOTLIGHT: LIVER FOR VITAMIN A

Liver is a nutritional gift, having among the highest nutrient density of all foods. Liver contains retinol (vitamin A), and according to the CDC, a deficiency in vitamin A is considered a main cause of childhood blindness in lower-income countries, though it is rare in the United States. Symptoms of vitamin A deficiency are night blindness, thinning of the cornea of the eye, and conjunctival metaplasia. Vitamin A is known as the anti-infective vitamin, as it is needed for immune function, tissue growth and repair, growth of bone, fertility and reproduction, and normal fetal development.

METHYLATION. Deficiency in vitamin B12 and folate during pregnancy and nursing is being researched in relation to proper brain development. Sixty to 70% of people in the United States carry a single mutation, called MTHFR; 30 to 35% have a double mutation in this gene. There are myriad studies that correlate reduction in MTHFR activity with diseases including cardiovascular disease, cancer, neurological symptoms, diabetes, depression, bipolar disorder, and many others. Methylation also plays a role in allergies, as an inability to methylate histamine can lead to a buildup of allergy symptoms. If you know that you have an MTHFR mutation, we recommend supplements of both the activated form of folate (5-MTHF) and B12 (in either methyl or hydroxy form).

Note: Folic acid is synthetic and to be mainly avoided; folate is natural and the preferred form. Liver is the best source of B vitamins, including B12 and folate.

TOMATO SAUCE

Ripe, red tomatoes contain nutrients, particularly when organic and vine-ripened, that support reducing cardiovascular and other oxidative damage per the antioxidants, phytochemicals, phenolic acids, various B vitamins, and vitamin C. Their lutein and lycopene content makes them very helpful for your eye health and overall ability to battle oxidative stress and neutralize damaging free radicals (lycopene is thought to be a stronger antioxidant than vitamin C!).

2 tablespoons (28 g) ghee, butter, or coconut oil

2 tablespoons (15 g) tigernut flour (other flours, such as arrowroot starch, can be used as thickeners), *optional*

2 tablespoons (15 g) chili powder

½ teaspoon curry powder

¼ teaspoon cayenne pepper

1 cup (235 ml) Souper Stock (page 45)

1 can (15 ounces, or 425 g) organic tomatoes, or 4 to 6 large fresh tomatoes, chopped

1 teaspoon garlic powder

½ teaspoon onion powder

½ teaspoon Celtic sea salt

Over medium-low heat, heat the oil, tigernut flour, and chili powder together in a large pot. Allow to cook for a minute or two, stirring to form a paste and making sure that the flour doesn't burn.

Add the remaining ingredients and bring to a slow simmer. Allow to cook for at least 30 minutes, stirring occasionally. Add more spices as desired, including cumin or cinnamon.

YIELD: 2 cups (490 g)

MASA (CORN) BREAD

Mainly, we won't highlight corn (a grain, not a vegetable) in our program; however, we recognize it is important in some cultures. Masa harina is corn flour that has been treated with lime water, a process called nixtamalization. This increases the value of the corn's nutrients and allows for the digestive system to be able to absorb the nutrient niacin (B3), which prevents deficiencies, including pellagra (a severe form of B3 deficiency). Soaking also changes the texture so that the finished dough (masa) is more elastic and workable. The key word to look for is "masa" to indicate the corn is nixtamalized.

1 cup (235 ml) filtered water

1 tablespoon (15 g) raw yogurt

½ cup (120 g) masa harina (nixtamalized corn flour)

1 farm-fresh, organic, pastured egg

4 tablespoons (60 ml) melted butter, ghee, fat, or oil, divided

1 to 2 teaspoons Celtic sea salt

1 teaspoon freshly grated ginger

½ cup (64 g) arrowroot starch

1 teaspoon aluminum-free baking powder

YIELD: 4 to 6 servings

Mix the water, yogurt, and flour together in a bowl. Cover and let sit overnight.

In another bowl, beat the egg and mix with half of the fat and the flour mixture.

Add the remaining ingredients and mix until a wet dough is formed.

To cook the dough, you can either fry it or bake it.

To fry the dough, drop tablespoon-sized (15 ml) balls into a skillet with the heated remaining fat. Depress with a spatula or a food press, flip, and cook on the other side. Serve warm or cool and freeze any extra for later use.

To bake the dough, pour into a greased loaf dish (glass or ceramic) and bake at 350°F (180°C, or gas mark 4) for 45 minutes, or until a knife comes out clean from the center.

NOTE

If you can't find masa harina, you can:

- Substitute gluten-free grains (millet, teff, amaranth, or sorghum)
- Make your own masa. Per *Nourishing Traditions*, add 2 quarts (1.9 L) of water to a 1-inch (2.5 cm) layer of pickling lime powder at the bottom of a 2-quart (1.9 l) jar. Shake, seal, and leave out overnight. (Don't re-shake the jar.) Pour out 2 cups (475 ml) of this lime water (the pickling powder sediment should stay at the bottom) into 2 cups (275 g) of cornmeal (it is best if it is freshly ground) and soak for 7 to 8 hours.

EGGROLLED LEFTOVERS

These eggrolls make a great lunch to enjoy at home or take on the go and can be fun to serve to guests. While some effort is involved, these end up being a different and delicious way to use up leftovers of meat and veggies.

1 to 3 cups (235 to 700 ml) melted coconut oil and/or ghee, or other animal fat (such as bacon grease, lard, or chicken drippings) or a combination

3 to 4 cups (weight will vary) leftover meat and veggie combinations, diced

1 to 2 farm-fresh, organic, pastured eggs

1 cup (120 g) grated raw cheese, such as cheddar, *optional*

8 to 10 (1 package [8 ounces, or 225 g]) brown rice–based eggroll or spring roll wrappers (such as from Star Anise Foods)

Heat the fat in a 13-inch (33 cm) or larger cast-iron pan or stockpot over medium-low heat. A drop of water will sizzle when ready.

Combine the cooked meat and veggies with the beaten egg and cheese, if using.

Submerge the wrap in a bowl of water for 3 to 5 seconds, carefully remove, and lay on a flat surface.

Load with ¼ to ⅓ cup (weight will vary) diced leftover combinations. Wrap one edge over the filling and then fold up the right and left sides and roll, ensuring little to no air remains.

Place in the pan with the hot oil. Allow to cook until the bottom edge is crisp. Turn with tongs and continue cooking and turning until fully crisp. Repeat with the remaining wraps.

YIELD: 8 to 10 eggrolls

QUICHE WITH A BROWN RICE CRUST

Eggs, nature's most perfect protein, provide a high-quality array of amino acids (all nine essential), vitamins, and other nutrients. Eggs are a good source of phosphatidylcholine and choline (a methyl donor, homocysteine regulator, and supporter of neurotransmitter synthesis). Studies suggest that the need for choline increases during pregnancy. Some research links lower levels of choline in pregnancy to risk for neural tube defects. Choose eggs that are from free-range chickens that have had a natural diet, resulting in a healthy ratio of omega-6 to omega-3 fats. As a nursing mom, you should be eating two or more eggs daily to provide Super Nutrition for your baby.

CRUST

¼ cup (40 g) brown rice

3 cups (710 ml) Souper Stock (page 45)

2 tablespoons (28 g) organic lard or ghee, divided

⅓ cup (33 g) grated raw, organic, grass-fed hard cheese (such as Parmesan)

¼ cup (40 g) chopped green onion

1 organic, pasture-raised egg white

FILLING

5 organic, pasture-raised eggs and 1 yolk

1 cup (110 g) grated raw, organic, grass-fed cheese (such as Swiss)

⅔ cup (160 ml) raw cream, coconut cream, or raw milk

Celtic sea salt to taste

½ teaspoon garlic powder

1 teaspoon minced onion

2 cups (weight varies) cooked broccoli, asparagus, spinach, or kale

Cook the rice according to the package instructions, substituting Souper Stock for the water.

Preheat the oven to 325°F (170°C, or gas mark 3). Prepare a pie pan by greasing it with 1 tablespoon (14 g) of the lard or ghee.

In a small bowl, combine the cooked rice, cheese, green onion, egg white, and remaining 1 tablespoon (14 g) fat. Press the rice mixture into the bottom of the pie plate and up the sides, making sure to cover the entire surface.

Bake the crust for 6 to 10 minutes.

Meanwhile, in a bowl, beat the eggs and egg yolk until foamy. Stir in the remaining ingredients and pour into the prepared pie shell.

Bake for 50 minutes, or until a knife inserted comes out clean.

NOTES

- Be creative! Use different vegetables and cheeses. Add cooked chicken, sausage, or bacon for flavor and tomatoes, peppers, mushrooms, and cauliflower for variety.
- Serve with a side of puréed pumpkin or sweet potato, warmed and dolloped with farm-fresh butter or ghee and cinnamon.
- You can find raw cheese at US Wellness Meats (https://grasslandbeef.com) or through realmilk.com.

YIELD: 4 to 6 servings

DRUGSTORE FORMULA DOESN'T CUT IT

Better Options Than Commercial Alternatives

Commercial formula is commonly accepted as the safest—and only—alternative to breastfeeding for infants. The nutritional, developmental, and other health benefits conferred by mom's milk are second to none, but even breastfed babies may, for a variety of reasons, be fed infant formulas at some point.

If you won't be exclusively breastfeeding, you need better options than just the commercial formulas. This chapter will provide you with several alternatives so that you can better balance your baby's nutritional needs with your time, resources, and budgetary constraints.

Note: The American Academy of Pediatrics recommends human milk first and foremost as the best source of sustenance for infants and babies, then cow's milk formula, then hydrolyzed protein formula, and only in specific situations (such as galactosemia and hereditary lactase deficiency) should soy formula be considered.

The Very Real Risks of Commercial Formula

The formula for "formula" still isn't perfected, and several risks are involved in commercial formula feeding.

UNHEALTHY INGREDIENTS

Reading the label on most formula containers might set off health-conscious warning bells, as many of the ingredients are clearly not nutritious choices: corn syrup, inflammatory oils, genetically modified foods, and synthetic nutrients.

UNACCEPTABLE SAFETY STANDARDS

In the United States, formula ingredients must only be declared Generally Recognized as Safe (GRAS) by the manufacturer. This is a category that was developed to regulate food ingredients for the general population, "*not* for infants who are a more vulnerable population," [emphasis added] as is stated in a report prepared for the FDA and Health Canada in 2004, "Infant Formula: Evaluating the Safety of New Ingredients."

LACKING IN LIVING ORGANISMS

Commercial formula lacks probiotics, prebiotics, enzymes, and the living immune cells found in mom's milk that support the gut and the immune system. Though some formula manufacturers have begun to add probiotics to formula, testing frequently proves them to be inactive and therefore of no benefit. Further, *all* commercial formulas contain glyphosate (see page 114), a chemical that destroys healthy gut flora.

Healthy gut flora is important to prevent allergies; studies show that infants with cow's milk allergy are deficient in specific good bacteria (that create butyrate) compared to infants who don't have allergies who have more good bacteria in their guts. Another study showed that the likelihood of developing an allergy to cow's milk (to hydrolyzed casein-based) formula was reduced with probiotics containing *Lactobacillus rhamnosus* GG bacteria.

WRONG SUGARS CAN HINDER DIGESTION AND BRAIN DEVELOPMENT

Lactose is the main carbohydrate source in human milk, cow's milk, and cow's milk–based formula. Lactose is the easiest sugar for your baby to digest; it breaks down into glucose and galactose, which is instrumental in brain development.

Lactose is the only sugar your infant should ingest. Mom's milk contains lactose and comes replete with lactase, the enzyme that digests lactose. Your baby makes lactase too, but still depends on some digestive help from mom's milk. Lactose-free formula exists because formula has no active enzymes to support its digestion and some babies' lactase production is insufficient. In the absence of mom's milk, lactose-containing formula is preferred, but there will be a pancreatic burden. Despite this, we still recommend lactose-containing formula, as lactose-free formula does not provide galactase, needed for your baby's brain.

Different from lactose, which releases energy steadily, soy and lactose-free formulas use other sugars (like corn syrup) that cause blood sugar and insulin spikes, followed by crashes that are disruptive to the body. Other sweeteners, like high fructose corn syrup (also found in soda), don't offer any galactose and instead break down into glucose and fructose.

COMPETING NUTRIENTS

Formula's nutrients can block each other, making the formula not as nutritious as it reads on the label. Also, adding new ingredients to formulas can change the requirements for competing nutrients. For example, iron was added to soy formula because soy's natural phytic acid blocked iron from being absorbed. Then, because non-heme iron absorption was still poor in babies fed soy formula, vitamin C was added as an attempt to improve absorption. Iron and vitamin C together then blocked both copper and zinc. Formula companies are now adding more zinc to try to compensate. Though minimum nutrient standards exist, no testing is required to ensure that all necessary nutrient levels are reached. Most often, formula manufacturers overlook such nutrient relationships. Surprisingly, the FDA does not approve infant formulas before they are put on the market.

COMPOSITION COMPARISON

According to Pediatric Clinics North America's article "Human Milk Composition: Nutrients and Bioactive Factors" (Ballard and Morrow, 2013), human milk "contains many hundreds to thousands of distinct bioactive molecules that protect against infection and inflammation and contribute to immune maturation, organ development, and healthy microbial colonization." New components are still being identified and the functionality of those components are under active investigation in many laboratories worldwide.

Of the hundreds of separate molecular compounds in mom's milk, many cannot be simulated or made synthetically.

INGREDIENTS YOU DON'T KNOW ABOUT

Mass manufacturing of commercial formula too often results in residues, pollutants, infestations, and other contaminant problems that have led to recalls.

Contaminants and Recalls

The CDC states: "Powdered infant formula is not sterile." The past few years have seen recalls of Similac varieties, Enfamil Newborn formula, and Sammy's Baby Formula (powdered). In April of 2016 the CDC warned of Cronobacter in powdered infant formula. Coronobacter bacterial infection can be fatal to infants, causing severe blood infections or meningitis. The CDC is informed of four to six infant Coronobacter infections each year, but because federal reporting of such occurrences is not required, the true number of cases is unknown. The CDC recommends that the number one way to prevent Cronobacter infection is to breastfeed.

Toxins

In 2008, one of China's infant formulas was found to have melamine contamination, sickening more than 50,000 babies and resulting in four deaths; traces were found in formula in the United States, as well, putting babies in danger of significant kidney disease. In 2009, the CDC discovered perchlorate—a toxic compound used in rocket fuel—in fifteen brands of infant formula, including the two best-selling brands.

Even the packaging isn't safe. The inside lining of formula containers often contains bisphenol A (BPA), an endocrine-disrupting toxin linked to learning disabilities and reproductive system and development changes. The European Safety Authority warns that canned commercial formula can expose infants daily to dangerous BPA. While in adults, BPA is eliminated from the body through a detoxification process in the liver, this process is underdeveloped in infants. Several studies have found levels that exceed the EPA's suggested safe limit figure. The FDA banned the use of epoxy resins in infant formula packaging, as well as BPA in baby bottles and sippy cups (July 2012), but there are

likely many other unknown toxins that persist in processed foods, including formula.

Soy formula contains additional toxic ingredients, including 10 times the manganese found in cow's milk formula (50 to 75 times that in mom's milk), as well as toxically high quantities of aluminum and fluoride. Aluminum competes with calcium for absorption. The AAP states that soy-based formula "may contribute to the reduced skeletal mineralization (osteopenia)" issues seen in preterm babies fed soy formula.

Dairy-based formula also contains soy and corn, because cows are primarily fed corn and soy. Corn and soy are high in inflammatory fats and are almost always genetically modified. Heavy use of pesticides, herbicides, and insecticides on soy and corn results in these toxins in all dairy products, including cow's milk–based infant formula. The massive doses of chemicals used on GMO foods adds to the significant toxic burden born by babies consuming infant formula based on soy or dairy. For more on pesticides and toxins, see chapter 5.

Note: Mom's milk can also contain toxins, from their own exposure and accumulation through food, proximity to commercial farms, and recent vaccinations. American moms have 760 to 1,600 times higher levels of glyphosate, which is the toxin found in the pesticide Roundup, in their milk than levels allowed in European water.

Damaged Proteins

The high-heat processing of all formulas (whether powdered or liquid) denatures proteins. This means that when exposed to high temperatures, the tertiary "3-D" molecular structure of proteins is damaged, and they lose their natural ability to function normally, potentially rendering them unfit for human consumption. When proteins are damaged in this way, they are more likely to be

DEEP DIVE INTO GMOS

It is estimated that 70% of the food sold in grocery stores in the United States contains Genetically Modified Organisms (GMOs). Approved GMO foods in the United States include varieties of corn, soy, cotton, tomato, rapeseed (canola), and potato, as well as papaya, squash, beet, alfalfa, rice, rose, flax, apple, plum, sugar beet, tobacco, and salmon. Unless you are using organic formula, your baby is consuming GMOs through dairy-based or soy-based formula. Two strains of apples have been approved by the USDA in 2015, and are sold in the Midwest, having been genetically altered to reduce enzyme content to slow down or stop bruising, spots, and food spoilage.

Research indicates that GMOs may cause genetic changes, allergies, or other serious harm to your health. There could also be unforeseen consequences, traits scientists can't test for yet, or scenarios reviewers haven't considered.

- GMO products, including maize, cotton, and soybeans, are engineered to contain their own insecticides. The mode of action of some GMO proteins is not fully understood and some of these proteins are known to be toxic to isolated human cells.

- The GMO process uses a bacterium chemically similar to anthrax, and the insecticides produced share structural similarities with ricin. Chemicals with similar structure to anthrax or ricin should be thoroughly tested.

- The Chinese have created genetically engineered low-fat pigs who are engineered to maintain their own temperature and weigh less so that "farmers" can pay less in heating and feeding costs, which means that pigs, very intelligent animals, might be kept in the cold and underfed. As yet, the FDA has not approved these GMO pigs for import or use in the United States.

- AquAdvantage Salmon, however, *has* been approved by the FDA, despite intense opposition. This genetically modified fish, which grows to market weight much faster than natural fish, is in grocery stores and restaurants already.

Lab animals show fertility problems and early signs of cancer when fed GMO foods. Consuming GMO means you're getting more toxic exposure from pesticides since those crops are sprayed directly with pesticides, herbicides, etc. Many workers who harvest the GMO plants have severe allergic reactions and experience high rates of asthma, allergies, and skin rashes. Further, mutated genes in GMO crops, when eaten, have been shown to incorporate into human cells and are suspected of creating increased immune reactions, antibiotic resistance, allergies, fertility problems, and cancer.

Many people argue that vegetarian GMOs will prevent food shortages by accelerating crop yield and extending shelf life, but we have a realistic, safe, and reasonable solution. Consuming all parts of animals, including bones for broth, marrow, and organs including liver, kidneys, tripe, and in some cases skin (as in poultry and fish), means that one food-animal would feed many, over a longer period of time. Genetic modification, genetic engineering, and genetic editing are not the path to the future, but the path to manipulating nature, taking us even further from natural, traditional, whole foods that heal and protect.

As there is no research to prove GMOs are safe and there are significant reasons for concern, we place them in our CRAP category. We are not alone in our concerns; GMO cultivation (planting) or imports are restricted or banned in 37 countries. On occasion, a country will ban the cultivation, but will import GMO feed for their animals. In that way, they are protecting the sanctity of their fields, seeds, and environment from cross-pollination. The United States, however, takes an innocent-until-proven-guilty stance, requiring no testing to prove they are safe and no labeling required for the public. In fact, Bayer, which purchased Monsanto (perhaps to more easily move underutilized GMO-related capital to the United States, where it is easier to research, approve, and sell GMOs), is moving its agricultural research division from Europe to the United States due to relaxed rules in the United States. Approvals for GMO food imports in the United States require an average of only 686 days compared to 995 days in the EU.

We're taking a shockingly large risk to unleash GMOs, and to consume them, for not much benefit, other than the revenue enjoyed by the agribusiness giants. That revenue is so attractive to the large food businesses that they dedicate millions to changing consumer perception. In fact, their lobbyists have been so successful it was recently approved to use our own U.S. taxpayer dollars to convince us. Three million dollars is being spent by the FDA on "consumer outreach and education regarding agricultural biotechnology," as reported by the *Washington Post* in 2016, targeting messages on genetically engineered food and crops, attempting to convince consumers that there are environmental, nutritional, food safety, economic, and humanitarian benefits. Do not be fooled. We urge you to take this issue seriously and to take action.

The good news is consumers have power. We can speak with our buying preferences. Dollars matter, and where you spend them makes a difference. Choose organic, and talk to your friends and family about GMO concerns. Demand non-GMO foods from your grocer. Question your legislators: should taxpayer dollars be spent to advance the agendas of agribusiness multinational companies?

This information, and so much more, is provided by the hard work and dedication of Jeffrey Smith at http://responsibletechnology.com, the Institute for Responsible Technology.

hard on the digestive system, allergenic, and can even be toxic. (Separate, but notable, pasteurization is a high-heat process.)

MISSING FATS, WRONG FATS, IMBALANCED FATS, AND DAMAGED FATS

The fat blends used in infant formulas completely lack cholesterol. Babies *require* cholesterol because it supports cell membrane function, nerve transmission, hormone creation, and brain development. The fact that mom's milk contains plenty of cholesterol and supplies nutrients that *increase* cholesterol's absorption underscores its importance.

Brain-building omega-3 fats are necessary for healthy and normal brain development. Mom's milk contains more fats and specific fatty acids than formula. To compensate, some formula manufacturers add DHA (docosahexaenoic acid) and ARA (arachidonic acid), often obtained from fermented fungus and algae, using a neurotoxic chemical solvent. These fatty acids are easily damaged by light, time, heat, pressure, and the chemical treatments to which they are exposed during processing, packaging, distribution, and storage, resulting in the added fats being oxidized, rancid, and damaged.

DEEP DIVE INTO SOY: A TROUBLEMAKER AT ALL AGES

Once promoted as a panacea of health, soy products (including tofu, soy formula, vegan cheese, veggie burgers, edamame, "vegetable" oil, and countless others) have become popular to the point that they appear in nearly every processed food, from "health" foods to factory-farmed animal products. Without even trying, the average American gets nearly 1 out of every 10 calories from soy alone—not many other single foods have such a high percentage of daily intake (except for corn and sugar)! Despite being depicted as and called a vegetable (as in veggie burgers, vegetable oil), soy is a bean (in the legume family, along with peanuts and navy, kidney, lima, string, pinto, and garbanzo beans; lentils; peas; and licorice), not a vegetable.

Soy is a health hazard, not only as a GMO, laden with pesticides, but also due to inherent digestive, nutrient, and hormonal disruptive capabilities. Studies have shown that soy can:

- Block and damage the thyroid (soy isoflavones are goitrogens and genistein reduces thyroid peroxidase); healthy thyroid function is critical for fat metabolism and energy production, and thus particular caution should be taken with babies who have congenital hypothyroidism

- Hinder protein breakdown, which can lead to malnourishment and food allergies
- Disrupt the endocrine system (glands such as the pituitary and thyroid)
- Lead to an increased risk of cancer (particularly breast cancer)
- Irritate the pancreas and digestive system, causing digestive distress
- Alter neurotransmitters, possibly leading to neurological and psychological disorders

Further, soy:

- Can cause excessive blood clotting
- Contains oxalates (most kidney stones are caused by high-oxalate foods)
- Increases the need for vitamin B12, because soy blocks B12 absorption
- Blocks mineral absorption, reducing key minerals like iron, zinc, magnesium, copper, and calcium.
- Contains excessive manganese (linked to brain damage in infants)

Soy in Infant Feeding

In addition to general concerns about soy, there are specific concerns related to soy-based infant feeding. Statistics published in 2006 in the *Environmental Health Perspectives* journal state that 1 in 4 to 5 babies in the United States and Canada are given soy formula during their first year. According to research published in *PLoS One* (2014), there is a 2.6-fold higher rate of febrile seizures (in both genders), a 2.1-fold higher rate of epilepsy diagnosis, and a 4-fold higher rate of simple partial seizures in male autistic children fed soy-based formula.

Severe GI effects from soy. The AAP reports, "Severe gastrointestinal reactions to soy protein formula have been described for greater than 30 years." Complications include severe bloody diarrhea, ulcerations, and acute and chronic inflammatory bowel disease.

Allergenic likelihood. Soy is one of the eight foods that cause 90% of food allergies. According to the National Institute of Allergy and Infectious Disease, U.S. Department of Health and Human Services, soy allergies particularly affect infants. Allergic reactions range from mild to life-threatening anaphylaxis.

Mineral deficiencies. Infants around 6 months of age have a critical need for iron and zinc. Soy-based formula contains phytates that block their absorption. Soy is an even bigger no-no for preemies. The AAP clearly warns, "Soy formulas are not recommended for preterm infants." This conclusion stems from studies showing that soy formula feeding could lead to the mineral deficiency–related disease osteopenia and other health complications.

Reproductive and hormone disruption. According to the National Institutes of Health, soy's isoflavones (phyto-, or plant-based, estrogens that mimic human estrogen) can cause "adverse effects on development." Genistein (an isoflavone in soy) has been found to trigger reproductive abnormalities, including a rare form of uterine cancer. Women who were fed soy formula as babies have been shown to have more menstrual discomfort, cycle irregularities, and uterine fibroids.

Babies fed soy formula receive daily doses of phytoestrogens that are 3,000 times more than found in mom's milk from mothers eating soy. The Weston A. Price Foundation reports that exclusively soy-fed babies have 13,000 to 22,000 times more serum estrogen compounds than do babies fed cow's milk formula.

During development, baby boys normally have a dramatic increase in testosterone during their early months. Soy's high amounts of estrogen have the potential to hinder characteristically male behaviors and normal physical development. For girls, the AAP reports that puberty is starting earlier than ever before. Animal studies suggest that this might be related to overall exposure to soy. NIH states, "Infants are more likely than adults to be vulnerable to the estrogen-like effects of the phytoestrogens in soy."

EXCEPTIONS TO THE NO-SOY RULE

Soy is not good for anyone at any age, but it's particularly bad for pregnant and nursing mothers, infants, and children. However, soy in its fully fermented form is an exception. Health benefits abound with vitamin K2 (menaquinone) and in its bacterial MK-7 form it is found in highest amounts in fermented soybeans, known as natto. Tamari soy sauce, though not a source of K2, is another form of fermented soy that is safe to use sparingly.

It is important to note that fermented soy such as natto has beneficial K2 yet it also has an increased goitrogen effect—thyroid blocking. Therefore, the benefits must be considered along with the potential negative impact to the thyroid for those who might have underactive thyroid. Consumption of soy should be limited to fermented soy only—particularly natto—or small amounts of gluten-free fermented soy sauce (e.g., tamari).

BETTER OPTIONS THAN STORE-BOUGHT FORMULAS

Donated Human Milk

Human milk is far better for human babies than the milk of another species. But we're far more socially accepting of using a cow's "donor" milk rather than a human's donated milk.

The United Nations Children's Fund (UNICEF) and the World Health Organization say that the best food for a baby who isn't fed his mother's milk is human milk from another healthy mother. Additionally, both the American College of Pediatricians and the Centers for Disease Control recommend pasteurized human donor milk if mother's own milk is unavailable. Benefits include fewer infections, higher intelligence scores, better development, and healthier babies.

Better even though it's pasteurized. The human milk obtained through most of these milk banks requires a prescription and the milk is pasteurized. This minimizes harm to beneficial bioactive components, while ensuring that bacterial contaminants are inactivated. It kills all pathogens, but it also damages and reduces effectiveness of some of the beneficial components of the milk. Even pasteurized, though, this option is better than commercial formula.

Pasteurized Donor Human Milk (pDHM) is considered to be the best replacement for mom's milk and is preferred by professionals to nourish preterm and at-risk infants. As such, pDHM has earned its nickname "liquid gold," as it is life-saving for premature and at-risk infants. Many milk banks are established to support neonatal intensive care units (NICUs). There are heart-breaking yet inspiring stories of moms who, after the loss of their own baby, will continue to pump and provide precious milk to help others in need. One article in the *Journal of Pediatrics* (January 2017) stated, "The primary benefit of pDHM may be the avoidance of formula." Even though pDHM is the best replacement, because of pasteurization, numerous components in mom's

Super Nutrition Food Categorizations for 0 to 6 Months	
SUPER POWER	**PURE**
• Mom's milk • Mom's friend's or relative's milk	• Human donated/donor milk (depending on pasteurization methods) • Homemade formula
OKAY	**CRAP**
• Enriched formula	• Commercial formula, especially soy based

milk that are thought to reduce sepsis, chronic lung disease, and neurodevelopmental benefit are reduced or absent in pasteurized donor human milk, and results show that pDHM does not demonstrate a reduction in those specific health risks. Truly, mom's milk is best; next best is mom's friend's or relative's milk, then pDHM.

Where would I get human donated milk? First, consider the milk of family members, friends, play group moms, or neighbors. Collect pumped milk from one or more lactating, healthy mamas that can be fed immediately or frozen. It is our experience that nursing mothers are sympathetic to other moms who experience difficulties with nursing, and they are likely very willing to help a baby in need. It doesn't hurt to ask.

The Human Milk-Banking Association of North America, www.hmbana.org, is a nonprofit association of donor human milk banks. Donors are not paid for their milk, reducing the potential of donors providing inaccurate health information or diluting or tampering with milk. Although the number of milk banks is growing, more awareness of this lifesaving practice is needed. Currently only 40% of the NICUs in the United States have access to DHM, and in other countries (UK, Brazil, and Germany) where milk banks are integrated with hospitals, it may be difficult to receive milk outside the hospital.

There is a rise in community-based milk sharing, a global network supporting families called Eats on Feets (http://www.eatsonfeets.org), a play on Meals on Wheels. They have established four pillars of safe breast milk sharing: informed choice, donor screening, safe handling, and home pasteurization. These organizations are allowing more access to health-giving mom's milk for all. Information is abundant online and they are increasing the popularity and social acceptance of sharing one of the greatest health advantages for our children, human milk.

Homemade Formula

Both the AAP and the FDA discourage homemade formula because, *if done carelessly or incorrectly*, it can lead to potentially dangerous nutrient deficiencies, particularly if cow's milk or goat's milk *alone* is given. Although we acknowledge the risk, we also know that correctly made homemade formula is *by far* the best alternative when mom's milk or donated milk are not viable options.

In making homemade formula, the FDA cautions "great care" is required and "safety should be a prime concern." If a scientifically based recipe meeting all nutritional needs is not followed to the letter, potential problems could be "very serious and range from severe nutritional imbalances to unsafe products that can harm infants." However, don't let this discourage you. There are potentially more serious risks involved with commercial formula than homemade. *You* are the best person to ensure your baby's safety and well-being. Increasing numbers of parents are making homemade formula, resulting in many health benefits (over commercial formula) for their babies. Look for an online or local community to exchange tips and experiences.

If you are unable to pay vigilant attention to making homemade formula, then we urge you *not* to do it, but rather enrich conventional formula (see page 79). If, however, you are motivated and willing to learn, and will be cautious, careful, and fastidious in taking on this responsibility, then homemade formula will provide a PURE food option for your baby.

Practical Feeding Tips for Newborns

When making homemade formula for your baby, you are taking steps to provide ultimate nourishment second only to mom's milk. The bottle-feeding experience can be improved, as well, by applying some guidelines and practical considerations.

Close contact during feeding. Human contact is important for baby's health. Fed by bottle or breast, your baby should be cuddled, preferably with skin-to-skin contact, eye contact, and emotional interaction. This sense of security will ease any discomfort and provide reassurance, relaxation, and peace of mind so that your baby can focus on swallowing, digesting, and utilizing nutrients optimally. Skin-to-skin contact has also been shown to promote newborn emotional connection, energy consumption, glucose levels, respiration, and brain development. Holding your baby during bottle-feeding (as opposed to propped bottles) will support optimal hormonal levels (including cortisol, oxytocin, and vasopressin), reduce stress and pain, and improve digestion and social development.

On cue. Begin to prepare your baby's bottle when she shows the first signs of being ready to eat (wakefulness, alertness, rooting or sucking motions, or bringing hands to mouth). It is especially important to heed early hunger cues due to the additional preparation time needed for a bottle.

How much to offer? The standard "rule" for full-term babies is about 1 ounce (28 ml) per hour. Thus, if your baby sleeps 3 hours and wakes hungry, expect to feed him 3 ounces (90 ml). As he grows, your baby will take more. If he sucks the bottle dry, put an additional ½ ounce (14 ml) in the next bottle at the next feeding and keep increasing by ½ ounce (14 ml) until a little remains. Always plan on wasting a little at the end of each feeding. If he drinks it all, it wasn't enough. Never force your baby to finish a bottle.

Bottle and nipple preparation. Before first use, wash bottles and nipples with soap and then boil for 5 minutes to reduce chemicals. For routine sterilization, either wash bottles and nipples in a dishwasher that reaches 180°F (82°C) or boil for 10 minutes.

Water matters. The American Dental Association supports not using water with fluoride for babies' formula "to reduce the risk of fluorosis." Well water should also be filtered and routinely tested for toxins and bacteria. "City" tap or municipal water also has "water treatment by-products," including chlorine and various chemicals like arsenic and perchlorate, which further contribute to nutrient deficiencies and the mental decline of future generations.

An ideal water to use is reverse osmosis (RO)–filtered water because it removes fluoride, chlorine, and other toxic materials. The concern with RO water is that both good and bad minerals are removed; with the removal of healthful minerals (calcium and magnesium), the water's pH can be acidic. You can add minerals back in through a colloidal or ionic mineral supplement. There are some alkaline waters for sale at health food stores. Ideally, water will be of a neutral or slightly alkaline pH.

FORMULA RECIPES THAT PROVIDE OPTIMAL NOURISHMENT FOR GROWING BABIES

The three homemade formulas in this chapter were developed by (and are used with the permission of) members of the Weston A. Price Foundation (WAPF), including doctors, scientists, and other nutrition and traditional-foods experts, such as Mary Enig, Ph.D.; they provide the healthiest ingredients for your baby when it comes to formula.

Breast Milk and Homemade Formulas Nutrient Comparison Chart

The Weston A. Price Foundation (WAPF) has compiled a nutrient-comparison chart, reprinted here with permission, for their three formula recipes and mom's milk. WAPF notes, "These nutrient comparison tables were derived from standard food nutrient tables and do not take into account the wide variation in nutrient levels that can occur in both human and animal milk, depending on diet and environment." For more information, visit www.westonaprice.org. Select "order materials" and choose the "Breast Milk/ Formula Flier." It is based on 36 ounces (1 L).

In order to make your own formula, you'll need to do some legwork to get all the ingredients, but that's the hardest part. Once you've gotten everything and made formula once, it gets easier.

The following recipes are printed verbatim from the Weston A. Price Foundation. Do not vary *at all* from these recipes.

Breast Milk and Homemade Formulas Nutrient Comparison Chart per 36 ounces (1 Liter)

NUTRIENT	BREAST MILK	COW'S MILK FORMULA	GOAT'S MILK FORMULA	LIVER-BASED FORMULA
Calories	766	856	890	682
Protein	11.3 g	18 g	18 g	15 g
Carbohydrates	76 g	79 g	77 g	69 g
Total fat	48 g	52 g	54 g	36 g
Saturated fat	22 g	28 g	30 g	16 g
Monounsaturated fat	18 g	16 g	16 g	12 g
Polyunsaturated fat	5.5 g	5.6 g	5.7 g	5.6 g
Omega-3 fatty acids	0.58 g	1.3 g	1.2 g	1.0 g
Omega-6 fatty acids	4.4 g	4.2 g	4.4 g	4.5 g
Cholesterol	153 mg	137 mg	166 mg	227 mg
Vitamin A*	946 IU	5,000 IU	5,000 IU	20,000 IU
Thiamin (B1)	0.15 mg	1.05 mg	1.1 mg	0.19 mg
Riboflavin (B2)	0.4 mg	1.2 mg	1.2 mg	1.9 mg
Niacin (B3)	1.9 mg	2.5 mg	4.4 mg	14.2 mg
Vitamin B6	0.12 mg	0.51 mg	0.60 mg	0.65 mg
Vitamin B12	0.5 mcg	1.9 mcg	2.8 mcg	39 mcg
Folate	57 mcg	236 mcg	284 mcg	159 mcg
Vitamin C	55 mg	57 mg	59 mg	62 mg
Vitamin D	480 IU	450 IU	525 IU	460 IU
Vitamin E**	9.9 mg	6.2 mg	4.7 mg	4.9 mg
Calcium	355 mg	532 mg	548 mg	NA***
Copper	0.57 mg	0.38 mg	0.58 mg	1.9 mg
Iron	0.33 mg	1.4 mg	2.2 mg	5.4 mg
Magnesium	37.4 mg	91.3 mg	96.1 mg	34.5 mg
Manganese	0.29 mg	0.034 mg	0.12 mg	0.24 mg
Phosphorus	151 mg	616 mg	729 mg	344 mg
Potassium	560 mg	949 mg	1228 mg	750 mg
Selenium	18.8 mcg	15.4 mcg	18.7 mcg	31.1 mcg
Sodium	186 mg	308 mg	320 mg	NA***
Zinc	1.9 mg	2.8 mg	2.7 mg	2.5 mg

* Vitamin A levels in human milk will depend on the diet of the mother. Nursing mothers eating vitamin A–rich foods such as cod liver oil will have much higher levels of vitamin A in their milk. Commercial formulas contain about 2,400 IU vitamin A per 800 calories.

** Vitamin E values are derived from commercial vegetable oils. The vitamin E levels for homemade formulas will be higher if good-quality, expeller-expressed oils are used.

*** Calcium and sodium values for homemade broth are not available.

RAW MILK BABY FORMULA

Our milk-based formula takes account of the fact that human milk is richer in whey, lactose, vitamin C, niacin, and long-chain polyunsaturated fatty acids compared to cow's milk but is leaner in milk protein. The addition of gelatin to cow's milk formula will make it more digestible. Use only truly expeller-expressed oils in the formula recipes; otherwise, they may lack vitamin E.

The ideal milk for baby formula, if he cannot be breastfed, is clean, whole raw milk from old-fashioned cows, certified free of disease, that feed on green pasture. For sources of good-quality milk, see www.realmilk.com or contact a local chapter of the Weston A. Price Foundation.

If the only choice available to you is commercial milk, we, and WAPF, recommend the meat-based formula (page 78) as your best alternative.

Starting no earlier than 4 months, depending on your baby's ready-to-eat signs, babies fed only commercial formula benefit from earlier feeding of nutritious first foods (see chapter 4). Those getting mom's milk are better off delaying first foods.

1⅞ cups (440 ml) filtered water

2 teaspoons gelatin

4 tablespoons (52 g) lactose

2 teaspoons virgin coconut oil

¼ teaspoon high-vitamin butter oil, *optional*, but highly recommended

2 cups (475 ml) whole, raw milk from organic, grass-fed Jersey cows

¼ cup (60 ml) liquid whey (Do NOT use powdered whey from the store or whey from making cheese. See the recipe for Homemade Whey from Store-Bought Dairy, page 80.)

¼ teaspoon *Bifidobacterium* powder

2 tablespoons (28 ml) good-quality raw or pasteurized cream (not ultrapasteurized) (Use 4 tablespoons [60 ml] if the milk is from Holstein cows.)

½ teaspoon unflavored, fermented cod liver oil or 1 teaspoon cod liver oil ("Salty cod" is the one you want, but plain or antioxidant-free cod liver oil can alternatively be used.)

1 teaspoon expeller sunflower oil

1 teaspoon organic, extra-virgin olive oil (in a dark bottle)

2 teaspoons Frontier nutritional yeast flakes

¼ teaspoon acerola powder

MOM-TO-MOM

WHY FRESH, RAW MILK?
Using raw, grass-fed, unpasteurized milk from a trusted, clean dairy, with a few tweaks necessary to make it optimally nutritious for your baby, results in an infant formula that is much closer to human milk than anything else could possibly be. See chapter 1 for more on raw milk.

If using tap water from the faucet, use only cold water to make formula. Never use warm water from the faucet, as warm water leaches lead solder from pipes. To further minimize lead in the water, always flush out the pipes each morning by running the faucet for 30 seconds before making formula. Alternatively, you can use mineral-rich spring water.

Note: Reverse osmosis (RO) water is great for limiting toxins, but requires remineralization to retain neutral to slightly alkaline pH.

Fill a 2-cup (475 ml) glass measuring cup with the filtered water and remove 2 tablespoons (28 ml) (this will give you 1⅞ cups [440 ml] water). Pour about half the water into a (nonaluminum, preferably stainless steel) saucepan and put over medium heat.

Add the gelatin and lactose and let dissolve, stirring occasionally. Once dissolved, remove the saucepan from the heat and add the rest of the water to cool it slightly.

Stir in the coconut oil and butter oil, if using, until melted.

Put the remaining ingredients in a glass blender. Add the water mixture and blend for about 3 seconds until everything is combined.

Place the formula in very clean glass bottles or a glass jar and refrigerate.

Before giving to baby, warm a glass bottle in a pan of hot water or a bottle warmer. (Never heat formula in a microwave oven!)

NOTES

- Mixed formula ideally should be made daily and can last 24 hours in the refrigerator. It can be left at room temperature for a few hours.
- Though formula should be made fresh daily, freezing it in individual 4- to 9-ounce (120 to 250 ml) serving sizes is fine. It may be stored in the freezer for 2 to 3 months. After defrosting, add ¼ teaspoon of probiotics per day. Be aware that after defrosting, the cream's consistency may change. If frozen, warm formula by setting jars in warm water to thaw.
- Add probiotics only after heated milk has cooled.

YIELD: 36 ounces (1 L)

VARIATION: GOAT'S MILK FORMULA

For some infants, the goat's milk protein is easier to digest than that found in cow's milk. WAPF instructs: Although goat milk is rich in fat, it must be used with caution in infant feeding as it lacks folic acid and is low in vitamin B12, both of which are essential to the growth and development of the infant. Inclusion of nutritional yeast to provide folic acid is essential.

To compensate for low levels of vitamin B12, if preparing the raw milk–based formula (at left) with goat's milk, add 2 teaspoons finely grated organic raw chicken liver, frozen for a minimum of 14 days, to the batch of formula. Be sure to begin egg-yolk feeding at 4 months.

NOTES

- Mixed formula ideally should be made daily and can last 24 hours in the refrigerator. It can be left at room temperature for a few hours.
- Liver can, alternatively, be boiled in Souper Stock (page 45).

LIVER-BASED FORMULA

The following recipe is for meat-based formula, which is considered hypoallergenic as it does not contain milk proteins from goats or cows. It is extremely important to include coconut oil in this formula, as it is the only ingredient that provides the special medium-chain saturated fats found in mother's milk. As with the milk-based formula, all oils should be truly expeller-expressed.

2 ounces (55 g) organic liver, cut into small pieces

3¾ cups (887 ml) Souper Stock (page 45)

5 tablespoons (65 g) lactose

¼ teaspoon *Bifidobacterium infantis* powder

¼ cup (60 ml) homemade liquid whey (see recipe for Homemade Whey from Store-Bought Dairy, page 80)

1 tablespoon (14 g) coconut oil

½ teaspoon unflavored high-vitamin or high-vitamin fermented cod liver oil, or 1 teaspoon regular cod liver oil (Use only recommended brands.)

1 teaspoon unrefined sunflower oil

2 teaspoons extra-virgin olive oil (in a dark bottle)

¼ teaspoon acerola powder

YIELD: About 36 ounces (1 L)

Simmer the liver gently in the broth until the meat is cooked through.

Liquefy using a handheld blender or in a food processor.

When the liver broth has cooled, stir in the remaining ingredients. Store in a clean glass or stainless steel container in the refrigerator.

To serve, stir the formula well and pour 6 to 8 ounces (175 to 235 ml) into a clean glass bottle. Attach a clean nipple and set in a pan of simmering water until the formula is warm but not hot to the touch. Shake well and feed to baby. (Never heat formula in a microwave!)

NOTES

⊙ Lactose, coconut oil, unrefined sunflower oil, extra-virgin olive oil, and acerola powder are available from Radiant Life (see Resources, page 260). Refer to Resources for other ingredients and supplies to make this formula.

⊙ Beef or lamb liver are the best early options. When your baby is older than 6 months, chicken or buffalo liver can be substituted.

While it's best to make formula fresh each day, once mixed, these formulas can be stored in the refrigerator for 2 to 3 days. Formulas can be left at room temperature for a few hours; however, once formula (even commercial) touches your baby's lips, it should be discarded within 1 hour.

"ENRICHED" COMMERCIAL, ORGANIC, COW'S MILK FORMULA

If it's not possible to make any of the formulas (exactly as stated) in the previous recipes, your next best option is to "improve" commercial formula by adding a few key ingredients that will make it more digestible and more nutritious for your baby. This formula can also be used as a stopgap in emergencies or when the ingredients for homemade formula are unavailable. WAPF has formulated this recipe, reprinted with permission, for improving upon commercial formula. When purchasing an off-the-shelf commercial formula, look for an all organic, coconut oil-containing formula that contains lactose. Any company that provides assurances relative to the protection of DHA and ARA (easily damaged and rancified fatty acids) and probiotics (which can often die due to storage techniques) is preferred.

1 cup (235 ml) milk-based powdered formula*

3⅝ cups (29 ounces, or 852 ml) filtered water

1 large farm-fresh, organic, pastured egg yolk

½ teaspoon unflavored high-vitamin or high-vitamin fermented cod liver oil, or 1 teaspoon regular cod liver oil (Use only recommended brands of cod liver oil, as noted in Resources, page 260.)

Place all ingredients in a blender or food processor and blend thoroughly. Store in a very clean glass jar in the refrigerator.

To serve, put 6 to 8 ounces (175 to 235 ml) of formula in a clean glass bottle. Attach a clean nipple to the bottle and set in a pan of simmering water until the formula is warm but not hot to the touch. Gently shake well and feed to baby. (Never heat formula in a microwave oven!)

NOTES

- Mixed formula should ideally be made daily and can last 24 hours in the refrigerator. It can be left at room temperature for a few hours.
- You can opt to first boil the egg as descried on page 99 for 3½ minutes (especially if you have low-quality eggs that are not free range and organic).
- For this recipe, it is essential that the egg yolk be the absolute highest quality.

YIELD:
About 35 ounces (1 L)

HOMEMADE WHEY FROM STORE-BOUGHT DAIRY

Homemade whey is easy to make from good-quality plain yogurt or from raw or cultured milk. See other whey recipes, page 106, or use this recipe from the excellent nutritional and culinary resource *Nourishing Traditions* by Sally Fallon.

2 quarts (1.9 L) organic plain yogurt

or

2 quarts (1.9 L) organic raw or cultured milk

You will need a large strainer that rests over a bowl.

If you are using yogurt, place 2 quarts (1.9 L) in the strainer lined with a tea towel. Cover with a plate and leave at room temperature overnight. The whey will drip out into the bowl. Place the whey in clean glass jars and store in the refrigerator.

If you are using raw or cultured milk, place 2 quarts (1.9 L) of the milk in a glass container and leave at room temperature for 2 to 4 days until the milk separates into curds and whey. Pour into the strainer lined with a tea towel and cover with a plate. Leave at room temperature overnight. The whey will drip out into the bowl. Store in clean glass jars in the refrigerator.

NOTES

- See Resources, page 260, for ingredients and supplies for homemade whey.
- Homemade Mom's Milk Whey, page 106, is a great option custom-designed to be optimally nutritious for your baby.

YIELD:
About 5 cups (1.2 L)

FROM FAKE FLAKES TO REAL FOOD

Meeting Nutrient Needs with First Foods

(6 TO 8 MONTHS)

Many parents are eager for their babies to try new foods as soon as they're able. But we urge you not to rush it. It's important that your baby is ready—developmentally, physically, and digestively—before you begin feeding him first foods. By waiting, you'll be ensuring better digestion and intestinal health.

Developing Digestion

If you feed your baby solid foods before he can digest them, he won't benefit from their nutrients. In the early months of life, his pancreas doesn't make many of its own digestive enzymes. Also, he is still building up friendly flora (probiotics) along his intestinal wall, which will eventually make digestive enzymes too. He relies on mom's milk (or formula) as a source of "predigested" food and digestive enzymes.

Enzymes are the "keys" that unlock the bonds in food molecules, allowing them to be broken down into their building blocks for digestion. It is the building blocks that are usable by his body for growth, biochemical processes, and energy. If foods aren't fully digested into their elemental building blocks, they simply aren't useful in growth and development, and undigested or partially digested foods are the impetus for food-allergy development.

Even worse, undigested foods can cause health troubles, including food allergies, digestive distress (pain and irregular bowel movements), autoimmune conditions (like diabetes and celiac disease), toxic overload, overstimulation of the immune system, nutrient deficiencies, inflammation, cognitive complications resulting from neurotoxicity, and other health problems.

Critical Nutrients at 6 Months

At around 6 months, your baby will have some very particular nutrient needs that are best met by introducing solid foods, though his digestive system isn't yet fully developed (a feat reached around 2 years of age). His caloric intake needs are growing, too. He needs to supplement mom's milk or formula, which should remain his primary source of nutrition.

Babies accumulate plenty of iron and zinc while in utero, but by 6 months old, much of these stores has been used up. Mom's milk offers absorbable iron and zinc, but often not enough to meet the monumental nutrient demands of rapid growth between 6 and 12 months.

IRONCLAD BLOOD AND BRAIN ARE BEST.
Babies need iron for normal neurologic development. In babies who don't get enough, doctors find irreversible cognitive and motor damage. *The scariest part is that even if iron is replenished, the damage may be permanent* and *irreversible.* Iron-deficiency anemia is tragically common; your best course of action is to include foods rich in absorbable iron—that is, animal foods—in your baby's diet on a regular basis. Note that while pediatricians check for anemia through bloodwork, studies show damage to the brain can occur *before* low iron shows up on such tests.

DEEP DIVE INTO AVOIDING FOOD ALLERGIES

Each year there are 30,000 emergency room visits and 150 deaths for allergy-related anaphylaxis to food allergens in the United States. One in 12 children in America have food allergies (a 50% increase between 1997 and 2011), and of this food-allergic population, 1 in 6 have experienced anaphylaxis (life-threatening symptom of allergen exposure).

For some time, it was believed that these allergies were developing due to early introduction of allergenic foods. This has been refuted and in 2017, the National Institute of Allergy and Infectious Diseases (NIAID) (with the help of the American Academy of Allergy, Asthma & Immunology [AAAAI] and 24 other organizations) stated that early peanut introduction (between 4 and 6 months) for "high risk" infants is recommended. (High risk was defined as infants with severe eczema, egg allergy, or both; the second highest risk group was characterized by mild to moderate eczema, with the lowest risk group showing no signs of eczema.) Any introduction of allergenic foods to high-risk babies should be done under a doctor's supervision.

We caution that legume proteins, such as soy and peanut, are hard to digest at such a young age, and, rather, we believe that nourishment, development, and maintenance of the gut along with choosing and ensuring the digestibility of foods will prevent food allergies, along with other specific aspects of our Super Nutrition program.

In fact, food allergies come from 1) undigested protein and 2) "open," or "leaky," gut walls. In the early months, your baby has openings in his intestinal lining—a normal state called "open" gut. This allows antibodies (protective proteins produced by the immune system) from mom's milk to pass through his gut wall easily into his bloodstream, where they can protect him. Later, these openings in the gut wall will close to keep whole and partial proteins from crossing his gut lining into his bloodstream. When this happens, his immune system is maturing, and doesn't require as much help from mom's antibodies. This is when solid foods can be added, between 6 and 9 months of age.

However, if food proteins are introduced while the gut lining is still "open," undigested foods/proteins can get into the bloodstream through the gut wall's openings, where the immune system views them as invaders and attacks. The food is then put into the immune "memory bank," so the next time that undigested food makes it into the bloodstream, the immune system will attack again, but with more force. This is a food allergy. Common symptoms of food allergies in babies are colic, abdominal distention, gas, spitting up, rash/eczema/hives, congestion, swollen mouth, cough, and/or difficulty breathing.

Food intolerances exist when a food's corresponding digestive enzyme isn't made by the body. For example, lactose intolerance exists in people who do not make lactase, the enzyme that breaks down milk sugar (lactose). Children make lactase up to an average age between 4 and 7, and many continue to produce lactase as adults. (Raw milk contains lactase, which is why it is digestible even by those with a lactase-enzyme deficiency.) Babies can develop both food allergies and food intolerances when solid foods are introduced too soon.

Eight foods are required by law in the United States (Food Allergen Labeling and Consumer Protection Act of 2004) to be specifically labeled for allergy awareness. They are: milk, eggs, fish, crustacean shellfish, tree nuts, peanuts, wheat, and soybeans. *Note:* The FDA does not regulate poultry, most meat, certain egg products, and most alcoholic beverages, but does regulate food labeling for all other food. These 8 account for 90% of allergic reaction.

Introduce new foods one at a time. If you notice or sense your baby is reacting, stop any new food. It may by that your baby's digestive system is not yet ready for it. Try it again in a month or two; if he reacts again it might be a food allergy and you'll want to avoid that food until his gut can further mature. Ensure you are serving him the most digestible form of each food to avoid development of long-lasting food allergies. If there is any sign of difficulty in breathing or swelling of the tongue, call 911 for emergency aid immediately.

Prevention of allergies, in short, stems from introducing foods when digestive and immune capabilities are mature enough to handle solid foods, introducing foods that are packed with enzymes (naturally occurring in very specific raw foods or through fermentation), including sources of gut-protective probiotics, and avoiding highly allergenic foods (soy, pasteurized casein, gluten in grains, etc.).

Additional protection is provided by raw dairy. As published in *Current Opinion in Gastroenterology*, "Maternal and infant consumption of unprocessed cow's milk has repeatedly been associated with protection from childhood asthma and allergies." And, studies have shown that children raised on raw milk have half the risk of developing hay fever. In September 2011, Reuters Health reported on a study published in the *Journal of Allergy and Clinical Immunology*, announcing: "Kids who drink raw milk have less asthma, allergies." The GABRIELA study of more than 8,000 children showed that raw milk consumption was inversely related to asthma, atopy (allergies), and hay fever! (No such benefit is conferred by pasteurized dairy.)

ZINC IS THE LINK FOR IMMUNITY, GROWTH, AND LEARNING. Zinc contributes to the health of your baby's immune system, digestive capabilities and intestinal mucosal lining, skin health, bone health, physical activity, growth, and cognitive development. If levels of zinc are too low, growth will slow, acid reflux and diarrheal disease can be more common, immune function will be impaired, and eczema may develop.

According to a study in the *American Journal of Clinical Nutrition*, zinc stimulates healthier bones, and low zinc is shown to stunt growth. Animal foods have the highest zinc content in the most absorbable form; therefore, it is no surprise that vegan children, especially boys, tend to be shorter. In fact, according to current research, having enough zinc from birth through age 5 can metabolically program your child's height.

Higher zinc levels might also lead to improved cognitive development. In a randomized, controlled study, cited by the *Journal of Pediatric Gastroenterology and Nutrition*, researchers compared introducing meat or iron-fortified cereal for exclusively breastfed infants. Results showed the meat-fed infants had substantially higher zinc levels than did cereal-fed infants, had a higher rate of brain growth, and demonstrated likely trends "toward other developmental advantages."

WATCH FOR BLOCKERS. Some foods contain iron and zinc *blockers*, which decrease the availability of these minerals. Blocker-containing foods include soy, grains, legumes, tea, and antacids (given for reflux).

DON'T RELY ON PLANT OR "FORTIFIED" FOODS. "Fortified" foods and plant sources have a form of iron called *non-heme*, which has a very low absorption rate—so even if you eat plenty, your body can use only a small fraction (about 4%) of it, and plant-based zinc absorption is also poor. Plus, when an inorganic-form iron is added as a means to "fortify" certain foods, it further blocks zinc absorption! (However, natural forms of animal-based iron do not block zinc.)

ANIMAL FOODS ARE THE BETTER CHOICE TO ENSURE CRITICAL NUTRIENT NEEDS ARE MET. The highly absorbable form of iron, called heme iron, is absorbed at 37% to 40%, and it is only found in animal foods. Easily absorbable zinc, too, is found only in animal foods. The animal foods' versions of these nutrients are so well absorbed that even if they are consumed with blockers, much can still be absorbed.

A HIGH-FAT DIET IS CRITICAL FOR BABIES

Saturated fat and cholesterol are absolutely *necessary* in a baby's diet! In fact, mom's milk has a caloric makeup of 50% to 60% fat, over half of which is saturated fat, with hefty doses of cholesterol. One of the early enzymes your baby produces is lipase, which enables him to absorb critical fats. Additionally, your mammary glands secrete a substance that ensures your baby best absorbs cholesterol from your milk. It might interest you to know that your baby's rapidly growing brain is 60% fat—being built by fats in his diet.

Science supports that babies need most of their calories from fats in the first year, and U.S. governing agencies such as the Food and Drug Administration (FDA) and American Academy of Pediatrics (AAP) agree that babies should not be on any kind of fat-restrictive diet for at least the first 2 years. (In fact, experts in the United Kingdom recommend higher-fat diets for the first 5 years, during which time 80% of brain growth occurs.)

THE TRUTH ABOUT SATURATED FAT AND CHOLESTEROL. Eating cholesterol doesn't clog arteries; rather, it serves to help your body by covering damaged areas, such as inflamed arteries. Arterial damage isn't from the Band-Aid (cholesterol) but stems from root causes of inflammation (such as dietary sugar and rancid, inflammatory fats) that actually *cause* the damage to arteries. A low-cholesterol diet forces your body to work harder to make more.

Cholesterol is necessary to aid in important metabolic functions, and is also:

- An antioxidant that fights lipid peroxidation (brain tissue degradation)

- Important for cellular, nervous system, and brain communication

- Needed to make hormones and for vitamin D metabolism

- Necessary to protect the nervous system and brain

- Critical for proper digestive health, intestinal wall integrity, and leaky gut prevention

Fats, meanwhile, have also been falsely blamed for poor health. Four main classes of fats exist: saturated, monounsaturated, polyunsaturated, and trans fats. The first three each serve natural health benefits and offer unique fatty acids required for optimal health. Thus, it is good to include each in your diet, including saturated fats. Trans fats, however, have a man-altered molecular structure that is harmful to health and must be avoided.

Saturated fat is necessary for, among other things:

- Cell structure and integrity of all the cell walls that make up your baby's body
- Absorption and use of fat-soluble nutrients (vitamins E and K1, beta-carotene, lycopene, zeaxanthin, lutein, CoQ10, etc.)
- Ensuring mineral activators (vitamins A, D3, K2) get assimilated and therefore minerals are absorbed
- Proper brain development
- Building nervous system communication components
- Absorption, conversion, and use of key nutrients
- Unique source of short-, medium-, and long-chain fatty acids (including MCTs)
- Feeding the heart
- Supporting health of lung tissue
- Ensuring bone strength and health
- As a source of antimicrobial and antiviral agents in the digestive tract
- *Reducing* your need for as many omega-3s to do important inflammatory work because saturated fats make omega-3s more efficient

Contemporary First Foods Challenge Your Baby's Health

Most pediatricians, family members, and friends recommend first foods to be rice cereal, yellow then green vegetables, then fruits and other grains, like oatmeal. Yet, these common "baby" foods don't contain enough of the specific nutrients that babies at this age absolutely require.

Furthermore, they don't provide adequate energy and are rough on babies' still-developing digestive systems.

BABIES ARE FUNCTIONALLY GRAIN INTOLERANT

Your baby's body is not ready to digest grains. He doesn't yet make enzymes to digest the necessary carbohydrates. Between 8 months and 1 year of age, babies begin making useful amounts of amylase (and until then, mom's milk supplies some, but a more complete set of carbohydrate enzymes won't be present until approximately 3 years of age). Some carbohydrates (like fiber) can never be digested by humans, since we don't ever produce the right enzymes; thus, we must rely on our friendly intestinal flora (probiotics) to digest them for us.

So babies (prior to toddlerhood) are functionally grain intolerant. They don't effectively make starch-digesting enzymes. As they have not yet built up sufficient beneficial bacterial colonies, babies are also fiber intolerant.

RICE CEREAL ISN'T RIGHT

Rice cereal flakes are a refined grain, stripped of natural nutrients. Such cereal is hardly more than sugar to your baby's body. Iron-fortified cereal offers only a 4% absorption rate for iron, and that form of iron makes zinc absorption worse. Rice flakes don't provide the critical nutrients and calories your baby needs.

In general, whole grains are better than refined. But in addition to being very hard to digest, they block critical mineral absorption. According to a study in the *Journal of Nutrition*, low levels of zinc are most often found in diets that have a lot of whole grains (wheat, corn, rice, oatmeal) and legumes, like soy. Such foods contain an antinutrient called phytic acid, which blocks not only zinc but also calcium, magnesium, and iron from being absorbed.

FRUITS AND VEGGIES ALONE WON'T DO

The other common choice for initial feeding is fruits and veggies. Although these foods do have antioxidants and other nutrients, they contain significantly fewer amino acids, vitamins, and critical minerals than do animal-based foods and therefore shouldn't be relied on solely to provide optimal, protective nutrition for babies. Also, as low-calorie foods, they're a poor choice for the *increasing* caloric demands of growing babies.

Traditional First Foods Offer Super Nutrition

Ideally, your baby's first foods will contain protein, fat, cholesterol, and plenty of absorbable iron and zinc—just like mom's milk! Such nutrients are found all together in only one type of food: animal-sourced. *Nutrition in Pediatrics: Basic Science, Clinical Applications* states, "Incorporating animal source foods . . . is often the only way to supply . . . [adequate] nutrients through natural foods." The AAP likewise recommends animal foods as first foods and suggests "puréed meats as good first foods because they contain ample protein, iron, and zinc."

But despite research and the AAP's recommendations, parents are still most often instructed to feed their babies rice cereal, fruits, and veggies as first foods.

HEALTH BENEFITS OF ANIMAL FOODS AS FIRST FOODS

Animal foods are higher in age-critical minerals than are grains, fruits, and veggies. Research from the *Journal of Nutrition* confirms, "Animal source foods can provide a variety of micronutrients that are difficult to obtain in adequate quantities from plant source foods alone." Animal foods are so nutrient dense, they require *fewer* calories to provide rich nutrition compared to plant foods. In addition, they contain the following.

Proteins and amino acids.

Proteins are chains of amino acids. These structures can be denatured (damaged) by heat, such as pasteurization. Nine amino acids are considered essential to humans because the human body cannot synthesize them. Foods that have these nine, in the right levels and amounts for optimal absorption and use, are called "complete" proteins.

Essential amino acids.

Your baby needs not only these 9 *essential* amino acids from his diet but also an additional 3, because babies and children can't synthesize cysteine, tyrosine, and arginine well. These are necessary in making heart, lung, and intestinal tissue, other muscles, antibodies, hormones, neurotransmitters, enzymes, bones, ligaments, tendons, cell membranes, and more! All 12 are found together in ideal proportions in animal foods, but *not* in plant foods. The quantity and variety of non-animal foods required to make sure all amino acids are available at the levels required by your baby's accelerated growth would exceed his capacity to eat and digest them (in terms of quantity of food required).

Unique nutrients not found elsewhere.

Animal foods, not plants, supply taurine, carnitine, CoQ10, vitamin A (retinol), B12, conjugated linoleic acid (CLA), butyric acid, carnosine, long-chain super-unsaturated fatty acids (AA, EPA, and DHA), cholesterol, and vitamin D3. A plant-based diet has *none* of these health-giving nutrients, and has less of most amino acids.

Bioavailable form of nutrients.

Animal foods also offer nutrients, like B6, iron, zinc, magnesium, copper, and calcium, in a way that is most easily absorbed and used by your baby, as opposed to the plant-based versions that lack sufficient bioavailability and therefore require conversion (resulting in much less of that nutrient being available to the body for benefit and use than what was consumed).

Antioxidants.

Animal foods supply powerful antioxidants, including superoxide dismutase, alpha-lipoic acid, carnosine, carnitine, glutathione, arginine, selenium, omega-3 fatty acids, and CoQ10. Antioxidants serve to stop the damage to cells and organs throughout the body caused by free radicals, and can also protect against environmental toxins, pollution, radiation, medication, and cigarette smoke. Oxidative stress occurs when too many damaging toxins accumulate, and the body doesn't have sufficient antioxidants to combat them. Reducing oxidative stress can prevent, lessen, or improve disease conditions.

ANIMAL FOODS ALLOW FOR LOWER CALORIES TO MEET NUTRIENT NEEDS.

Animal foods provide more nutrition in fewer calories and significantly smaller quantities. Per calorie, animal foods (particularly organ meats) are more nutrient dense than plant foods, so much so that to compete nutritionally, you'd have to spend all day eating plant-based foods. Your baby may only take a few bites per meal; therefore, packing a powerhouse of nutrient richness in each bite is important.

ANIMAL FOODS ARE BETTER DIGESTED.

The first readily available digestive enzymes your baby makes are those for digesting protein, fat, and cholesterol. Meanwhile, your baby is missing the enzyme amylase, which digests starch.

MAKE IT A LIVER AND SWISS; HOLD THE SUPERSIZED BROWN RICE AND BROCCOLI

To meet the RDA for calcium (1,000 mg) you can eat 50 cups (9.8 kg) of brown rice (10,800 calories), 100 ounces (2.8 kg) of tofu (1,500 calories), 3 cups (435 g) of almonds (2,225 calories), or just under 4 ounces (112 g) of Swiss cheese (482 calories).

The RDA for iron (8 mg for men, higher for women) can be met by 20 cups (600 g) of spinach (140 calories), 25 cups (1.8 kg) of broccoli (775 calories), 5 cups (775 g) of edamame (945 calories), or only 5 ounces (140 g) of liver (240 calories).

Feed Animal Foods for Strong, Smart, and Social Children

Numerous studies reveal that animal-source foods are integral to adequate growth, musculature, activity levels, and cognitive development in growing children. Specifically, a study reported in the *Journal of Nutrition* found that children eating meat had 80% greater increase in upper-arm muscle. The meat-eating group also scored higher on intelligence tests, which has been corroborated by several studies to date. The meat eaters were also "more active on the playground, more talkative and playful, and showed more leadership skills."

Further research demonstrates that children eating animal foods also grow stronger bones and are taller and even leaner. Milk and meat significantly increase height, making children grow faster, and can even correct stunted growth.

Comparing Nutrient Richness of Produce to Animal Foods				
NUTRIENT	APPLE (100 G)	CARROTS (100 G)	RED MEAT (100 G)	BEEF LIVER (100 G)
Calcium	3.0 mg	3.3 mg	11.0 mg	11.0 mg
Phosphorus	6.0 mg	31.0 mg	140.0 mg	476.0 mg
Magnesium	4.8 mg	6.2 mg	15.0 mg	18.0 mg
Potassium	139.0 mg	222.0 mg	370.0 mg	380.0 mg
Iron	0.1 mg	0.6 mg	3.3 mg	8.8 mg
Zinc	0.05 mg	0.3 mg	4.4 mg	4.0 mg
Copper	0.04 mg	0.08 mg	0.18 mg	12.0 mg
Vitamin A	None	None	40 IU	53,400 IU
Vitamin D	None	None	Trace	19 IU
Vitamin E	0.37 mg	0.11 mg	1.7 mg	0.63 mg
Vitamin C	7.0 mg	6.0 mg	None	27.0 mg
Thiamine	0.03 mg	0.05 mg	0.05 mg	0.26 mg
Riboflavin	0.02 mg	0.05 mg	0.20 mg	4.19 mg
Niacin	0.10 mg	0.60 mg	4.0 mg	16.5 mg
Pantothenic acid	0.11 mg	0.19 mg	0.42 mg	8.8 mg
Vitamin B6	0.03 mg	0.10 mg	0.07 mg	0.73 mg
Folic acid	8.0 mcg	24.0 mcg	4.0 mcg	145.0 mcg
Biotin	None	0.42 mcg	2.8 mcg	96.0 mcg
Vitamin B12	None	None	1.84 mcg	111.3 mcg

Reprinted with permission from Chris Kresser's nutrition information blog, https://chriskresser.com.

Note: 100 grams is just under 1 cup of apple (1 cup = 125 grams), under a cup of carrots (1 cup = 128 grams), and is about 3.5 ounces (1 ounce = 28 grams) of ground beef or liver.

VEGETARIANISM ISN'T THE "HEALTHIEST"

But aren't diets based on plant foods the best? The answer is emphatically no! A vegetarian diet is *not* nutritionally adequate for your growing baby. This being said, vegetables do play a significant role in your child's diet and we strongly recommend they be given at every meal.

Plant-based diets have mineral blockers, enzyme inhibitors, protein digestion blockers, poorly absorbed minerals, and digestive irritants; are often inflammatory; tend to be high in sugars; and are nearly always deficient in nutrients critical for healthy growth and development.

Diets free of animal foods have low levels of, or less available, nutrients, including:

- Vitamin A and D (fat-soluble activators), resulting in poor mineral usage

- Body-ready essential fatty acids (AA, EPA, and DHA, necessary for brain and cognitive development, immune support, and anti-inflammation)

- CoQ10 (necessary for fighting free radicals; aids the cardiovascular system)

- Cholesterol (necessary for brain development and cellular communication)

- Body-ready B6 (necessary for several conversions of happiness neurotransmitters and aids in detoxification pathways; also helps B12 and folic acid convert harmful homocysteine— a risk factor in cardiovascular disease)

- B12 (soy consumption further increases the need for B12)

- Body-ready zinc and iron

- Amino acids carnitine and carnosine and taurine (an amino sulphonic acid, necessary for fighting free radicals and inflammation; helpful for cardiovascular health, fat metabolism, treating depression, and cellular energy production; and protective of the eyes and the brain)

According to the *American Journal of Clinical Nutrition*, "Iron and zinc are . . . minerals of greatest concern when considering the nutritional value of vegetarian diets. With elimination of meat and increased intake of phytate-containing legumes (the nutrient-blocking effects of phytates are discussed on page 225) and whole grains, the absorption of both iron and zinc is lower with vegetarian than with nonvegetarian diets."

Several researchers have found that animal foods are so important in ensuring proper growth and height, strength, and intelligence, they argue that it is unhealthy *not* to include animal foods in children's diets. After extensive research on the criticality of animal foods in children's health, Lindsay Allen, Ph.D., professor at the University of California, Davis, states, "There's absolutely no question that it's unethical for parents to bring up their children as strict vegans." Consequently, for vegan or vegetarian nursing mothers, we strongly recommend supplementation and beginning your baby on animal-based foods between 4 and 6 months old.

We respect the beliefs of many vegetarians and are certainly appalled by the cruel and unjust treatment of factory-farmed animals. By procuring animal foods from pastured farms, you will both be supporting animal breeding and raising that is humane, healthiest, and least stressful for the animals *and* be providing foods with superior nutritional content.

BRAIN-BUILDING OMEGA 3S: ANIMAL FOODS GIVE THE GIFT OF BRAIN DEVELOPMENT

Omega-3s are well known for their critical anti-inflammatory and antioxidant capacities; they are the good guys in the fight against inflammation and toxins. In *The Omega-3 Connection*, Andrew M. Stoll, M.D. says, "Without large amounts of DHA, the long-chain omega-3 commonly found in fish, we might not have evolved [as a species, from primate] at all." Further, DHA deficiency causes significant negative impact on brain development in infants, beginning in the last trimester and first year of life, most critically. Both DHA and EPA are omega-3s, and are found only in animal foods.

Consuming plant-based sources of omega-3s does not produce best brain development for two reasons: 1) plant-based omega-3s are difficult for the human body to convert to the bioavailable brain-building forms: DHA and EPA, and 2) the amount of fats in plants is so low you wouldn't be able to eat the quantity of plant foods you'd need for adequate brain building. See the table below for details.

CHOOSE PASTURED ANIMAL FOODS

We *strongly* advocate procuring animal foods for your baby from pastured sources, where the animals are not confined, but free to roam, get sunlight (activating their vitamin D), and eat their natural diet (grass, clover, bark, foliage,

FOOD	TYPE	TYPICAL SERVING SIZE	IN GRAMS	ALA	DHA
Salmon	ALA/EPA/DHA	3.5 ounces	99 grams	0.867 gram	1.5 grams
Cod liver oil	EPA/DHA	1 tablespoon	13.5 grams	negligible	1.5 grams
Walnuts	ALA	1 ounce	28 grams	2.5 grams	0.1 gram (converted)
Flaxseed	ALA	1 tablespoon	13.5 grams	6 grams	0.24 gram (converted)
Grape leaves	ALA	1 cup	14 grams	0.12 gram	0.005 gram (converted)

To get the same amount of DHA in 3.5 ounces of salmon (206 calories) or 1 tablespoon of cod liver oil (135 calories), one would have to consume:

- 15 ounces of walnuts (2,775 calories, ~210 walnut halves)
- 6.25 tablespoons of flaxseed (750 calories)
- 300 cups of grape leaves (3,900 calories)

(Note: Per Weston A. Price Foundation, children 3 months to 12 years are best served with a dose of cod liver oil that provides DHA and EPA omega-3s.)

bugs, small animals, etc.) based on their instincts. Pastured animal foods have a higher EPA and DHA content than do animal foods fed soy and corn, not to mention an overall higher nutrient profile, including minerals, vitamin E, and beta-carotene.

Real Foods Offer Super Nutrition

Real foods are in whole form, grown naturally, preferably local and seasonal, vine ripened, recently harvested, raw and not pasteurized, pastured and not factory farmed, and without additional chemicals. With the recipes that follow, we'll take you far from fake flakes to real, nourishing, digestible foods for your baby.

PRACTICAL FEEDING TIPS AT THIS AGE

Most medical and scientific experts recommend feeding babies only mom's milk, or formula, until age 6 months. The World Health Organization and the AAP state not to introduce *any* solids before 4 months of age.

Before 6 months your baby:

- Doesn't make enzymes needed to digest first foods

- Has underdeveloped kidneys, not yet ready to handle waste from solids

- Is lacking sufficient beneficial bacteria required for digestion

- Has an "open" gut (see page 84)

Super Nutrition Food Categorizations for 6 to 8 Months	
SUPER POWER	**PURE**
• Mom's milk • Grated frozen liver • Soft-boiled egg yolks (warm but runny) from organic, pasture-raised hens • Marrow, from grass-fed organic bones • Souper Stock (page 45), from pasture-raised organic animals • High-quality cod liver oil	• Soft-boiled, organic egg yolks • Organic soup stock–braised vegetables • Organic peeled, stewed, puréed fruits with fat • Organic banana • Store-bought, organic bone broth • Organic avocado • Grass-fed, organic meats
OKAY	**CRAP**
• Organic baby food jars (stage 1 to 2) • Nonorganic avocado • Nonorganic banana • Nonorganic vegetables (washed, prepared in stock)	• Teething biscuits • Rice flakes • Brown rice flakes • Oatmeal or other grains • Soy anything • Nonorganic baby food • Juice (organic and nonorganic)

For these reasons, it is best to wait until at least 6 months of age *and* until your baby shows all the below signs that he's ready for solids.

- Sits unassisted or with minimal support
- Opens his mouth when something comes toward it
- Can indicate disinterest in further feeding by turning his head away
- Closes lips around a spoon when introduced to mouth
- Seems interested when others are eating, watching food travel from plate to mouth

Continuing to nurse provides additional digestive support as he begins to digest solids.

Very first meals. First meals can simply be offered between regular feeding times or after a shortened nursing session or a smaller bottle. You don't want your baby to be starving and frustrated, nor too full, to be interested.

Consistency and texture. "Solid" foods shouldn't be solid. Use mom's milk, formula (chapter 3), or Souper Stock (page 45) to thin foods to the right consistency for your child. Adjust the thickness and texture as your baby seems ready.

Water? Extra water to drink isn't necessary during 6 to 8 months of age, as your baby should get enough fluid from mom's milk or formula. If it is hot and others are thirsty, 1 or 2 ounces (28 to 60 ml) of water can be offered from a cup or bottle. Your baby should be nursing about 6 to 8 times a day or drinking 28 to 32 ounces (805 to 950 ml) a day of homemade or enriched formula to ensure adequate hydration.

What's enough? Let your baby be the guide in what and how much he wants to eat. When he turns away or is no longer interested, the meal is over.

Slow introduction. Introduce new foods every 3 to 4 days and give new foods earlier in the day (rather than before bedtime) so that you can observe any possible allergic reactions.

Pattern, not schedule. Establish a repeatable pattern, such as nursing upon waking, mid-morning meal, nursing before afternoon nap, dinner with the family, and nursing before bed. Following a *pattern*, as opposed to randomly feeding or being on a strict, clock-based *schedule*, will give your baby a critical sense of meal reliability, while still allowing some flexibility in your day. This also allows for adaptability as your baby changes and grows.

Recipes for Real Foods Offering Optimal Nourishment

For the initial foods, we present "very first foods" that adequately aid digestion, provide optimal nutrition, and should not cause intestinal distress. After a few weeks of these foods, you can introduce additional "first foods."

PATTERN	FIRST HALF OF 6TH MONTH
Early AM	Mom's milk/homemade formula (upon waking)
Midmorning	Very first foods
Midday	Mom's milk
Afternoon	Mom's milk (before nap)
Evening	Mom's milk
Nighttime	Mom's milk (before bed)

PATTERN	SECOND HALF OF 6TH MONTH
Early AM	Mom's milk/homemade formula
Midmorning	New foods (every 3 to 4 days) + already-introduced food
Midday	Mom's milk/homemade formula
Afternoon	Mom's milk/homemade formula (before nap)
Evening	Already-introduced food
Nighttime	Mom's milk/homemade formula (before bed)

FEEDING VERY-FIRST FOODS AT 6 MONTHS

As you begin your baby on food, continue nursing or feeding homemade or enriched formula (see chapter 3). Provide regular feedings, as before, with a shortened session at the new "meal" times. In the first few weeks of feeding, you can introduce soft-boiled egg yolk, puréed liver, Souper Stock (page 45), and some minimal cooked, puréed meat with the stock. For a complete list of acceptable foods at this age, see the Food Introduction Timeline on page 255.

And don't worry, babies instinctually love uber-nutritious liver.

FEEDING FIRST FOODS AT 6½ MONTHS

In the second few weeks of feeding, you can introduce avocado, banana, and poultry-based Souper Stock. Continue the already-introduced foods from the previous two weeks, possibly adding some small amounts of additional braised meat with the Souper Stock.

FEEDING FIRST FOODS AT AROUND 7 MONTHS

After about 4 weeks of feeding (around 7 months old), tropical fruits and lacto-fermented and braised or baked vegetables with healthy fats can be added to the menu. For super-digestive nutrition, sweet potatoes and taro can be lacto-fermented (see page 104).

VERY FIRST FOOD: LIVER

Vegetarianism and veganism are popular diets these days. Babies, however, are designed to consume animal foods, from mom's milk to other easy-to-digest, body-ready, and bioavailable nutrient-supplying animal foods.

That being said, we only support the highest quality animal foods, where animals were pasture raised, able to forage, follow their instincts, and live a natural, low-stress, low-pain life. Factory farming and the industrialization of agricultural farming stands in stark opposition of this. It is for these reasons that many conscientious individuals embrace vegetarianism or veganism, to take a stand against the mistreatment of farm and food animals. We agree with this. However, avoiding animal foods doesn't make the same impact as does only eating pasture-raised animal foods and never eating animal foods that aren't supporting the humane animal treatment desired.

LIVER

Grated liver from a trusted, grass-fed, organic source, is a great first food. Grated liver should be frozen for at least 14 days.

2 ounces (55 g) raw liver (grated if frozen, or finely minced if refrigerated)

Very little liver is needed for a super nutrition boost—start with just ½ to 1 teaspoon. Serve liver raw (most nutritious) or cooked in Souper Stock (page 45).

If you're headed over to a friend's house for dinner, bring frozen, puréed meat in a glass container with a few frozen Souper Stock cubes. Heat up a pan of water and place the container inside. When liquefied, taste for temperature, and you've got your baby's dinner.

YIELD: 1 serving

Regenetarians, a term coined by David Bronner, a long-term vegetarian turned regenetarian, are vegans or vegetarians who never eat factory-farmed meat or dairy products, but will consume *strictly* only grass-fed beef, grass-fed dairy, and other grass-fed or pastured products. As Lierre Keith instructs in *The Vegetarian Myth*, life of any kind cannot survive without the loss of other life; she refers to the circle of life, in which plants grow in soil, which feed herbivores, herbivores feed omnivores and carnivores, and those animals then die, and their bones and blood feed the soil, which feeds the plants. . . . Such is the food chain and circle of life.

LIVER PATE

Providing a small taste of coconut oil or lard with previously introduced foods is prudent, as is providing liver and egg yolk (page 99) separately a few times. When all ingredients have been sampled and well tolerated by your baby, you can create this great and healthful pâté.

2 ounces (55 g) raw liver (grated if frozen, or finely minced if refrigerated)

1 tablespoon (14 g) coconut oil or (13 g) lard

2 tablespoon (28 g) soft-boiled egg yolk (see page 99)

2 tablespoons (28 ml) Souper Stock (page 45)

Sauté the liver in coconut oil over low heat for 1 to 2 minutes—the liver should be a pinkish brown when done. Take off the heat and mash the liver into the egg yolk and thin with the stock to the desired consistency. Bullet blenders or the chopper attachment that come with some hand blenders work great for puréeing these small amounts.

Serving Options: Mix the liver into mom's milk (or with other foods as you add them) for a fortifying, nutritionally superior meal. For more early baby-feeding information, including using grated liver for your baby, visit www.westonaprice.org and enter "Nourishing a Growing Baby" in the search engine.

NOTES

⊙ Due to the high quantity of vitamin A found in liver, limit your baby to either 1 chicken liver or 1 ounce (28 g) of beef/calf liver every other day; or 10 to 15 grams of liver (⅓ to ½ ounce) per day on average, particularly if you're providing cod liver oil.

⊙ Contrary to commonly held beliefs, healthy liver does not store toxins but rather processes and converts toxins so they can be excreted. A fatty liver from a sick animal, however, *will* contain toxins, since toxins are stored in fatty tissue, whereas healthy livers are lean.

⊙ As noted on the Weston Price Foundation website, we should consume liver from healthy animals—cattle, lamb, buffalo, hogs, chickens, turkeys, ducks, and geese. The best choice is liver from animals that spend their lives outdoors and on pasture. If such a premier food is not available, the next choice is organic liver.

⊙ If you can't get clean liver, another option is to add powdered, desiccated liver to your baby's meals or mix with mom's milk or formula. Find grass-fed, desiccated liver capsules at www.radiantlifecatalog.com. Six capsules is equivalent to 1 ounce (28 g) of liver.

YIELD: 1 serving

VERY FIRST FOOD: SOFT-BOILED EGG YOLK

Mom's milk and egg yolks provide the "perfect protein" for babies, containing an ideal suite of vitamins, minerals, and amino acids, along with the enzymes to help break them down.

Why serve egg yolks soft-boiled? Animal foods are very rich in heat-sensitive enzymes, but overcooking destroys them, reducing their digestibility and making the food more allergenic. Also, cooking the yolk until firm makes it dry and chalky, and your baby won't swallow it as easily as a warm, runny yolk.

1 farm-fresh, organic, pastured egg

Pinch (less than ⅛ teaspoon) of Celtic sea salt

NOTE

⊙ Eggs are one of the more allergenic foods. If your baby develops a rash around his/her mouth or vomits after eating egg yolk, your baby is not ready for eggs. Reintroduce egg yolk in a month. For most, a little more maturity is all that is needed. But for some, true allergies persist. See Deep Dive into Avoiding Food Allergies on page 84. If your baby reacts to any food with mouth/tongue swelling or difficulty breathing, call 911 immediately.

YIELD: 1 egg yolk

In a small saucepan, bring water to a boil. Using a spoon, slip the egg into the boiling water. Cook the egg for 3½ to 4 minutes.

Remove the egg from the water with a spoon and drop it into a bowl to crack it. When the egg is open, peel away some white, which is semihard. The yolk should slip out in a malleable ball. Scoop up the yolk with a spoon and put it into a different small bowl, leaving all the white behind.

The yolk should be warm and soft, not firm or "dry." Add sea salt to supply additional trace minerals and improve the taste (see discussion of salt in chapter 6). Spoon-feed it to your baby.

DOES THE KIND OF EGG MATTER?

Eggs from pastured chickens on a local farm have as much inflammation-fighting omega-3s as wild-caught salmon, and more vitamin A, more beta-carotene, and more brain-building long-chain fatty acids that support mental development and sharp vision. On the contrary, soy- and corn-fed hens in captivity (the source of most eggs) are high in un-heart-healthy omega-6 fats.

Choosing the highest-quality, organic, *pasture-raised*, freshest eggs will substantially decrease the already-low chances of salmonella contamination and provide 30% to 40% higher DHA, an omega-3 fatty acid recognized for its benefits in infant cognitive development and functioning.

MASHED AVOCADO

Avocados are a fabulous source of monounsaturated fats and contain the enzyme lipase, which predigests the avocado's fat as it ripens—great for your baby's developing digestive system. Choose a soft avocado with dark brown skin.

1 avocado

Mom's milk or homemade formula, *optional*

Slice the avocado in half all the way around; then, holding each half in your hands, twist the halves apart. Cut away any brown spots.

Place a peeled quarter (or less) in a bowl and mash with a fork. Add mom's milk or homemade formula (see chapter 3) to thin, if necessary.

Store the part that "held on" to the pit—it will keep better with the pit in. Cut the remaining half in another half and peel it. Store the other quarter.

YIELD: ½ to ¾ cup (115 to 172 g)

VARIATION: MASHED BANANA

Bananas' high enzyme content means that they can digest themselves; thus, there's less work for your baby's digestive system to do. Bananas also contain fructooligosaccharides, which are food for the good bacteria in your gut. Choose organic, brown-spotted bananas—they taste the sweetest and are the easiest to digest.

¼ banana

Mom's milk or homemade formula, *optional*

Mash ¼ peeled banana with a fork and thin with mom's milk or homemade formula (see chapter 3), if necessary.

YIELD: 1 serving

For day care, thaw frozen cubes of puréed meats and broth overnight in the refrigerator. Day cares can reheat them or other individual servings of food you prepare, but insist that they do not put them in the microwave! Avocado and banana can also be served at day care from frozen after at-home preparation, or fresh.

VARIATION: TROPICAL FRUITS

At 7 to 8 months, tropical fruits such as passion fruit, guava, papaya, pineapple, kiwi, and cantaloupe can be introduced (you should wait until at least 8 months for mangoes). They are enzyme rich and when ripe are close to predigested for your baby. Predigested foods tax the pancreas less, allowing certain enzymes to serve the immune cells better and faster.

Assorted tropical fruit

Mom's milk or homemade formula, *optional*

Peel and mash the fruit, leaving more soft lumps depending on your baby's readiness to spoon feed, or chop these fresh, ripe fruits into small pieces for finger food.

YIELD: ½ to 1 cup (75 to 150 g)

NOTES

- Pineapple is very sweet and should not be given too often or in large quantities.
- When giving your baby kiwi, cut out the white central core.

IRON-RICH ORGAN PURÉE

Organ meats have a wide range of health benefits, including high concentrations of bioavailable forms of vital nutrients such as zinc, iron, and B vitamins, alongside specialty nutrients that are difficult to obtain from other foods: Heart, for example, is the best food source of B vitamins, heme iron, copper, CoQ10, phosphorus, and selenium; kidney contains an incredible amount of vitamin B12, folate (vitamin B9), retinol (vitamin A), niacin (vitamin B3), pantothenic acid (vitamin B5), and zinc; and liver provides more nutrients bite for bite than any other food and is particularly rich in choline, vitamin B12, folate (vitamin B9), and retinol (vitamin A).

4 ounces (113 g) kidney from grass-fed animals

4 ounces (113 g) liver from grass-fed animals

4 ounces (113 g) heart from grass-fed animals

1 tablespoon (14 g) lard or coconut oil (for browning meat)

½ to 1 cup (120 to 235 ml) Souper Stock (page 45)

To prepare the kidneys, slice in half and cut out the fatty white cores. For the liver and heart, remove any membranes. Finely slice the organ meats.

Heat 1 tablespoon (14 g) of fat in a skillet over low heat, add the meat, and brown it. The inside can be slightly pink.

Alternatively, simmer for 5 to 8 minutes in Souper Stock until the meat is tender.

After using either method to cook the meat, cool it completely.

For babies 6 to 7 months: Purée to a smooth consistency, adding Souper Stock or mom's milk for the right consistency. As your baby ages, gradually reduce the amount of liquid to allow more texture and thickness over time.

For babies 8 to 9 months: Serve chopped as a finger food.

NOTES

⊙ Your baby will only need a few teaspoons (20 g) a day for all the benefits this Super Nutrition POWER food provides. Also, this purée can be added to other foods.

⊙ Freeze the organ purée in an ice cube tray for perfect size meals. Purée can be added to other recipes that use ground beef or other ground meats.

⊙ Serve with Radiant Roots (page 104) or other vegetables for a balanced baby meal.

YIELD:
1¼ cups (300 g) purée,
or 1¾ (200 g) chopped

COD LIVER OIL

In 2011, the AAP journal, *Pediatrics*, reported on the importance of DHA (an essential omega-3 fatty acid as found in cod liver oil) for infants and its critical role in reducing infant morbidity (deaths)! Cod liver oil (CLO) not only provides DHA, but also has a super combination of the special fat-soluble vitamins A (retinol) and D3 (necessary for utilizing minerals), as well as inflammation-fighting fatty acids. DHA supports the nervous system and cellular communication, as well as assisting in the colonization of probiotics in the gut.

Vitamin K2, critical for bone and dental health, can also be found in butter or ghee from grass-fed animals or supplemented as drops. Dr. Weston Price found the combination of fat-soluble vitamins A (retinol, not beta-carotene), D3, and K2 were a remarkable blend of healing nutrients that restored health in sick children.

DOSING

½ to 1 teaspoon high-quality cod liver oil, starting with smaller doses and graduating to 1 teaspoon

Administration: It is of the utmost importance that you either mix it in pumped breast milk or formula or give gently by spoon. *Never* squirt oil into your baby's mouth since oil aspiration is very dangerous. Unless mixed in breast milk or formula, don't give CLO before sleep; never give oil to a child who is screaming or fighting; and avoid giving oil to a baby who frequently spits up. Keep babies upright for 15 to 30 minutes after giving them oil.

NOTES

- Give CLO particularly on days your baby is not consuming liver or fish roe.
- If you are breastfeeding and taking CLO yourself, your baby will not need supplemental CLO. However, if your baby already has a 3C condition, such as eczema, then giving additional to your baby is recommended.
- If you are making homemade formula (see chapter 3), the correct amount of CLO is already within the formula.

RADIANT ROOTS

Starchy root vegetables are a great way to obtain fiber and nutrients along with some complex carbs important for growing children and are known for being "slower-burning carbs." According to many large studies, like one that appeared in the *European Journal of Clinical Nutrition* in 2012, higher root vegetable intake is even associated with a reduced risk for diabetes. We presume this is because root vegetables contain fiber and nutrients and hopefully displace simpler starches such as refined flour, chips, and fast food.

¾ to 1 pound (340 to 455 g) taro or sweet potato

½ tablespoon Celtic sea salt

1 tablespoon (28 ml) whey (see page 80)

Mom's milk or homemade formula, marrow, and coconut oil, *optional*, for serving

YIELD:
4 to 6 baby servings

Preheat the oven to 325°F (170°C, gas mark 3).

Puncture the taro or sweet potato with a fork and bake for 1½ hours (or until soft). Once cool, peel. Add the salt and whey to the sweet potato or taro and mash.

Place the mashed tuber in a glass bowl and cover. Leave for 24 hours on the counter and then move to a glass container and store in the refrigerator.

Thin to the appropriate consistency with mom's milk or homemade formula (see chapter 3) and then mix with marrow or coconut oil.

NOTES

⊙ Lacto-fermented root vegetables will last at least 1 to 2 weeks in the refrigerator.

⊙ Carrot, radish, or beet can be substituted for sweet potato or taro.

INGREDIENT SPOTLIGHT: TARO

Along with sweet potatoes, taro is a great option for introducing lacto-fermented foods (see Mom-to-Mom sidebar at right) into your baby's diet because it is soft and starchy.

Hawaiian poi is a staple and common baby food made from fermented taro corms. According to the USDA, "Taro is good for people allergic to milk or cereals and can be consumed by children who are sensitive to milk (Roth and et.al., 1967) . . . taro flour and other products have been used for infant formulae in the United States and have formed an important constituent of proprietary canned baby foods." Compared to grains, taro is lower in phytic acid, but higher in oxalates (which are higher in taro roots that remain in the ground for longer periods of time). Taro can be cooked well (to combat the acridity, which can cause itchiness in the mouth and throat if not cooked well) and served without being lacto-fermented, though introduction to lacto-fermentation is important relative to digestibility and nutritional enhancement.

MOM-TO-MOM

Lacto-fermented foods aid digestion, provide enzymes, and offer increased nutrients, in addition to being a natural source of probiotics. Fermented or cultured food often needs a "starter" or catalyst for the fermentation process. Lacto-fermentation typically uses whey as the starter.

Sometimes called pickling, lacto-fermentation provides many nutritionally beneficial factors all at once. Fermentation is the process of good bacteria breaking down natural sugars in foods. This amazing process neutralizes antinutrients, increases enzymes, greatly increases nutrient content, produces even more good bacteria, and literally predigests food. For centuries, foods were preserved via fermentation.

Lactobacillus, the bacteria that causes pickling, is the most pervasive and ubiquitous good bacteria known. It is in the air we breathe, the surfaces we touch, and the foods we eat. It is a common probiotic supplement—you'll see several strains that begin with *L.* (such as *L. acidophilus*). The *L.* stands for *Lactobacillus*.

Second to pickles, sauerkraut is probably the best known lacto-fermented food, though in some Asian cultures, kimchi is common. Cabbage, water, and salt, along with the lacto-bacteria, can "create" sauerkraut through the lacto-fermentation process.

CURDS AND WHEY: THE MOMMY WAY

Whey is a wonderful constituent of milk, its quality based on the bovine diet (grass-fed, ideally) and living conditions (pasture-raised, hopefully), and contains three amino acids that are uniquely used by the body to make glutathione, a master detoxifier and powerful antioxidant, critical for good health. Cysteine, glycine, and glutamate are rarely found in such perfect combination and condition (they are damaged by pasteurization and heat treatment), making whey from raw milk the perfect recipe for fighting inflammation, toxins, cancer, oxidative stress, and much more.

HOMEMADE MOM'S MILK WHEY

Mom's-milk whey is actually the best option for making lacto-fermented foods for your baby. If you express your milk (even just 3 ounces [90 ml]) and allow it to sit at room temperature (or optionally in the refrigerator) for approximately 1 to 2 days in a clean, sealed container, the milk will separate into a cream layer with yellow liquid beneath (whey). Cool in the refrigerator so the cream "firms up" and remove the cream layer (which can be mixed with fruits as a custom "dessert" for your baby). The remaining yellow liquid is whey and can be used to lacto-ferment vegetables for your baby. It's just another way to provide the natural goodness of your milk! Homemade whey can last 2 to 3 months in the refrigerator.

Not much is needed, just a few teaspoons (10 ml) of whey to lacto-ferment the small servings of root vegetables. For example, if you have only 2 teaspoons of whey, just use ½ to ¾ cup (5½ ounces or 152 g) of cooked root. (You can use your milk in other recipes, too, as it is definitely a super food for your baby!)

NOTE

- While your milk is best to create custom whey for your baby, you can elect to use bovine, sheep, goat, or camel milk that is raw, organic, pasture-fed, and from a trusted dairy to create whey for its health and digestive benefits.

HOMEMADE RAW DAIRY WHEY

Aside from mom's milk for your baby, generally, the best lacto-fermentation "starter" is whey from grass-fed, raw (unpasteurized) cow's milk or yogurt. Otherwise, you can procure whey directly from a pasture-based farm cooperative. In most cases, if raw milk products are not available, whey can be made from organic whole-milk yogurt in a process similar to what follows.

Whey is rich in calcium, phosphorus, and potassium (a blood pressure–regulating nutrient), and is a good source of zinc, magnesium, and selenium, as well as vitamins B2, B5, and B6.

1 pint (475 ml) raw milk or raw yogurt

Curds and whey can be made from raw milk or raw yogurt that has separated. Raw milk can be used up to one month and raw yogurt up to 3 months. Allow the sealed container of milk or yogurt to sit out at room temperature for a few days. It will separate into whey (the yellow liquid you often see on top of yogurt) and milk solids (curds).

Pour the separated dairy through several layers of cheesecloth or a coffee filter lining a mesh strainer. The whey will filter through, and the curds will be captured over the course of 16 to 24 hours.

Curds will peel easily off the cheesecloth or filter and will vary in color from white to pale yellow.

Whey lasts 6 months in the refrigerator, sealed in a clean container. It can also be frozen and thawed for use.

Curds can be stored in the refrigerator for 1 month. Curds can be used in recipes as a much healthier substitute for store-bought cream cheese or to mix with fruit for a treat. See Raw Cheese Blintzes on page 237. It even makes super creamy cheese cake. Spoon curds into date halves for a great finger food dessert or snack.

ALLAYING COMMON FEARS. When *raw* dairy (human, cow, or goat) "sits out" at room temperature, wonderful and healthy things happen. Its probiotics and enzymes set to work. Enzymes predigest the sugars in the milk, probiotics multiply (making the cultured dairy or lacto-fermented end-product richer in enzymes and probiotics), and they increase the overall antioxidant and nutrient content. Lactic acid, which helps digestion, is also produced. Different than pasteurized dairy, which sours if left out of the refrigerator for too long, raw dairy's nutrition is enhanced by a day or two at room temperature. (And don't worry about making whey during the warmer months— hotter temps actually speed up the process.) We do caution, however, that when preparing whey, ensure that your hands, containers, and surfaces are clean so as to avoid pathogenic bacterial contamination.

NOTES

⊙ Other options for lacto-fermentation starters are:
  » Homemade Mom's Milk Whey (see opposite)
  » Pasteurized dairy
  » Celtic sea salt (1 tablespoon or 15 g)
  » Culture starter (see Resources, page 260).
  » If your family has a history of 3C conditions, Homemade Mom's Milk Whey is the best option.

⊙ Do not feed raw yogurt or cow's milk (raw or pasteurized) to your baby until 9 months, but the whey from raw dairy can be used to lacto-ferment foods that your baby can eat now.

YIELD:
1¼ cups (295 ml) whey and
¾ cup (165 g) curd

MARROW AND MASH

Marrow has long been a delicacy, even for early Paleolithic man, according to anthropological and archaeological evidence. More recently, it has fallen out of favor, as have other organ and offal dishes, despite their nutrition benefits. You can still find marrow at upscale restaurants, including French and Middle Eastern eateries. Theories abound about the benefits of marrow, from postulating that its absence in modern diets may contribute to blood and marrow diseases such as leukemia to brain-oxidation protection capabilities—though more tests are needed to be conclusive. Marrow is particularly delicious and usually more palatable for those unused to organ meats as staples, providing unique benefits coveted by humans for millennia.

½ pound (225 g) marrow bones

1 to 2 tablespoons (14 to 28 g) coconut oil (or other cooking fat, see Fabulous Fats, page 38)

½ pound (225 g) dark meat poultry

¼ teaspoon Celtic sea salt

¼ cup (28 g) finely chopped cooked carrots

¼ cup (56 g) mashed cooked sweet potato

Preheat the oven to 425°F (220°C, or gas mark 7).

Place the marrow bones on a stainless steel cookie sheet (if oblong, the cut side goes up).

Bake for 20 to 25 minutes, until the edges bubble and the marrow easily separates from the bone. *Note:* If the bones are frozen, this will likely take 45 minutes.

Carefully scoop the marrow from the hot bones either with a spoon or a small butter knife.

While the marrow bones are cooking, heat the coconut oil in a cast-iron or stainless skillet over medium heat. Add the dark meat poultry and sea salt, cooking through for about 15 to 20 minutes, stirring frequently.

Mix the marrow, poultry, carrots, and sweet potato into a delicious and nutritious marrow and mash.

Optionally, add other age-appropriate herbs and spices for more flavor and antioxidant benefits. See the Allowable Foods list on page 255.

YIELD: 1½ cups (338 g)

INGREDIENT SPOTLIGHT: BONE MARROW

Some culinary experts in gourmet cuisine suggest that bones with intact marrow (sliced in circle or oblong half-cylinders) be soaked in cold water with a teaspoon of vinegar or sea salt for several hours, frequently replacing the water. You can do this before baking in the oven, or the Weston A. Price Foundation suggests covering the bones with water and slowly bringing to a boil, simmering for 20 minutes. Carefully scoop the marrow out of the hot bones. Alternatively, when using marrow bones to make Souper Stock (page 45), when cooked, marrow can be scooped from the bones or stock (sometimes it escapes the bones and is floating in the liquid). Mix the marrow with soft, cooked vegetables such as cauliflower, broccoli, carrots, or sweet potatoes.

DEEP DIVE INTO FARM COOPERATIVES AND CONSUMER-SUPPORTED AGRICULTURE (CSA)

While health food stores or even your local grocery store can provide grass-fed animal foods, often a better place to get your animal foods is from a local, trusted, pasture-based farm.

Farm co-ops are available in most areas, where simply emailing in a weekly or monthly order allows you to meet at the drop spot, cut a check, and take home your nutritious, fresh food. You can find local, pastured, organic animal foods, as well as trusted raw dairy farmers, near you by contacting your local chapter of the Weston A. Price Foundation (www.westona-price.org) or by searching "buy fresh buy local" with your location on the Internet.

For produce, we recommend joining a CSA (visit www.localharvest.org to find one near you). Getting fresh, local, seasonal, and organic produce from a CSA saves money, supports your local economy, increases variety, and provides nutritional benefits. Due to very short transportation routes, fruits and vegetables are vine ripened, enabling them to get a last infusion of nutrition from the soil (unlike foods from your grocery store, which ripen on the shelf). Additionally, produce is often harvested the same day that it is delivered, substantially increasing the enzyme content of the food.

FIRST FRUIT SAUCES

Apples and pears are good first fruits for your baby; they are easily digestible when stewed and offer fiber and vitamins. Pears contain vitamin C, vitamin K1, potassium, and copper. Apples contain antioxidant phytonutrients, including epicatechin, which is a flavonoid (also found in dark chocolate) associated with reduced death from cardiovascular disease and improved cognitive function. Apples of a deeper red color also contain some cyanidin, an antioxidant that is stronger than vitamins C and E and resveratrol. The quercetin that apples contain is mainly in the peel. Even better sources of quercetin include capers, elderberries, juniper berries, cilantro, fennel, lovage leaves, red onion, and yellow hot peppers. Studies have shown that a higher intake of quercetin-rich foods yields lower incidences of lung and stomach cancer.

1 to 2 pounds (455 to 910 g) unpeeled apples or pears

1 to 2 teaspoons coconut oil (unrefined, virgin, organic)

Core and chop the fruit.

Cook with the coconut oil in a saucepan on the stove over low heat until the fruit is soft, about 20 minutes.

Purée the cooked fruit for a young baby; mushy lumps can be left as your baby grows older and tolerates the change in texture. For early introduction, thinning with mom's milk or formula works well. Cool and serve.

NOTE

⊙ Adding cinnamon and nutmeg brings additional flavor to this dish for older babies (around 8 months).

PROCEED WITH CAUTION: Apples and pears are both on the Environmental Working Group's list of foods that have the most pesticides used on them if nonorganic (see the complete list in chapter 5). So, make sure you choose organic apples and pears to avoid the pesticides, if possible.

YIELD: 2 to 4 cups (490 to 980 g)

OH-SO-MUCH-BETTER THAN CEREAL O'S

Taking the Toxins Out

(8 TO 10 MONTHS)

This is an exciting time of beginning independence for your little one. Part of your baby's exploration of the world is the practice of bringing everything to her mouth (and if empty-handed, her own dimpled fingers or toes will suffice). Many parents are very concerned about how this behavior constantly exposes their babies to germs. Fortunately, most germs are helpful. You would, however, be wise to be wary of *other* unseen dangers: the ubiquitous toxins in her food and environment.

Toxins Take Stabs at Health

Due to our undeniably toxic environment, babies are born with a significant toxic load—before even taking their first breath of air.

Toxins should concern us for two reasons: 1) their effect on development, health, and the body and 2) their ability to influence genetics. Toxins can negatively influence genetic expression in ways we do not yet understand. *If genetics load the gun, the environment pulls the trigger.* See page 11 for a deep dive into epigenetics.

MORE TOXINS THAN EVER! Chemicals in our food, water, and environment are on a sharp upswing, and babies today face the greatest toxic burden ever known. Kenneth Bock, M.D., in *Healing the New Childhood Epidemics*, writes an impressive description of today's toxic realities, including hydrocarbons, pathogens, and waste in our drinking water; mercury, lead, diesel exhaust, and other pollutants in our air; mercury, garbage, and other poisons in our oceans; and chemicals, heavy metals, hormones, and antibiotics in our food.

Dr. Bock notes, "The total toxic burden on the average American [child] is measurably higher than it was even 10 years ago." In the nearly two decades since these words were written, our environment now contains even more toxins, including a proliferation of electromagnetic field radiation (EMF/"electronics"), glyphosate (the primary ingredient in Roundup), genetically modified organisms, and various other chemical cocktails.

Doing what you can to reduce toxins, while nourishing your baby as best as you can, will go far to help protect her from the reality of severe toxic attacks on health.

PROCESSED FOODS WITH TOXIC ADDITIVES. Processed foods in the Standard American Diet (SAD) are dismantled, refined, bleached, and deodorized. What nutrients they have are mostly synthetic and are poor replacements for the real thing. The FDA maintains a list of more than *3,000* additives, 80% of which have not been tested for carcinogenicity, immunotoxicity, or neurotoxicity.

DEEP DIVE INTO GLYPHOSATE

Glyphosate, found in Roundup, is increasingly linked with 3C conditions, and illustrates the damage and risk of all such toxic chemicals, many of which travel in packs with glyphosate.

Glyphosate, an organophosphate, is the most common agricultural chemical in use globally (as reported by *Newsweek*, February 2, 2016); Americans have dumped 1.8 million tons of glyphosate on crops and fields, and more than 9.4 million tons have been unloaded globally since its introduction in 1974, according to *Environmental Sciences Europe*. In the last 20 years, there's been a 15-fold increase in glyphosate use. This increase is attributed to the GMO crops ("Roundup Ready" corn and soybean) that can now tolerate staggering doses of Roundup pesticide.

Glyphosate is listed as carcinogenic by California's Proposition 65 (a list indicating known cancer-causing substances), and causes damage through endocrine (hormone) disruption, destruction of gut flora, severe depletion of manganese (required for antioxidant protection), and disruption of sulfation detoxification (a primary way to clear toxins), resulting in neurological diseases, such as autism and Alzheimer's, and can contribute to anxiety, depression, and Parkinson's disease. As reported by Drs. Seneff and Samsel, in *Surgical Neurology International*, "Our gut bacteria contains the same metabolic pathway found in plants that is targeted and disrupted by Roundup. Is it any wonder that leaky gut, inflammatory bowel disease, colitis, and other gastrointestinal diseases have spiked since the onset of Roundup Ready GMO crops?"

Roundup also contains a mixture of many other chemicals that, together, are much worse than glyphosate alone. According to *BioMed Research International*, "Roundup was [found to be] by far the most toxic among the herbicides and insecticides tested."

The pervasive use of glyphosate and other such chemicals means that you and your baby are exposed to dangerous amounts, even from foods previously thought to be healthy. For example, less than 2 parts per billion (ppb) of glyphosate is considered "safe," yet non-GMO Cheerios were found to have 1,100 ppb! Beyond its pesticide use, glyphosate is also used as a desiccant (chemical drying agent) on oats and wheat. It is also found in vitamins, medications, vaccines, tampons, and even water.

The best ways to limit exposure are to consume organic foods and limit processed food consumption. To counter the effects of glyphosate, include raw apple cider vinegar in your diet (it contains bacteria that helps remove glyphosate); eat probiotic-rich foods, such as unpasteurized sauerkraut, kimchi, pickles, and raw yogurt; and consume sulfur-rich foods, including cruciferous vegetables (cauliflower, cabbage, Brussels sprouts), onions, and garlic.

TOXINS FROM RADIATION-EXPOSED FOODS. Meats, produce, and seasonings are typically irradiated (treated with radiation) to extend shelf life, in addition to having been exposed to environmental radiation. In studies, animals fed irradiated feed experienced early death, reproductive problems, cancer, chromosomal abnormalities, liver damage, and vitamin deficiencies.

DEEP DIVE INTO ELECTROMAGNETIC FIELD (EMF) TOXICITY

Our baby's toxic exposure doesn't end with food; there are many toxins in our environment, including air, water, and beauty products. One invisible toxin increasing all around us is electromagnetic field radiation (EMFs).

According to the World Health Organization: "Exposure to electromagnetic fields . . . during the 20th century . . . has been steadily increasing . . . Everyone is exposed."

Our exposure to EMFs increases as fast as new technologies are introduced, including wireless networks, wireless devices, household electronics, baby monitors, televisions, microwave ovens, fluorescent lamps, Wi-Fi, and Bluetooth. Most dramatic has been our increased use of cell phones. Research published in 2018 conclusively links cell phone radio frequency waves to cancer, heart conditions, and DNA damage.

Specific to pregnancy, the WHO informs that typical environmental exposure to EMFs has been associated with health problems, prematurity, and low birth weight. And, according to WHO, "a number of epidemiological studies suggest small increases in risk of childhood leukemia with exposure to low frequency magnetic fields in the home."

The best thing you can do for your baby's health is to reduce exposure. Increase physical distance from EMF sources wherever possible, including locating Wi-Fi, routers, electric lines, smart meters, and breaker boxes away from your child's bedroom. Don't store your cellphone near your baby. Limit your child's time on electronics. Choose wired Internet and phones when possible, and turn off computers, routers, and Wi-Fi at night. Lastly, keep baby monitors as far as possible from his crib, as they, too, emit EMFs.

TOXINS FROM MAN-MADE DNA. *Seventy percent* of the foods consumed in the Standard American Diet are genetically modified. (See page 66.)

TOXIC SAD PRODUCE. Conventional farming today relies heavily on chemicals (pesticides, herbicides, fungicides, insecticides, and fertilizers). If you serve a nonorganic apple to your baby, you are also serving up an average of 16 different pesticides, applied at least 36 times.

TOXIC SAD WATER. Municipal (or tap) water has purposefully added toxic chemicals, like fluoride and chlorine, that kill friendly gut flora and disrupt metabolism. (See page 116.) Other, unintentional chemicals and toxins are also present in water—lead, hormones, antibiotics, and rocket fuel, to name just a few. Well water can contain chemicals that have leached into the ground or accumulated in rainwater.

TOXIC SAD ANIMAL FOODS. Most farm animals have it very rough these days. They are fed genetically modified, mold-ridden, inflammatory, pesticide-treated, GMO legume and grain-based "feed." They are kept in giant overcrowded warehouses, rather than allowed to naturally graze outside. This unnatural diet and confinement-based lifestyle makes the animals so sickly that they require frequent antibiotics. Drugs, like steroids and growth hormone, are used to put extra weight on or to keep cows lactating. In fact, *70% of big pharmaceutical companies' drug sales are made to our farm animals!*

DEEP DIVE INTO THE TRUTH ABOUT FLUORIDE: IT'S TOXIC

Fluoride has been added to the public water system since the 1940s. In January 2011, the U.S. Department of Health and Human Services lowered the maximum amount of fluoride allowed in water, demonstrating knowledge of the risks of fluoride.

DAMAGES TEETH AND BONES. According to Ruth Yaron, M.S., in *Super Baby Food*, 80% of American children have dental fluorosis (mottling and breakdown of the teeth) resulting from *too much* fluoride. And fluoride damage to teeth is an indicator of what is going on with bones.

The CDC cites an increased risk of dental fluorosis as children ingest higher levels of fluoride. Dr. Mercola and the Global Healing Center cite that decreased IQ, skeletal fluorosis, arthritis, and damage to the thyroid, pineal gland, and kidneys are consequences of fluoride ingestion.

POISONOUS. Fluoride is neurotoxic and damages more than 200 enzymes in the body. Further, according to David Brownstein, M.D., author of *Iodine: Why You Need It, Why You Can't Live Without It*, fluoride blocks iodine absorption, increasing the likelihood of thyroid disease and cancers. Iodine deficiency, he writes, "is the most common preventable form of mental retardation known."

NO HELP FOR DECAY. After all that, fluoride has never actually been proven to prevent cavities! In fact, a study presented in 2010 by the American Chemical Society explains that the "protective layer" produced by topical fluoride is so thin that it is quickly worn away by ordinary chewing.

TOXIC SAD FOOD PACKAGING. Foods are abundantly packaged, stored, and heated in plastics. Some packaging is aseptic, killing even the beneficial bacteria that should exist in foods, while others, like most aluminum cans, contain chemicals such as bisphenol A (BPA), an endocrine disruptor. These chemicals are often quite toxic to the human body. We urge you to reduce plastic food storage to whatever degree possible, opting for glass, stainless steel, or ceramic.

TOXINS IN VACCINATIONS. Whether the potential effectiveness of vaccinations outweighs the risk is for parents to decide, as is the schedule with which any vaccines are administered to their children, but no one disagrees that there are toxins within vaccines. See page 118.

COMBINED AND CUMULATIVE EFFECTS OF TOXINS. Individual toxins are harmful enough on their own, yet they are often *even more* harmful in combination. In fact, so many exist that the possible combinations in the environment are too numerous to count or properly test. Studies show that what one toxin could do alone is made much worse by the presence of another toxin—making the reality of combined and cumulative toxic effects today that much more worrisome.

THE EFFECT OF THESE TOXINS ON BABIES IS THE 3C CONDITIONS!

Toxins in the body contribute to the 3C conditions, especially autism, asthma, allergies, learning disabilities (like ADHD), and cancer. Experts from the National Institute of Environmental Health report that even very low exposure to toxins in early life increases risk of behavioral problems and autoimmune conditions. For example, a study published in *Pediatrics* showed that children with higher levels of organophosphate pesticides (like glyphosate) were twice as likely to have attention deficit hyperactivity disorder (ADHD).

Exposure to toxins early in pregnancy contributes to the likelihood of autism in unborn babies. From research published in *Current Opinion in Pediatrics* (April 2010), genetic variations account for "only a small fraction of [autism] cases." This leaves environmental exposures to be a major contributor to the development of autism.

Philip J. Landrigan, M.D., M.Sc., chair of the Department of Community Medicine at Mount Sinai School of Medicine and director of the Center for Children's Health and the Environment at Mount Sinai, provides several examples of toxins' causal role in disease. He states that asthma is exacerbated by air pollution; developmental delays are caused by lead in paint and contaminated drinking water; and pediatric cancers are caused by radiation and benzene.

When children can no longer handle the toxic burden, then one or more of the 3C conditions manifest. Depending on the child's inherent ability to handle the toxins, as well as to what particular cocktail of toxins she is exposed, the manifestation of toxic overload can be any of the 3Cs.

MOM-TO-MOM

At six months, with concern for dental health, doctors typically start recommending fluoride supplementation. We strongly disagree.

As discussed on page 116, fluoride is a known neurotoxin that can harm brain function. Paul Connett, Ph.D., toxicologist, and chemist states, "A variety of studies . . . have indicated that in communities with higher levels of fluoride, children have lower IQs."

A 2017 Mexican study, spanning twelve years, further indicates that fluoride should be avoided, even in pregnancy. Those with a higher prenatal exposure to fluoride were more likely to have children with lower IQs.

TO VACCINATE OR NOT VACCINATE:
INFORMED CHOICE

Whether to vaccinate your child according to the full recommended vaccination schedule, a customized version of that, or not at all carries a lot of controversy. Some experts believe that not one vaccine exists today that is worth the risks it poses. Others recognize that vaccines have contributed greatly to the near eradication of many diseases. What we do know is that vaccines contain inflammatory toxins, such as adjuvants (e.g., aluminum), preservatives (e.g., formaldehyde), and contaminants (e.g., glyphosate), and some vaccines contain human fetal cells (e.g., MMR, Varivax, and Hep A). In situations where babies carry a significant toxic burden, don't detoxify well, have an acute or chronic infection, and/or have gut dysbiosis, vaccines pose a greater risk.

We cannot urge you enough to do research when it comes to vaccinations. If you choose not to vaccinate at all, we suggest that you support your baby's immune system in other ways (see chapter 6). If you do vaccinate, we ask that you consider a few things: nutritional status of your child, evidence of 3Cs (see page 8), as well as immune, allergy, and gut health.

Remember: There are alternatives to the standard vaccine schedule, including not vaccinating and supporting the immune system through various methods (including those mentioned in chapter 6), choosing a select few vaccines, asking for vaccinations individually rather than in combined shots, and spreading out the timing of various doses. If and when vaccines are administered, refer to chapter 5 to support detoxification. We also advocate feeding your child with a predominance of nutrient-rich, digestible foods (per recommendations throughout the book) in order to foster strong nutritional status, which is protective for your child.

There are many sources of information on each vaccine and related disease(s). In addition to speaking with a doctor, we recommend that parents read the vaccine package insert, review the physician desk reference, or refer to the United States Centers for Disease Control and Prevention. We highly recommend the National Vaccine Information Center, an advocacy group that supports everyone's right to choose.

HELPFUL RESOURCES
To further aid you in your research and medical choice regarding vaccination, the following sources may be of use:

CENTERS FOR DISEASE CONTROL AND PREVENTION (CDC)
Table of excipients included in vaccines in the United States
https://www.cdc.gov/vaccines/pubs/pinkbook/downloads/appendices/b/excipient-table-2.pdf

NATIONAL VACCINE INFORMATION CENTER
(703) 938-0342
https://www.nvic.org

THE VACCINE-FRIENDLY PLAN
By Paul Thomas, M.D.
https://www.drpaulapproved.com/the-vaccine-friendly-plan.html

SUZANNE HUMPHRIES, M.D.
Dissolving Illusions (with Roman Bystrianyk)
http://www.dissolvingillusions.com/

VITAMIN C PROTOCOL FOR PERTUSSIS
http://drsuzanne.net/2017/10/sodium-ascorbate-vitamin-c-treatment-of-whooping-cough-suzanne-humphries-md/

AMERICAN ACADEMY OF PEDIATRICS STUDY ON VITAMIN A TREATMENT OF MEASLES
http://pediatrics.aappublications.org/content/91/5/1014

INSTITUTE FOR VACCINE SAFETY AT JOHNS HOPKINS BLOOMBERG SCHOOL OF PUBLIC HEALTH
Package Inserts and Manufacturers for some US Licensed Vaccines and Immunoglobulins
http://www.vaccinesafety.edu/package_inserts.htm

You may also review the vaccines references we find very informative on page 263.

REPORTING REACTIONS

Report adverse vaccine reactions to the Vaccine Adverse Event Reporting System (VAERS) at (800) 822-7967 or online at www.vaers.hhs.gov. If your child has a vaccine injury, your child may be eligible for compensation under the National Vaccine Injury Compensation Act. You can find out more information at www.hrsa.gov/vaccinecompensation.

PROTECT YOUR RIGHT TO CHOOSE

When there is risk, there must be choice. Therefore, it is critical that we act to retain the right to determine what is injected into our children's (and our own) bodies. Whether you fully vaccinate, alter the vaccine load or schedule, or don't vaccinate at all, the right to choose should be yours and yours alone.

A Better Way to Reduce Toxins and Their Effects

Dr. Landrigan explains that the 3Cs (he calls them the "new pediatric morbidities") are of "toxic environmental origin," and therefore *can* "*be prevented* by reducing or eliminating children's exposures to toxic chemicals in the environment" and in the diet [emphasis added].

ENVIRONMENTAL TOXINS. Take measures to reduce overall toxic exposure for your baby, paying attention to cleaning products, toys, bath soaps, sunscreens, lotions, clothing, and more. Ensure that soaps and products do not contain antibacterial agents, such as triclosan. Take shoes off when you enter your home (to avoid tracking in chemicals) and take great caution when your home is undergoing renovation.

MINIMIZE TOXINS IN WATER. We recommend filtered (and if filtered through reverse osmosis, ideally remineralized to reach a neutral or slightly basic pH level) water for all food and drink preparation. It is also best to use filtered water for bathing, either with a showerhead filter or whole house water filtration system.

MINIMIZE VACCINE TOXIC EFFECTS.

Vaccines and their toxins become more of a risk for undernourished children. Nutrient deficiencies, particularly vitamins A, B12, and B9 (folate), can increase the risk of side effects from vaccinations, explains Russell L. Blaylock, M.D., neurosurgeon, nutrition researcher, excitotoxin expert, and author of *Health and Nutrition Secrets*. In two poignant examples, vaccinating vitamin A–deficient children resulted in high mortality versus vitamin A–sufficient children; vitamin A, B12, and folate–deficient children demonstrated likelihood to develop a severe brain and spinal cord–damaging condition. Providing your baby cod liver oil, liver, and butter regularly should ensure protective levels of vitamin A, B12, and folate.

Additionally, healthy gut flora (good yeasts and bacteria) help detoxify the chemical adjuvants in vaccines, including mercury (thimerisol) and aluminum, to name just a few. Gut flora is kept strongest and most protective when we eliminate or minimize steroids, antibiotics, and antacids. Additionally, a diet rich in fermented, unpasteurized foods replenishes and supports the microbiome of our gut. Further, vaccination should be delayed during any period of illness, or after antibiotic or steroid use.

At higher risk for vaccine injury are children with an autoimmune condition; a mother who has an autoimmune disease; birth by C-section; children who are formula fed; and children with tics, learning disabilities, poor diet, allergies, eczema, or autism spectrum disorders.

An article in *Discover Medicine* (2010) suggested one potential mitigation strategy: "Perhaps, the assessment of autoantibody and HLA status prior to immunization will serve as a marker for individuals at risk. More research is required to identify those individuals with an increased risk to develop [vaccine-caused] autoimmune phenomena."

MINIMIZE TOXINS IN FOOD. Choose organic produce, particularly when consuming foods that are the most pesticide contaminated. (See page 125.) Washing produce with a vegetable/fruit wash containing grapefruit seed extract helps reduce external pesticides. Select organic grass-fed meat to consume the least pesticides and heavy metals, and to get the most nutritional benefits.

Also, minimize processed foods. In 2018, a study showed that polysorbate 80 and maltodextrin erode the healthy mucosal gut barrier, which shifts gut bacteria predominance in favor of the bad kind, which leads to leaky gut. Sticking with few- to single-ingredient foods will help you avoid industrial-food-processing residues, chemicals, preservatives, GMOs, and other toxins (including nitrates, heavy metals, dyes, flavorings, etc.).

CAUTION: MICROWAVES. Though many commercial baby foods are "microwavable," we absolutely do *not* recommend heating your child's food in the microwave. It can heat unevenly, resulting in possible scalding of your baby's mouth. It destroys many nutrients, including proteins, enzymes, and vitamin C. And if microwaved in plastic, the food will have toxins leached into it. Instead, remove from the container and place in a pan to heat.

LOAD UP ON NUTRIENTS. Nutrients and nutrient-rich diets can reduce toxic effects. Here are just a few examples from scientific research and medical studies demonstrating protective nutrition:

- Adequate B vitamins maintain sufficient glutathione and reduce oxidative stress to the brain (including impacting the brain's ability to recover from physical impact, such as sports concussions, as do sulfur, magnesium, zinc, vitamin D, and omega-3 fatty acids).

- Conjugated linoleic acid (CLA), found in grass-fed products, including ghee, increases antioxidant activity, combating oxidative stress.

- Sulfur, in foods like garlic, improves antioxidant status; the higher the sulfur content, the higher the antioxidant capability.

- Antioxidants substantially protect against radiation.

- Iodine reduces the toxic effects of fluoride, chloride, and bromine and helps the body excrete them. It also reduces risk of thyroid cancer from radiation exposure.

- Adequate vitamin C reduces toxicity of methylmercury and radiation, including air travel and X-rays.

- Adequate protein intake protects against methylmercury (the type we consume in food) and improves the ability to detoxify it.

- Selenium renders mercury markedly less lethal to the fetus.

- Molybdenum substantially decreases sensitivity to sulfites.

- Taurine protects the liver and testicles from the toxic effects of cadmium.

- The combination of sufficient vitamin D and its role in enabling the absorption of essential minerals together block the absorption of toxic minerals (such as lead, arsenic, aluminum, cobalt, and strontium).

- Vitamin B1 and molybdenum protect against acetaldehyde (which dulls the brain and is carcinogenic), which often accumulates in high-refined carbohydrate diets typical of most children and adults today, and studies have shown acetyladehyde plays a role in autism and learning disabilities.

- Calcium, zinc, and essential vitamins reduce the toxic effects of lead and excess manganese.

- Methionine, taurine, zinc, vitamin C, and glycine together prevent the learning and memory impairment from lead exposure. Taurine and thiamine (B1) can reverse lead neurotoxicity.

- Calcium, zinc, and essential vitamins reduce the toxic effects of lead.

- Saturated fatty acids protect the liver from medications.

In short: NUTRIENT-RICH SUPER POWER FOODS REDUCE TOXIC DAMAGE!

DETOXIFICATION. The ability to remove toxins once ingested, inhaled, injected, or absorbed relies on many biochemical pathways the body has to render toxins safe and eliminate them. Detoxification methods vary but all rely on coenzymes (vitamins and minerals) and enzymes, and many of these pathways involve the liver and kidneys. Toxins tend to be stored in adipose tissue, and are eliminated through conversion to non-harmful molecules, or through excretion, as in sweat, bile, urine, or feces. Antioxidants help in detoxification, as part of the process can result in dangerous free radical by-products that antioxidants can neutralize. The two phases of liver detoxification are significantly supported by the following nutrients: vitamins A, B-complex, C, D, and E, bioflavonoids, quercetin, herb milk thistle, amino acids, cysteine, glutamate, lysine, carnitine, taurine, glycine, mineral calcium, and sulfur metabolites. Given this, we know that proper detoxification requires a nutrient-rich diet.

Antioxidants help disarm toxins. They are necessary to prevent and reduce the consequences of toxins, such as brain damage and inflammation, both of which make organs and systems unable to function normally (leading to disease). According to Elizabeth Lipski, Ph.D., C.C.N., clinical nutritionist and author of *Digestive Wellness for Children*, "The average person is exposed to over 100 different chemicals [every day]. If we get enough antioxidants . . . from our foods, we can easily slough off most chemical toxins."

Fruits, vegetables, and greens contain important antioxidants such as vitamin C and bioflavonoids, but you might be surprised to learn that *animal foods* contain many key antioxidants and the raw "materials" (nutrients) for synthesizing more, as mentioned in chapter 4.

Furthermore, eating probiotic-rich foods and probiotic supplements reduces the amount of toxins that can gain access to your baby's bloodstream through his intestinal wall. When probiotic protection is adequate, heavy metals and other toxins are blocked by the probiotics, thus kept out of the blood, and will be excreted in the stool, as nature intended. As Robert Bernadini points out in *The Truth About Children's Health*, "The amount of . . . [toxins] that wouldn't harm well-nourished individuals may *poison undernourished* children" [emphasis added].

Common Sources of Environmental Toxins			
HOUSEHOLD TOXINS		**FOOD TOXINS**	
• Chlorine bleach • Chemical cleaners • Perfumes and fragrances • Building/construction materials and solvents • Fluoride (toothpaste, grapes, wine, processed chicken, medications) • Fabric softeners • Petroleum jelly and mineral oil • Plastic/phthalates— store in glass instead • Cookware—nonstick and aluminum and microwave • Plastic toys • Candles with lead wicks • Paints with VOCs—volatile organic compounds • Paint thinners • Adhesives • Fabric softener • Cigarette smoke • Styrofoam • Microwave ovens • Teflon pans—source of fluoride • Aluminum pans and foil • Detergents and chemical cleaners • Antibacterial products: soaps, gels, cleansers • Water with chlorine, chloramine, fluoride, and/or lead • Lead in dishware, pipes, or paint • Carpeting • Mildew and mold in the home	• Pesticide spraying • New cars (dashboard, upholstery) • EMFs (electromagnetic frequencies) • Dry cleaning • Bromine in furniture, electronics, mattresses, pools, hot tubs • Asbestos • Formaldehyde • BPA (bisphenol A) • Deodorant with aluminum • Triclosan (antibacterial agent) • Nail polish • Soaps with parabens • Hairspray, hair gels, mousses with phthalates • Makeup with phthalates, lead, synthetic ingredients • Lice-killing pesticides • Shampoos	• Artificial sweeteners (aspartame, sucralose) and artificially sweetened foods • Nitrites and nitrates— bacon, hot dogs, sausage, bologna • Sulfites—lettuce, dried fruits, fresh fruits and vegetables (especially in restaurants), processed potato products, corn by-products • Sorbic acid—cheese, frosting, dried fruit, dips • Colors and dyes (esp. yellow #5)—hundreds of processed, colored foods • Parabens—jelly, soda pop, pastry, beer, cake, salad dressing • Benzoic acid—soda pop, fruit juice, margarine, apple cider • Monosodium glutamate (MSG), also hydrolyzed vegetable protein and texturized vegetable protein—bouillon, Chinese restaurant dishes, chicken broth or flavoring; may also be in glutamate, sodium caseinate, calcium caseinate, hydrolyzed corn protein, autolyzed yeast, or yeast extract • EDTA—margarine, salad dressing, frozen dinners, other processed foods • Propyl gallate—frozen dinners, gravy mix, turkey sausage • Alginate—ice cream, salad dressing, cheese spread, frozen dinners	• Bromates/bromine— baked goods, bread crumbs, refrigerated dough • Growth hormone in foods • Preservatives • Flavorings • BHA and GHT • Annatto • Emulsifiers • Table salt and baking powder with aluminum • Artificial flavors (like vanillin) • Trans fats (all hydrogenated oils—fully or partially) • Farm-raised fish with PCBs • Time-released pharmaceutical drugs • Mercury in fish • Aluminum cans, often lined with plastic • Antacids with aluminum • Fluoride tablets • Artificial fats • Nonorganic poultry and rice (may contain arsenic) • Genetically modified food • Chlorine in water • Fluoride in water • Fluoride in baby foods—chicken nuggets, nonorganic grape juice, highest in baby food chicken • Glyphosate—oats, almonds, wheat, corn, soy, in most processed foods, even some organic, Cheerios and Oreos highest

Based on and adapted from *Nourishing Hope for Autism*, by Julie Matthews

Common Sources of Environmental Toxins

HIDDEN TOXINS		BABY CARE TOXINS	
• Heavy metals • Lead, cadmium, mercury, aluminum, arsenic; polluted air, water, soil, food • Lead in water supply from lead pipes • Aluminum in soy products, cookware, refined table salt, deodorants, antacids, baking powder, vaccines, IV solutions, IV medications, IV vitamins • Mercury-amalgam fillings, linked to Alzheimer's and a number of other disease conditions • Toxins produced by yeast and fungus in the gut, such as ethanol and acetylaldehyde • Toxins produced by pathogenic bacteria, such as sulfites (from sulphate-reducing pathogens) • Toxins created by incomplete protein digestion, such as gluteomorphin and casomorphin	• Pesticides, herbicides, insecticides, like glyphosate • Fluoride in medications: Prozac, antibiotics (Cipro), Prevacid, Flonase, Flovent, Lipitor, surgical anesthetics	• Infant sleepwear and pajamas that are flame retardant (antimony) • Toothpaste with fluoride and artificial ingredients • Vinyl and PVC toys and lunch boxes—also contain lead • Plastic water bottles, food storage containers, baby bottles • Teethers with phthalates • Diaper bags (triclosan) • Arsenic-treated wood in playgrounds or desks (green-tinted) • Polyurethane in changing pads (learning disabilities, cancer, and infertility) • Chlorine in portable cribs and bassinet mattresses (learning disabilities, endocrine problems, infertility) • Phthalates in vinyl bath toys and polycarbonate plastic bottles (endocrine problems) • Talc/asbestos in baby powder (mesothelioma, lung irritation, respiratory problems, coughing, vomiting, pneumonia) • Petroleum/propylene glycol in baby oil (lung irritation, allergies, immune system problems)	• Triclosan and chloroxylenol in fragrance, dyes, ammonia, formaldehyde, glycols, phenol, BHA/bhtare in antibacterial gels, soaps, and baby wipes (endocrine, immune, organ, and skin problems, cancer) • BPA and nitrosamines in teething rings and polycarbonate plastic bottles (brain, reproductive system, heart, and liver damage, cancer) • Formaldehyde in cribs, changing tables, mattresses, baby bedding materials, bubble bath (cancer) • Nitrosamines in bottles with latex rubber nipples (cancer) • Oxybenzone in sunscreens (allergies, hormone disruption, cell damage) • Parabens in bubble bath (cancer) • Fire-retardant chemicals, dyes, formaldehyde finishes, plastic (polyester, nylon, acrylic, Spandex) and cotton pesticides in baby clothes (cancer)

Common Baby Food Pitfalls

By simply making better-than-average choices regarding beverages and finger foods at this age, you'll go far to protect your baby's health.

JUICE IS JUST AN ILLUSION OF HEALTHFULNESS

The AAP reports that almost 90% of infants under 1 year of age are given juice—and some are consuming more than 16 ounces (475 ml) per day! Store-bought juice *is naught more than sugar water.* (Unfortunately, organic, 100% juice isn't any better because it is still mostly sugar, lacking the fiber, enzymes, and nutrients of whole fruit.) It is bad for your baby in several ways.

JUICE DISPLACES NUTRIENT-RICH FOODS. Babies often get full from juice, such that they are no longer hungry for nutritious foods and drinks. Moreover, the *addicting* nature of juice means that children keep asking for it.

JUICE IS AN IMPETUS FOR TOOTH DECAY. The American Academy of Pediatrics (AAP) recommends that infants younger than 12 months do *not* routinely have fruit juice "since it offers no nutrition benefit at this age" and is generally accepted as a contributor to tooth decay. Or at any age, we attest. The AAP also recommends babies and toddlers "not be given juice from bottles or easily transportable covered cups that allow them to consume juice easily throughout the day," and recommends whole fruits over juice, due to fiber and other nutrients found in the whole fruit.

THE DIRTY DOZEN AND THE CLEAN FIFTEEN

This list of foods, compiled by the Environmental Working Group (EWG), should always be purchased organic due to having the highest contamination. (For more information, visit the EWG's website, www.foodnews.org.)

THE DIRTY DOZEN

1. Strawberries
2. Spinach
3. Nectarines
4. Apples
5. Peaches
6. Pears
7. Cherries
8. Grapes
9. Celery
10. Tomatoes
11. Sweet bell peppers
12. Potatoes

Note: The current Clean 15, which are foods least contaminated and less critical to buy as organic, and therefore safer to consume at restaurants, include: sweet corn (though risk for GMO), avocados, pineapples, cabbage, onions, frozen sweet peas, papayas, asparagus, mangoes, eggplant, honeydew melon, kiwi, cantaloupe, cauliflower, and grapefruit.

JUICE WEAKENS IMMUNITY. Studies show that sugar in juice reduces immune function by disabling critical white blood cells for 5 to 7 hours after ingestion, which makes them less able to fight off infection. The immune system is effectively "stunned" by sugar, fructose, honey, and even *100% juice.*

JUICE CAUSES BELLYACHES AND DIARRHEA. The AAP warns that excessive juice consumption can be associated with diarrhea, flatulence, and abdominal distention and can lead to malnutrition. In *My Tummy Hurts,* Joseph Levy, M.D., warns that "juice abuse" causes diarrhea and promotes obesity.

JUICE IS A SOURCE OF HEAVY METALS. In 2010, a California study found that 80% of all juice (yes, organic too) contains the dangerous toxin lead! And since 40% of high fructose corn syrup (HFCS) samples contain mercury, juice made with HFCS is likely to contain harmful mercury as well.

We recommend only filtered water or Souper Stock (page 45) as additional beverages at this age. Offer them perhaps when hot outside and others are thirsty, in small quantities so as not to displace mom's milk or formula.

FINGER FOODS TO FORGO

Cereal (like Cheerios) is the most common finger food babies eat to practice their pincer grasp. But under further inspection, cereal proves to be a harmful CRAP food!

CHEMICAL: PROCESSED GRAIN PRODUCTS ARE A SOURCE OF TOXINS. Due to the processing they endure, cereals are sources of allergenic neurotoxins, created via a high-heat process called extrusion, which denatures proteins. Whole grains are even worse, as they contain more protein to be denatured.

Many cereals and teething crackers that babies and children consume today contain dangerous levels of glyphosate. Additionally, cereals contain a class 2A toxin: acrylamides, most with over 500 times the safe limit.

Further, the high-heat processing that cereal manufacturing requires damages delicate fatty acids, rendering them rancid and toxic, and even destroys many of the well-intentioned added vitamins and minerals.

REMOVES BODY'S NUTRIENTS: CEREAL IS SUGAR LOADED. Even "healthy" cereals contain some form of sugar. Refined grains themselves are sugars to the body, but most cereals have multiple forms of added sweeteners.

GRAINS ARE HARD TO DIGEST. At this age, your baby is barely making the starch-digesting enzymes needed to digest grains (see chapter 4). Gluten, a protein found in wheat, barley, and rye grains, is particularly hard to digest.

GRAIN FOODS LEAD TO AUTOIMMUNE DISEASES. Celiac disease is an autoimmune disease most closely associated with gluten ingestion, and it is becoming more prevalent. Early gluten introduction has been shown to play a role in the development of celiac disease, as well as other autoimmune disorders. According to *Interdisciplinary Toxicology*, an estimated 1 out of every 20 people in North American and European populations suffer from celiac disease. Toxins, leaky gut, and diet are at the root of this epidemic.

ADDICTIVE: CEREALS ARE A SOURCE OF DIETARY OPIATES. A special enzyme (called DPP-4) is needed to digest gluten. Because babies don't yet have this gluten-busting enzyme, the gluten can get "stuck" in a partially digested form. Called gluteo*morphin,* it acts similar to other opiates—morphine and heroin—clouding and fogging the brain, hindering development and perception, and altering behavior. Gluteomorphins *are just as addicting as other opiate drugs*, so your baby can get physically hooked on cereal and wheat.

When eating cereal with pasteurized milk, another potential dietary opiate enters the mix. A lack of DPP-4 can also lead to poorly digested pasteurized casein from the milk, which results in case*omorphins* (other dietary opiates). Flour-based foods and dairy products, together, increase the intake of sources of dietary opiates.

Souper Stock and fermented foods increase stomach acidity and thus stimulate digestive enzymes, like DPP-4. Also, the gelatin in Souper Stock eventually *increases* the amount and activity of enzymes that break down gluteomorphin and caseomorphin. Feeding your baby Souper Stock (and cultured foods) will pay off when grains are finally introduced—he'll be better able to fully break down potential dietary opiates into their "kinder" amino acid building blocks. *Limiting toxins* will further help, since toxins deactivate these important enzymes.

PROCESSED: PROCESSED, REFINED GRAINS. Flour used in cereals is typically refined, meaning the whole grain is broken apart, the nutrient-rich portions removed, and then it's "fortified" with *synthetic* vitamins and minerals, additional sugar, flavorings, colorings, and more franken-food constituents.

The toxic, depleting, inflammatory, allergenic, and addictive nature of breakfast cereals make them a very *poor* choice for babies, as well as for children and adults. Can you do better than "O's" for your baby? Absolutely!

Safeguard Your Child Against Toxins with Optimal Nourishment

Toxins are everywhere, but you *can* do something to help! *Toxins are rendered less damaging and effects are decreased in well-nourished children.* By providing a diet based on Super Nutrition, you are minimizing the impact that toxins will have on your child's health.

WHAT YOU CAN EXPECT AT THIS AGE

SELF-FEEDING. Between 8 and 10 months, your baby will develop the "pincer grasp," which means touching an opposing finger together with his thumb, allowing him to grasp smaller objects. It is now time for some finger-friendly foods, giving your baby a chance to practice this new grip and become more confident with self-feeding. Even if your baby isn't yet interested in feeding himself, let him get used to holding an extra spoon as well as touching, feeling, even squishing foods.

MORE TEXTURE. Even though your baby may not have teeth yet, his hard gums can mash foods, and he can eat more textured foods. At 8 months, food purées and mashes should be thicker than they have been so far, with very soft, squishy lumps. By 9 months, foods should be chunkier, though chunks should still be soft and smooshy. Once babies can tolerate these chunkier foods well, without choking (usually around 9 months), it is time to consider adding finger foods.

Super Nutrition Food Categorizations for 8 to 10 Months	
SUPER POWER	**PURE**
• Fish roe • Raw yogurt or kefir • Raw butter • Grass-fed, organic heart and liver • Lacto-fermented veggies, roots, and fruits • Organic animal fats	• Organic fruits • Organic vegetables • Organic pastured meats • Organic coconut milk • Organic yogurt and kefir • Organic butter • Organic eggs
OKAY	**CRAP**
• Organic baby food (stage 2 to 3) • Nonorganic, non–Dirty Dozen fruits and vegetables, washed • Non-processed, non-pastured meats • Nonorganic butter	• Breakfast cereal • Processed baby meats • Teething biscuits, crackers, cookies • Baby food with added sugar, juice, fruit concentrate, or anything other than fruit, vegetable, or meat • Juice (organic or nonorganic)

HOW MUCH? By 8 months, meal sizes will still vary based on your baby's hunger and nutrient needs, but on average will consist of 1 to 4 tablespoons (15 to 55 g) of a food (which is ¼ cup [55 g], or two frozen cubes). Some babies will be hungry enough at a meal to consume ½ cup (115 g) of food. Follow your baby's hunger signs and stop feeding when she loses interest.

Continue nursing about 5 times per day, or give 25 to 32 ounces (700 to 950 ml) of formula in 24 hours. By 9 months, meals become more important to satisfy nutritional needs, though nursing and bottles are still important for complete nutrition, comfort, bonding, and to satisfy your baby's suckling instinct. If your baby is not interested much in food, you may need to reduce the quantity of mom's milk or formula.

HOW MANY FOODS PER MEAL? During this age, meals will start to be made up of more than one food. Always serve an animal protein or fat with each meal. Continue to introduce new foods every 3 to 4 days.

Recipes to Help Protect Against Toxins

Between the ages of 8 and 10 months, nutrient needs remain ever critical. Requirements for absorbable iron, zinc, and copper are still high. Protein needs are not quite half met through nursing or formula intake, so animal foods continue to be a very important part of your baby's diet. For a more complete list of acceptable foods at this age, see the Food Introduction Timeline on page 255.

PATTERN	8 MONTHS
Early AM	Milk/homemade formula
Midmorning	Milk/homemade formula + snack
Midday	Milk (new food every 3 to 4 days)
Afternoon	Milk/homemade formula
Evening	Meal
Nighttime	Milk/homemade formula

PATTERN	9 MONTHS
Early AM	Milk/homemade formula
Midmorning	Bottle or nursing and small meal
Midday	Meal
Afternoon	Milk/homemade formula
Evening	Meal
Nighttime	Milk/homemade formula

FEEDING AT 8 MONTHS

At around 8 months of age, you can start introducing gelatin, fish roe, some new veggies, a few fruits, and a wide variety of meats cooked in Souper Stock (page 45). Meals usually continue at twice per day until 9 months. Often, they are still accompanied by nursing or bottles or are fit in between feedings. The above chart shows the feeding pattern we suggest.

Finger Foods at 8 months

- ⊙ Fish roe
- ⊙ Chunks of soft avocado
- ⊙ Chunks of very ripe banana
- ⊙ Jigglers (page 152)
- ⊙ Very ripe and soft cantaloupe, mango, or papaya chunks, slightly mashed
- ⊙ Cut up, cooked carrots or soft squash chunks

FEEDING AT 9 MONTHS

By the time your baby is around 9 months old, meals will usually progress to 3 times per day. They may now be made of multiple foods and aren't always accompanied by formula or nursing. The above chart shows the feeding pattern we suggest.

Finger Foods at 9 months, as your baby is ready:

- ⊙ Very, very ripe peeled pear or peach chunks
- ⊙ Baked sweet potato mashed with butter and rolled into easy-to-pick-up balls
- ⊙ Diced small, stewed apples or pears
- ⊙ Very ripe and soft cantaloupe, mango, or papaya chunks, slightly mashed
- ⊙ Cooked, peeled zucchini and parsnips
- ⊙ Chopped or minced liver

HEARTY STEW

Despite the trend toward lean meat preference, organ meats, while lean, are often disregarded. Many indigenous cultures include dishes of heart, tongue, liver, and kidneys. Native American lore includes the practice that like helps like; for example, to keep your cardiovascular system healthy, eat heart, and to keep your ability to detoxify well, eat liver.

Dietary heart is an excellent source of carnitine, taurine, B vitamins, and the antioxidant CoQ10, all of which individually show remarkable cardiovascular benefits, and they neutralize the toxic damage of free radicals (found in environmental toxins, secondhand smoke, and other pollutants), but packaged together, significantly improve cardiovascular and overall health. The combination of these nutrients have stunned researchers with their heart-health benefits.

Carrots, when cooked, have a better antioxidant supply, as reported in 2002 in the *Journal of Agricultural and Food Chemistry*, which states that cooking carrots increases their levels of beta-carotene. Other vegetables that have enhanced antioxidants through boiling, in particular, include spinach, mushrooms, asparagus, cabbage, and peppers.

2 medium carrots, chopped

½ medium onion, finely chopped

2 tablespoons (28 g) ghee, coconut oil, or lard

½ pound (225 g) beef heart, minced

½ pound (225 g) ground beef, *optional*

2 ounces (55 g) beef liver, *optional*

½ to 1 teaspoon Celtic sea salt

2½ cups (570 ml) Souper Stock (page 45)

Boil the carrots until soft and drain.

Brown the onion in the fat in a skillet over medium-high heat until the onions are mushy and well cooked, about 10 minutes.

Lower the heat to medium and add the meat. Cook 3 to 4 minutes or until brown, leaving the liver light pink inside. Add the carrots and sea salt and stir together.

Fill the pan with enough stock (or filtered water if stock is not available) to cover the meat. Lower the heat to low, cover the pan, and simmer until the meat is very tender, 2 to 3 hours.

Purée the meat with the vegetables and stock or, if your baby is ready, cut the meat into very tiny bites and serve with stock.

NOTES

- Note which foods in this recipe your baby has not yet had, and introduce them individually. Otherwise, omit untried ingredients and limit the stew to previously tolerated foods.

- If you've served beef before, introducing heart at the same time is fine since heart is also beef muscle meat.

- You can simmer chopped heart overnight in a slow cooker of Souper Stock, with carrots, celery (must be well cooked to mushy), and onion, along with a pinch of Celtic sea salt, marrow bones, and a small bit of vinegar.

- Additional seasonings like pepper and tarragon can be added at age 1.

YIELD: Dinner for family, or 3 to 5 servings for baby

GELATIN, JAM, JIGGLERS, AND CUSTARD

There's gelatin and then there's *gelatin*. The gelatin we are referring to is not the bleached, artificially colored, over-sweetened Jell-O brand to which you might be accustomed. Unprocessed gelatin is pure and whole and provides important amino acids, and serves as a fortifying and nourishing gift to the digestive tract. We recommend gelatin powder sourced from responsibly farmed, pastured (grass-fed) animals, such as Bernard Jensen, Great Lakes, and Vital Proteins.

The beauty of gelatin is you can vary the ratio of gelling powder to liquid to end up with different consistencies, from jams to gummies. The following table is a guide to get the result you desire. Remember to always allow the gelatin to bloom (let sit in a small amount of cold liquid for 10 to 15 minutes), which will make it easier to dissolve when added to the hot liquid. For babies at 8 months, we suggest jam to loose-jiggler consistency. Gummies are firmer and should be served when your baby is closer to 10 months or older.

Spend one morning or afternoon in the kitchen per week—doing prep, planning, making Souper Stock, etc. Those hours will pay off through the rest of the week, minimizing the time required each day. Set aside those 3 to 4 hours per week as strictly kitchen time, making it a priority on your calendar.

	GELATIN POWDER	LIQUID/FRUIT MASH
JAM	2 teaspoons (5 g)	2 cups (475 ml)
CUSTARD	3 teaspoons (7 g)	2 cups (475 ml)
JIGGLERS	6 teaspoons (14 g)	2½ cups (570 ml)
GUMMIES	8 teaspoons (18 g)	½ to ¾ cup (120 to 175 ml)

You can use filtered water, fruit mash, mom's milk, or homemade formula as the liquid to enhance nutrition. We have provided a few of our favorite recipes on the following page.

FRUITY JIGGLERS

2 cups (322 g) pears or (300 g) apples, peeled and cored and chopped

6 teaspoons (18 g) gelatin

Use a juicer to make fresh juice from whole fruit. Two pears or apples will be about 2½ cups (570 ml) juice. Simmer the juice, minus ½ cup (120 ml), in a saucepan over medium heat.

Add the gelatin evenly over ½ cup (120 ml) cool fruit mash or liquid (½ cup filtered water can be also used). Set aside for 10 minutes until the gelatin has absorbed the liquid. Stir to ensure it dissolves.

If you don't own a juicer, heat the fruit in a saucepan over medium-low heat, stirring occasionally, until liquefied, about 1 hour, then purée the apples and/or pears with an immersion blender, if needed. Slowly stir the gelatin mixture into the hot fruit liquid, ensuring the gelatin fully dissolves.

Pour into an 8 × 8-inch (20 × 20 cm) glass dish or other shallow glass container and refrigerate for at least 3 hours.

Slice into small finger-fun cubes for your 8-to-9-month-old baby. The jiggler should melt/dissolve easily in your mouth.

YIELD: Sixty-four 1-inch (2.5 cm) cubes

NOTES

⊙ Tropical fruits cannot be used to make gelatin; because they are so enzyme rich, their busy digestive activity will break down (predigest) the gelatin and it will never "set."

⊙ Use apples or pears and introduce berries at 10 to 12 months.

⊙ You can also use stock and veggies to make savory jigglers.

FRUIT GUMMIES

(AT AGE 18 MONTHS OR OLDER, WHEN YOUR BABY IS READY)

8 teaspoons (18 g) gelatin

½ cup (120 ml) fresh squeezed, homemade orange juice

In a small saucepan, sprinkle the gelatin over the chilled orange juice. Allow to sit for 10 minutes before heating. Slowly heat the mixture.

Continue stirring over low heat until the gelatin is completely dissolved—it will be thick and somewhat syrup-like. Remove from the heat and quickly pour into molds or even a small glass dish (grease with coconut oil).

Put in the freezer for 10 minutes to harden. Remove and pop out of molds or cut into squares if needed.

YIELD: 8 gummies

NOTES

⊙ Vitamin C powder, probiotics, and other vitamins or supplements can be added into the mixture during heating to make homemade vitamins.

⊙ We do not recommend using store-bought juice (see discussion on juice, page 125).

COCONUT CUSTARD

4 ounces (120 ml) coconut milk or coconut cream

3 teaspoons (7 g) gelatin

4 ounces (120 ml) mom's milk or homemade formula

Sample coconut milk individually first, to ensure it agrees with your baby. Sprinkle the gelatin over mom's milk and set aside. Heat the coconut milk in a saucepan. Bring to simmering over low to medium heat. (*Note:* If using mom's milk, do not heat.)

Once the gelatin has absorbed the liquid, scoop into the simmering mixture.

Pour into individual small dishes or a bowl and refrigerate.

The custard should be set after 3 hours and should be of firm but soft consistency.

YIELD: Four 2-ounce (57 g) servings

FANCY FISH ROE

Baby "caviar" has Super POWERs. Not just for yachts and villas, caviar has billion-dollar health benefits your baby can enjoy. In fact, fish roe is an ancient sacred food for preconception, pregnancy, nursing moms, and growing children.

Fish roe's small size, shape, and stickiness make them fun practice for the pincer grasp. She will be fascinated chasing them around her high-chair tray.

This super food packs a powerful punch for protection against toxins. These nutrient-rich eggs have vitamin A, K2, zinc, iodine, and DHA and are a very rich source of vitamin D. (If you're giving your baby additional vitamin D or are taking it yourself, you can skip your dose on the days you both consume roe. Some studies show 1 tablespoon of fish eggs contains 17,000 IU of precious vitamin D.)

In fact, fish roe is a Super POWER food:

- ⊙ **P—Protective**—builds the brain, supports the immune system and digestive health

- ⊙ **O—Optimal nutrition**—very nutrient dense

- ⊙ **W—Wisdom** of the ancients—a traditional food around the world

- ⊙ **E—Enriching**—mineral and vitamin rich, especially with vitamin D

- ⊙ **R—Regenerating**—a healing food, used for fertility and for growing optimally healthy babies

1 teaspoon fish roe (raw, frozen, or dried)

Fresh fish roe usually requires no preparation. If frozen, just thaw it. Some roe might require removing casings.

1 teaspoon is a good serving size for self-feeding.

Roe can also be stirred into a soft-boiled egg yolk (see page 99), mixed with mashed avocado, stirred into Souper Stock (page 45) meat meals, or served with puréed vegetables.

NOTES

- ⊙ Purchase only refrigerated roe, as shelf-stable caviar contains preservatives, or order online.

- ⊙ Salmon roe is largest and best for first finger foods.

- ⊙ Avoid domestic paddlefish caviar from the contaminated rivers of Mississippi, Ohio, and Tennessee.

YIELD: 1 serving

HOMEMADE GHEE

Ghee is prepared from butter, and using the highest quality, organic, grass-fed, cultured butter is advised. It is great for cooking or spreading and contains butyrate, which is a digestive aid. Ghee has not only vitamins A, D, and E, but also the coveted vitamin K2 (Weston A. Price's "X Factor"). Combined together, these nutrients can support strength in bones, supple arteries, and healthful endocrine function.

2 cups (450 g) unpasteurized, unsalted, organic, and grass-fed butter

Cut the butter into cubes and place in a medium-size saucepan.

Heat over medium heat until melted and then reduce the heat to a simmer for 12 to 15 minutes.

Watch for the butter to form a foam layer, then bubble, and then form a second foam layer. When the second foam forms, the ghee is complete and should be a golden color. You should see brown milk solids at the bottom of your pan.

Cool for a few minutes and then slowly pour through a wire mesh strainer lined with cheese-cloth (several layers will work better). Milk solids/protein are not to be poured into ghee (but you can eat them!).

Ghee will last up to 1 month at room temperature or up to 2 months in the refrigerator.

NOTES

⊙ By putting ghee in recipes and slathering cooked vegetables or fruit with this powerfully packed, nutrient-rich flavor enhancer, your child will get not only the nutrients in the ghee, but the additional ability to absorb and utilize fat-soluble nutrients in fruits and vegetables.

⊙ Without the remaining milk solids, ghee is less allergenic and resembles the high-vitamin butter oil that Weston A. Price had such success with when helping to regenerate the health of children and adults.

⊙ If raw butter is not available, pasteurized, organic, and grass-fed unsalted butter can be used.

YIELD: 1⅞ cups (440 ml)

YOGURT, KEFIR, AND YOGURT CHEESE

Milk that has been cultured is a good source of protein, as well as vitamins, minerals, and probiotics. Fermented dairy provides phenomenal health benefits, such as improving calcium absorption, boosting immunity, aiding digestion and detoxification, and helping to prevent and treat constipation, thrush, and yeast diaper rashes. Yogurt is fermented (curdled) milk. Kefir is similar to yogurt, but it's usually more liquid and has different microflora strains, including good yeast. Another way to get the benefits of cultured dairy is to strain the whey out of the yogurt and use the curds as a nutrient-rich "cream cheese." This soft cheese has the benefits of fermentation and raw dairy. It is also called fromage frais (fresh cheese).

2 cups (16 ounces, or 455 g) whole, plain, organic yogurt or kefir (preferably raw)

Let the covered raw yogurt or kefir sit out on the counter for 24 hours. It will separate into whey (the yellow liquid) and milk solids (curds).

Line a mesh strainer with several layers of cheesecloth (or a coffee filter) and set over a bowl. Pour in both layers of the yogurt or kefir.

Let the whey drip through the strainer for 24 hours (remaining on the counter if raw dairy is used and in the refrigerator if using pasteurized dairy); the curds will be captured in the cloth. (If you suspend the strainer higher over the bowl, you'll make "drier" cheese.) This resulting yogurt cheese will be similar to cream cheese in consistency.

Yogurt cheese will last for 2 weeks in the refrigerator.

The whey can be used for lacto-fermentation (see Homemade Curds and Whey in chapter 4).

YIELD: About 1½ cups (12 ounces, or 340 g) "cheese" and ½ cup (120 ml) whey

Spices should be introduced individually, as all new foods should be, to watch for any reactions that indicate your baby isn't ready for that food or spice. Spices that can be used at this age (and no earlier than 6 months) are: clove, green cardamom, nutmeg, and cinnamon—but not dry and loose, only stirred into a moist ingredient (and too much can create a burning sensation in the mouth, so use sparingly). Around 8 months, additional spices can be added, including coriander, cumin, dill garlic, ginger, and turmeric. Spicy seasonings shouldn't be introduced until into your child's first year.

Children exposed to many flavors prove to be adventurous eaters as adults. The best way to introduce new spices is to mix with cooked sweet potatoes, carrots, or other food that has already been part of your baby's regular fare. Once you've introduced and determined that a new spice is well tolerated, a mixed dish such as Turkish Liver (page 141) can be a great addition to your baby's menu.

NOTES

⊙ Raw yogurt and kefir are vastly preferred. (Check with local CSAs and farm co-ops.)

⊙ Commercial yogurt should say "live" and "active" cultures so that the beneficial bacteria is living—which is the only way it does you any good. If the label says "pasteurized," "stabilized," or "heat-treated after culturing," then the bacteria will have all been destroyed by the heat processing. See Resources, page 260, for recommended brands.

⊙ Choose whole-milk, unflavored yogurt, as fats make the probiotics hardier and healthier, and flavors usually have added sugar.

⊙ The yogurt cheese can be mixed with very soft fruits as a dessert or with soft vegetables for dinner.

ICED BANANA COCONUT CREAM

Coconut isn't a nut, but a healthy palm fruit and a seed. Allergies to coconut are rare. However, if you are concerned about allergies, put coconut oil on your baby's skin first to make sure there is no reaction. In some cultures, coconut has been a longstanding first food for babies starting at 6 months. This might be due to traditional wisdom, as coconut is second only to mom's milk in content of lauric acid. The body converts lauric acid into monolaurin, a potent antiviral constituent that is being studied to fight very strong viruses, including herpes and HIV.

½ ripe banana

¼ cup (58 ml) coconut cream, mom's milk, or homemade formula (if formula-fed)

Cut the banana in half. Peel and freeze the banana overnight.

Remove the banana half from the freezer and chop. Add the desired liquid and blend in a Vitamix or food processor.

Serve as a cold, sweet, healthy treat or as part of a meal.

NOTES

⊙ The recipe can be doubled.

⊙ For a larger serving, use 1½ bananas with ¾ cup (175 ml) of coconut milk.

YIELD:
2 to 3 baby servings

INGREDIENT SPOTLIGHT: COCONUT

The coconut's health benefits are many and there are plenty of products you can incorporate into your diet.

- *Copra, or coconut "meat,"* is a great source of fiber. Translucent meat from young green coconuts is easier to chew than mature white meat.

- Often called "nature's sports drink," *coconut water* is an excellent electrolyte solution. It also helps replenish lost fluids after illness or diarrhea.

- *Coconut milk* is very nutritious, offering minerals, vitamins, and healthy fatty acids. But it still falls short of the nutritional profile of animal milk.

- *Coconut cream* contains medium-chain triglycerides (MCTs). Known to support thyroid health and improve metabolism, these MCTs are key in promoting healthy ketosis, demonstrated to reduce the progression of Alzheimer's and some cancers.

- *Coconut oil* is a pure source of MCTs, as well as potent antiviral and antibacterial immune-boosting elements and antioxidants.

- *Coconut butter (or manna)*, made from mature coconut flesh, includes natural coconut sugar, nutrients, and lauric acid.

FRUIT MEDLEY

One of the favors the beneficial bacteria in our gut does for us is digest and break down fiber and other carbohydrates. Eventually, your baby will have built up her army of beneficial bacteria, but until then, most vegetables and fruits should be cooked before serving to make them more digestible and nutritious—and therefore protective against toxins. Cooking breaks down antinutrients that can impair digestion and also breaks down fiber, which, without plentiful probiotic friends residing in the gut, can be a digestive irritant if consumed raw.

½ cup (about 60 g) cherries, pitted and halved or quartered

2 peaches or nectarines, pitted and chopped

3 apricots, pitted and chopped

1 tablespoon (15 g) ghee or coconut oil

Cook the fruit in the fat in a saucepan over low heat until very soft and juicy, about 20 minutes.

Purée (use caution when puréeing hot liquids) if needed using a hand blender.

Cool and serve.

NOTES

⊙ Introduce each of these foods (via chopping, cooking, and mashing) individually if they have not been already.

⊙ Since apples and pears were already introduced in First Fruit Sauces (chapter 4), they are a great addition to the Fruit Medley.

⊙ As cherries, peaches, and nectarines appear on the list of the most pesticide-ridden foods (see "The Dirty Dozen and the Clean Fifteen," page 125), choose organic, if possible. (If organic is not available, wash well with a natural wash containing grapefruit seed extract.)

⊙ This dish makes a great "dessert" or celebration "treat" for your baby. There is no need to try ice cream or cake when nature provides abundant flavor and natural sweetness in fruits!

YIELD: 1½ cups (384 g) (or about 6 to 8 baby servings)

TURKISH LIVER

Liver is nutritious and in addition to the powerful retinol form of vitamin A it provides, it is also known as the best source of B vitamins (including B12). It also contains vitamin C (some of which is destroyed with cooking), vitamin E, copper, zinc, protein, phosphorus, iron, thiamin, CoQ10, and selenium.

1 pound (455 g) fresh calf or lamb liver

⅓ cup (50 g) lard, coconut oil, or ghee (for frying)

1 medium red onion, chopped

1 teaspoon freshly grated turmeric root

1 clove garlic, minced

2 tablespoons (2 g) finely chopped cilantro

Pinch of ground cloves, *optional*

Celtic sea salt to taste

Cut the liver into small cubes, removing any tough membrane.

Melt the oil in a large skillet and add the onion, turmeric, and garlic and cook well, about 10 minutes.

When the onions are cooked and the oil is hot enough for frying (a drop of water sizzles), add the liver cubes. Brown the cubes on all sides. Lower the heat to a simmer and add the cilantro, ground cloves, if using, and sea salt.

To serve to your 8-month-old, purée her portion with an immersion blender. As your baby approaches 10 months, she will be able to eat the soft liver cubes and mushy onion strands.

NOTES

⊙ For older babies, children, and adults sharing this meal, you can optionally add ½ teaspoon ground sumac to your portions. Some claim that sumac (*Rhus coriaria*), which is a red berry, ground, and altogether unrelated to poison sumac and part of the cashew family (Anacardiaceae), like mangoes, might be allergenic to those very sensitive to cashews, the same as with pink peppercorns.

⊙ It is best to introduce new spices one at a time with several days in between to watch for reaction. The spices that mom consumes while nursing will likely be tolerated because they have been introduced in mom's milk. Baby's first spices should be mild, easy on new taste buds, and simple to digest.

YIELD:
8 to 10 baby servings

SWEET POTATO POND SOUP WITH AVOCADO TURTLES

Sweet potatoes are an excellent source of beta-carotene (the precursor to retinol) and anthocyanins, which work in a complex way with other flavonoid components in foods and are currently being studied, but are believed to be potent free-radical scavengers and antioxidants. Adding fats, from coconut cream and ghee, as well as the fat-digesting enzymes in avocado, make for a healthful and colorful soup to consume.

1 onion or leek, diced

4 tablespoons (55 g) ghee or coconut oil

3 medium sweet potatoes, peeled and chopped into 1-inch (2.5 cm) cubes

2 to 3 teaspoons (5 to 7 g) ground cinnamon

2 cup (475 ml) chicken Souper Stock (page 45)

1 cup (235 ml) coconut cream

Celtic sea salt or Himalayan salt

In a medium-size pan, sauté the onion in the fat over medium-low heat until translucent, 5 to 10 minutes. Add the sweet potatoes and continue to sauté over medium heat until the potato chunks are soft, about 20 minutes. Sprinkle the cinnamon on top and stir to distribute evenly.

Add the stock, increase the heat, and allow to simmer for 10 minutes, or until the potatoes have cooked through. Blend in the pot with a stick/immersion blender or spoon into a regular blender and blend until smooth. Add the cream and return to a simmer. Season with sea salt.

Pour into two bowls and serve with Avocado Turtles.

AVOCADO TURTLES

1 large ripe avocado

Slice the ripe avocado in half, then into quarters. Discard the pit. Peel the avocado quarters and dispose of the peel. Cut the avocado into small chunks that are bite-size for your baby.

Drop some into your baby's soup. He will enjoy finding them with his spoon.

YIELD: ½ cup (120 ml)

POACHED FISH

Poaching preserves moisture and adds flavor to fish like albacore tuna, salmon, and sablefish/black cod. All three are classified as "Best Choice" by the Seafood Watch program. The USDA advises, "Babies need the omega-3 fatty acids found in fish for brain, nerve, and eye development. Most children don't get enough, especially when they switch from breast milk or formula to solid food. Additionally, children's food preferences largely develop by age five, . . . parents [are urged] to help their kids develop a taste for seafood early."

1 tablespoon (10 g) finely chopped white onion

2 cloves garlic, minced

1 teaspoon freshly grated turmeric

1 tablespoon (8 g) freshly grated ginger, *optional*

3 tablespoons (42 g) ghee, coconut oil, or (45 ml) cultured butter

2 large carrots, finely diced

1 zucchini, finely diced (can substitute yellow squash)

3 cups (700 ml) Souper Stock (you can make a fish/seafood stock or use chicken Souper Stock, page 45)

2 to 3 tablespoons (28 to 45 ml) Homemade Mom's Milk Whey (page 106), *optional*

4 to 6 fillets (6 ounces, or 170 g each) wild-caught Atlantic mackerel, pollock, herring, or salmon

Celtic sea salt to taste

In a skillet over medium heat, sauté the onion, garlic, turmeric, and ginger in the desired fat for 5 to 10 minutes or until the onion is transluscent.

Add the carrot and zucchini and cook until the veggies are soft, about 5 to 10 minutes.

Add the stock and bring to just below a boil.

Reduce the heat and simmer for 10 minutes. Reduce the heat and add the whey, if using.

Slowly add the fish into the hot liquid, making sure it is submerged.

Raise the heat back to a simmer and cover with a lid. The fish should be poached in 6 to 8 minutes, depending on the thickness of the fish. The cooking liquid should remain just below boiling.

Remove the fish and purée, thinning with mom's milk, formula, Souper Stock, or the poaching broth to the right consistency for your baby. The vegetables can be removed and puréed or given as finger food. Season with salt to taste.

YIELD: 4 to 6 servings

NOTES

- Fish was once off the list for younger babies due to allergenicity; however, recommendations to wait on allergenic foods have been reversed, and for the most part, we agree. Some good fish to try early on with babies include wild-caught salmon, herring, and sardines.

- *For sardines:* Add sardines to the warm liquid. Purée into a spoonable meal for your baby. Choose sardines such as Wild Planet brand, wild-caught, non-GMO, in water with no salt added.

- When choosing fish, refer to the sidebar "Deep Dive into Choosing Seafood Wisely" page 203.

RECONSIDER BABY FOOD JARS AND NOODLE STARS

Bolstering Immunity with Nutrients and Foods

(10 TO 12 MONTHS)

When your baby is 10 to 12 months old, you can work through new flavors faster and relax a bit in terms of foods' consistency. Along with new foods, your baby will be putting everything else he can get his little hands on into his mouth. While that's fine most of the time, you will need to consider raising his defenses against potential illnesses.

Your baby's expanded social schedule also comes with increased exposure to bacteria and viruses. While such exposure is important for your baby's developing immune system, it is important to fortify your baby with powerful immune-boosting foods to ensure that he has everything he needs to win the battles against those infectious agents. This is the hallmark of the third pillar (immune boosting) of Super Nutrition.

True Culprits of Illness

Your baby is constantly exposed to germs. But whether he gets sick is based on the strength of his immune system, not germ exposure alone. In fact, most bacteria are helpful. Ultimately, microbial exposure serves to strengthen immunity by *helping* your baby's gut develop a strong barrier against agents that could make him sick.

A weak immune system is the true culprit behind illness. Struggling immunity comes from poor diet, sugar, toxins, antibiotic overuse, nutrient deficiencies, low omega-3 and high omega-6 fatty acids, protein deficiency, and lack of good bacteria.

THE OUTSOURCING OF OUR IMMUNE SYSTEM. With antibiotics being such a quick fix, we've forgotten the importance of strengthening and fortifying our natural immune system. But with new antibiotic-resistant bugs that these drugs can no longer fight for us, we need to take our immunity back into our own hands. Protection from infection should only be "outsourced" (to medicines) rarely and in times of extreme illness.

What to Feed Your Baby for Optimizing Immune Strength

Eighty percent of our immune system is actually found in the gut. So the best way to keep your baby healthy is by focusing on his gut. Healthy intestines discourage infection. Feed him foods that nourish intestinal tissue, support the mucosal lining (which coats the gut), and provide him plenty of good bacteria in his diet and environment. By building these layers (intestinal tissue, mucosa, good bacteria), you'll be ensuring that he's got a thick and strong barrier against infecting agents and toxins.

The immune system uses nutrients to fight off invaders and infection. It relies on protein; several specific vitamins, minerals, and antioxidants; as well as probiotics, the right ratio of good omega fatty acids, and help from antimicrobial fats (for example, those in grass-fed butter, meats, and coconut oil). *Even a single* nutrient deficiency will suppress the immune system, disarming it, and will allow infection to embed more easily.

THE SUNSHINE VITAMIN HELPS IMMUNE PERFORMANCE

Vitamin D is intimately involved with the immune system. According to a study published in the *American Journal of Respiratory and Critical Care Medicine*, a single dose of vitamin D can stop pathogenic bacteria. Vitamin D insufficiency is related to higher rates of common colds, influenza, and the respiratory infection RSV. It likely contributes to the increased rate of illness during darker winter months.

Although sunshine exposure is the best way to acquire sufficient vitamin D, it is also important to get some vitamin D from foods or supplements, especially during the winter months in northern climates. Vitamin D–containing foods include fish roe, fish liver oils, wild-caught fish and shellfish (after your baby reaches 18 months), sun-exposed pastured animal fats (particularly from chickens and pigs), as well as liver and egg yolks.

POWER UP IMMUNITY WITH PLENTIFUL PROBIOTICS

According to *Pediatric Gastroenterology and Clinical Nutrition*, "The primary cause of infection is not due to the presence of unfriendly bacteria, but is actually due to insufficient friendly bacteria." Bad bugs don't so much cause illness as a lack of good bugs!

Good bacteria are *bad* microbes' natural enemy. They fight illness-causing strains of bacteria, yeast, parasites, and *even viruses (like cold and flu)*. According to a study in the journal *Pediatrics*, beneficial bacteria are effective in *preventing* childhood colds and flus. Giving probiotics twice a day to 3- to 5-year-olds during 6 months reduced fever incidence by 72%, coughing by 62%, and runny noses by 58%! The groups getting probiotics also used fewer antibiotics and missed fewer days of school. Such significant findings imply that *chronic runny noses, coughs, and viral illness in children could actually be caused by a probiotic deficiency*.

Supplemental probiotics are very helpful for the immune system and overall health. In *Digestive Wellness: How to Strengthen the Immune System and Prevent Disease through Healthy Digestion*, Elizabeth Lipski, Ph.D., reports on studies that show "supplemental *Lactobacillus acidophilus* and *L. casei* decreased the severity and incidence of bronchitis and pneumonia in babies aged 6 months to 2 years."

The kind of bacteria your baby is exposed to early on can influence whether he will later develop 3Cs. In a 2011 study, reported in the *Journal of Allergy and Clinical Immunology*, led by John Penders of Maastricht University, 2,700 babies were followed through age 7. Researchers found that a baby's early exposure to bad bacteria resulted in a higher likelihood that he would have immune-mediated health problems, such as food sensitivities, eczema, and/or wheezing in childhood. Exposure in the absence of sufficient good bacteria will help lead to these health issues.

Your baby's intestinal tract is essentially sterile at birth. You want good bugs to take their rightful place as rulers of his gut ecosystem, establishing a hierarchy that keeps bad bugs at bay. Nature designed the first exposure to be through the vaginal canal, during birth. Next, your baby is dosed with even more beneficial bacteria when you nurse because your colostrum and milk are packed with healthy probiotics.

Early exposure to such healthy bacteria serves him well by protecting against infection (as well as facilitating digestion, getting rid of toxins, making vitamins, and more!). Also, as Penders's study showed, babies with healthy bacteria (known to actively crowd out bad bacteria) are not as likely to have allergies and asthma in childhood, as are those babies born via C-section who have pathogenic bacteria taking up residence in their intestinal tract. If your baby had a C-section delivery or is not being nursed, it is critical to supplement directly with probiotics and to include lacto-fermented foods and raw and cultured dairy early on in his diet to ensure adequate exposure and colonization of beneficial bacteria. (*Note:* Also take extra care to avoid using antibacterial agents.)

Babies born via C-section can benefit from vaginal seeding, in which swabs from the birth canal allow some of the benefits of a natural birth to be conferred to your baby. For more information, ask your doctor about this process.

Lacto-fermented foods (for example, unpasteurized pickles, sauerkraut, and kimchi) and beverages (kombucha), fresh (raw) dairy, and cultured dairy (e.g., yogurt and kefir) are sources of probiotics as well as lactic acid, which is very helpful for intestinal (and therefore immune) health.

In the *Journal of Medicinal Food* in 2014, it was reported that kimchi, a Korean dish made by adding lactic acid bacteria (such as lactobacillus) to vegetables, has numerous health benefits. They state, "Health functionality of kimchi, based upon our research and that of others, includes anti-cancer, antiobesity, anticonstipation, colorectal

DEEP DIVE INTO DISINFECTING: IT'S A DISASTER

Science from two centuries ago taught us to fear all germs. Now, though, we know that germs are mostly *helpful*. Microbes live in our bodies as friendly helpers that act together as another "organ" upon which we rely. These friendly flora *protect* us from heavy metals, other toxins, and infectious agents; and they create nutrients for us and help us digest foods properly.

Being "sterile" by using disinfectants doesn't mean being safe. Antibacterial cleansers, wipes, and sanitizing gels can *kill off* your baby's army of protective microbes, making bad bugs even stronger and your child's defenses even weaker.

Specifically, beware of antibacterial products with agents like triclosan, a registered pesticide, which accumulates in your child's tissues and has been linked to higher rates of allergies, immune diseases, organ damage, endocrine malfunction, and eroded immune systems.

This has led several experts, including Dr. Matthew Greenhawt, M.D., Infectious Diseases in Children editorial board member, to question antibacterial practices. He ponders, "In our clean modern-day society, where we protect our children from infection through methods ranging from an aggressive vaccination program to a seemingly omnipresent availability of instant hand sanitizer, one must wonder if our rising rates of allergy and atopic disorders parallel our efforts to *reduce* microbial exposure."

Don't try to make your baby too clean for his own good. Studies show that mild early-life illness and immune system engagement can create lifelong immunity and ward off autoimmune conditions later in life. *Let him fight his own microbial battles;* he'll be healthier and stronger for it—all his life.

health promotion, probiotic properties, cholesterol reduction, fibrolytic effect, antioxidative and antiaging properties, brain health promotion, immune promotion, and skin health promotion."

ENABLE ENZYMES TO ENGAGE THE ENEMY

Strive to supply your baby with enzyme-rich foods as a great way to fortify his immunity. Enzymes support white blood cells and other infection-fighting agents, while directly fighting pathogens, too. Fortunately, many of the probiotic-rich foods are also enzyme-rich foods. Fresh, raw milk is an excellent source of enzyme-based pathogen

killers. Tropical fruits, like pineapple, kiwi, and papaya, and lacto-fermented foods and beverages, like sauerkraut and cultured dairy (yogurt), provide enzymes as well.

A WELL-ROUNDED TRADITIONAL-FOODS DIET STRENGTHENS IMMUNE FUNCTION

By feeding your baby plenty of good fats—particularly saturated fats—you'll provide him with antiviral, antibacterial, and antimicrobial fatty acids that will help him stay healthy. The Weston A. Price Foundation reports that butter contains glycosphingolipids, which specifically protect against intestinal infection, especially in the very young. Butter fats, as well as the fats in coconut oil, have antimicrobial constituents that are active against pathogens and yeast, while feeding good bacteria. An adequate supply of dietary docosahexaenoic acid (DHA) is critical for human nutrition, but is particularly critical during infancy, during which time low DHA intake has been associated with an increased risk of chronic diseases, including asthma and allergies.

Protein- and nutrient-rich foods are broken down into amino acids and contain an array of vitamins and minerals that your baby's body will use to build his immune army (antibodies). There is a reason chicken soup is a panacea of healing—the protein, fats, highly absorbable minerals, and gelatin in soup (made from bones) are restorative and supportive to the digestive system and thus critical to immunity. Protein deficiency stunts the body's ability to build enzymes and antibodies, both of which are necessary for immune function and fighting off illness.

The process of slow cooking meat, as is done for meats in soups, provides nutrients that we do not get in our convenience, fast-food-based diets. We exist on foods from quick preparation methods, such as grilling, broiling, and frying, so we reach for predominantly muscle-based cuts of meat that align to such cooking techniques, such as steaks, chicken breasts, and lean ground beef. Consistently sticking to such cuts and cooking styles results in the absence of collagen and gelatin that are inherent in dishes such as pot roasts, boiled dinners, soups, and stews. For more information on the nutrients found in collagen and gelatin, *Deep Nutrition* by Catharine Shanahan, M.D., is an excellent resource.

What *Not* to Feed Your Baby for Optimizing Immune Strength

Avoiding flour- and sugar-based foods and other inflammation-causing foods will increase the chances that your baby's immune potential will be reached.

SUGAR: NOT SO SWEET FOR PROTECTION FROM INFECTION

Sugar, particularly, increases the body's susceptibility to infection. Jerry Kartzinel, M.D., pediatrician and coauthor of *Healing and Preventing Autism*, states, "The best way to get . . . [the] immune system to improve is to DECREASE . . . SUGAR INTAKE!" [emphasis *not* added]. As published in the *Journal of Clinical Nutrition*, sugar of all kinds (honey, juice, table sugar, etc.) *significantly* reduces your baby's immune system's ability to destroy pathogenic bacteria.

Sugar and white flour are the favorite sustenance of many bad bugs and harmful yeasts. These pathogenic flora feed on such simple carbs and ferment them in the gut, causing gas, diarrhea, toxic by-products, and intestinal illness. Bad yeast, in particular, can cause sugar cravings, leaky gut, ADHD, anxiety, and depression. By eliminating refined carbohydrates in your baby's diet, you reduce these sickness-causing flora by starving them.

FOODS THAT FEED THE FIRES OF INFLAMMATION

Foods that cause inflammation weaken your baby's immune system, making it hard for good flora to make a home in his gut. Inflammation is by and large affected by the ratio of essential fatty acids you get in your diet. Omega-3 fatty acids directly reduce inflammation and thin the blood in the body, whereas most omega-6 fatty acids cause inflammation and platelet stickiness. While both are integral to health, it is the *ratio* of omega-3 to omega-6 fatty acids, as well as the "nutritiousness" of the fat they come in, that is most important.

Russel L. Blaylock, M.D., reports on studies showing that inflammatory-inducing omega-6 fats reduce immune capabilities. He notes, "We now know that omega-6 oils profoundly suppress immunity . . . as a result they also promote infections."

In our modern diet, there are far too many unhealthy omega-6s (found in vegetable oils and from grain- and soy-fed animal foods) and far too few omega-3s (fish oils, flaxseed oil, grass-fed/pastured animal foods), resulting in an inflammatory imbalance. (Most Americans get 20 to 50 omega-6s for every one omega-3.) A traditional-foods diet, however, will naturally provide the correct omega-fatty-acid ratio that is closer to 3:1.

If Your Baby Does Get Sick

It is inevitable that sometimes your baby *will* get sick—and *should*, on occasion. Today's typically fed babies are reported to catch 7 to 10 colds per year, which is more frequent than one would expect in a traditionally nourished baby. Providing Super Nutrition should improve your baby's immune capability and minimize infection frequency, as well as severity. When your baby does get sick, honor his instincts to eat (or not), but ensure that he drinks and stays hydrated.

CHOOSE BEVERAGES WISELY

Coconut water is a natural source of nutrient-rich hydration and is an excellent way to replace lost electrolytes during illness. Another premier electrolyte solution is Souper Stock (page 45). We recommend alternating coconut water (see page 138) with Souper Stock during illness. (For nursing babies and young children, mom's milk is the very best fluid during illness, with homemade formula being second best. See page 75.) Coconut water or mom's milk can also be frozen into ice pops to soothe sore throats and provide hydration.

FATS FOR FEVER

The old adage "starve a fever, feed a cold" has some scientific credence. Studies suggest that children often instinctually choose not to eat during illness; and 36- to 48-hour fasts actually result in significant improvement in immune strength and infection-fighting capabilities. Temporarily not feeling hungry and therefore not eating much while sick might allow our immune system to function better. Don't make your baby fast, but if he's not eating for a day or two, as long as he is drinking, you need not be worried.

During such time, offer him fats, such as marrow, ghee, butter, or tiny spoonfuls of coconut oil, but don't worry if he's not interested. Fats such as these are rich in natural antimicrobial, antiviral, and antibacterial agents, and just small amounts can be satiating. Also, a fat-rich diet lessens dehydration risk.

Fever is the body's natural response to infection. Raising the body temperature means the heart beats faster, pushing nutrient-carrying blood to the scene and enhancing enzyme function, which helps destroy microbes. Further, with increased temperatures, microbes are less able to multiply, keeping infections in check. While it may seem frightening, the fever is your child's best way to fight infection.

Further, use of common fever-fighters comes with risk. Acetaminophen (brand name: Tylenol) is used far too frequently. Very real risks are involved with the use of Tylenol, including liver toxicity (making detoxification harder among other serious health risks) and reduced antioxidant capabilities (through lowering glutathione levels throughout the body), which results in increased risk for asthma, ADHD, and autism. Several studies show that the risk of asthma is dose-dependant on the use of Tylenol. Even pregnant mothers should consider Tylenol risk, as some research shows an increased risk for autism and attention issues in children. Of concern is the common practice of medical practitioners to recommend use of Tylenol when vaccines are administered, as the reduced ability to detoxify means that your baby will be less able to clear vaccine toxins (immune-irritating adjuvants and chemicals) and is therefore at higher risk of harm from them if Tylenol is used. This is supported by at least one study that demonstrated an increase in autism occurrence related to the acetaminophen given after MMR vaccines.

DEEP DIVE INTO TRUSTING THE WISDOM OF THE BABY BODY

In the 1920s and '30s, pediatrician Clara Davis, M.D., did a 6-year feeding experiment with babies. In 1939, she published her results, entitled "The Self-Selection of Diets by Young Children," in the *Canadian Medical Association Journal*.

She provided the babies with nutrient-dense, real foods, including soured milk, sea salt, bananas, orange juice, barley, cornmeal, peaches, bone jelly (gelatinous bone stock), tomatoes, beets, meats, bone marrow, raw lettuce, cooked and raw eggs, oatmeal, wheat, peas, cabbage, apples, cooked glandular organs, lamb, and chicken. Babies could choose as much as they wanted of whatever was before them.

Though their individual choices varied widely and changed over time, all the babies were hale, hearty, and "throve." None were noticeably fat or thin. There were no nutrient-deficiency diseases, constipation issues, vomiting, diarrhea, or serious illness, though once the group did get a fever. (Interestingly, during this illness, most chose unusually high amounts of *raw* beef, carrots, and beets.)

The babies self-selected foods in the right quantities and variety to ensure they had all essential nutrients, adequate energy, and proper digestive health; some were noted to select foods that corrected nutrient-deficiency disease (e.g., rickets) and when cured, no longer showed preference for those former favorites. All babies were of remarkable and superb health. Dr. Davis called this "the wisdom of the body," though she warned, "self-selection can have no . . . value if the diet . . . [is] selected from inferior foods" (by which was meant: white flour and sugar, which Dr. Davis said were "nutritional evils").

Your baby, too, has such wisdom of his body—and you *can* trust it.

Alternative options include homeopathics and holding your baby (to elicit endorphin pain relief) to provide relief. If medication is used, ibuprofen may be the lesser of two evils, compared to Tylenol/acetaminophen. Ibuprofen carries some risk to the kidneys during severe dehydration or where preexisting kidney problems exist. Medications may be warranted if your child is unable to sleep, is too uncomfortable to take in liquids, or fever exceeds 105°F (40.5°C). For fever greater than 100.4°F (38°C) in babies under 3 months, we recommend that you notify your doctor.

REBALANCE GUT ECOSYSTEM AFTER ANTIBIOTICS TO AVOID REPEAT INFECTIONS

Antibiotics damage the immune system by killing good bacteria and creating the right environment for bad microbes to thrive. This leaves your baby's immune system in a weakened state, more susceptible to repeat infections, and allows for overgrowth of antibiotic-resistant bacteria and other microbes, like damaging yeast. After antibiotics, it is very important to rebuild healthy flora and regain a favorable balance in the intestinal ecosystem by providing your baby's body with probiotic-rich foods and supplements (see page 148). When antibiotics are necessary, be sure to supplement with probiotics, according to package directions, and incorporate lacto-fermented foods and beverages (see chapter 2) daily, for at least 2 months after antibiotic treatment.

Stave Off Infection by Steering Clear of Baby Food Jars and Pasta Pitfalls

If you *only* provide your baby with meals of nutrient-rich, real, whole foods, you need not stress about quantity and variety; your baby will eat when hungry and in need of nutrients. If, however, his diet includes sugar, white flour, or juice, you cannot rely on his hunger cues and preferences, since these foods can be addictive and make him feel full without providing enough nutrition.

We, along with the AAP, recommend introducing *many* different foods by the end of the first year, as there is nutritional value in variety. Additionally, variety in the diet helps broaden children's palates and helps instill positive eating habits early. Offer a new food 8 to 30 times before giving up, as it takes time for babies to become familiar with new tastes and textures.

REFINED VS. REAL: We recommend avoiding refined salt and sugar for babies this age. Refined salt, like table salt and the kind you find in packaged foods, is simply sodium chloride. This kind of salt is disturbing to the body because most of the naturally occurring minerals found in whole salt are stripped away during refining and processing.

Unrefined, whole salt, however, is good for your baby (and for you!). Adding a pinch of high-quality sea salt to water makes it an electrolyte solution, and adding sea salt to Souper Stock (page 45) means it is rich in both *macro* minerals from bones and *micro* minerals from the salt. Whole, unrefined salt is essential for life and good for health, which is likely why it is so pleasing to the palate. This kind of salt is made of *80* highly absorbable trace minerals that occur naturally in proportions that make them work best together

PATTERN	10 MONTHS
Early AM	Mom's milk/home-made formula, then meal (shortly after waking)
Midmorning	Milk/homemade formula
Midday	Meal
Afternoon	Milk/homemade formula (before nap)
Evening	Meal
Nighttime	Milk/homemade formula (before bed)

and in the body (so the health problems often seen with refined salt are not seen with sea salt). Particularly, unrefined salt is important for proper digestion and nutrient assimilation and thus serves to bolster the immune system. Celtic sea salt and Himalayan salt are our preferred types, being richest in mineral content. Redmond Real Salt is also mineral rich. Whole, unrefined salt should have color—usually beige, gray, or pink.

PRACTICAL FEEDING TIPS AT THIS AGE

FASTER INTRODUCTION, THICKER CONSISTENCY. New foods can now be given every 1 or 2 days, rather than every 3 or 4. Also, foods can now be of a much chunkier consistency and need not be thinned down. Though many commercial baby foods are "microwavable," we absolutely do *not* recommend heating your baby's food in the microwave.

Your baby still isn't ready to handle chewing and swallowing like a grown-up. Choking is a risk, so never leave your child unattended while eating.

PATTERN	11 MONTHS
Early AM	Mom's milk/home-made formula, then meal (shortly after waking)
Midmorning	Snack
Midday	Meal
Afternoon	Milk/homemade formula (before nap)
Evening	Meal
Nighttime	Milk/homemade formula (before bed)

Super Nutrition Food Categorizations for 10 to 12 Months

SUPER POWER	PURE
• Lacto-fermented fruits and veggies • Coconut kefir • Grass-fed, raw cheese • Kidneys and other organ meats • Cod liver oil • Animal fats from grass-fed animals • Mom's milk	• Organic tropical fruits • Coconut water, unsweetened • Onion, garlic, beets, and other organic fruits and vegetables • Organic meats, eggs, and other animal foods

OKAY	CRAP
• Organic baby food (stage 3) • Nonorganic, non–Dirty Dozen fruits and vegetables, washed • All-natural meats, eggs, and other animal foods • Nonpastured, non-organic animal fats and butter	• Pretzels, crackers, cookies, bars • Prepared baby "meals" • Noodles and pasta dishes • Sweetened baby foods • Juice • Pasteurized dairy • Canola oil, soy oil, corn oil

FAMILY MEALS. Around this age, your baby's meals will align with family mealtimes. We advise you to eat with your baby starting from an early age. A bite for baby, then a bite for you—if possible. Despite the mess, keep offering your baby a spoon. The added weight and thicker texture of these new foods may make it easier for your baby to use it!

WATER. Hydration is tantamount to proper bodily function and detoxification. Offer water (preferably filtered, remineralized) in between meals. However, refrain from offering too much at meals, as it can reduce stomach acid, which is necessary for proper protein digestion. Souper Stock, mom's milk, cultured mommy milk, or formula can be offered in a cup throughout the day or with meals.

FOODS AND FLUIDS. Babies normally take between 18 and 24 ounces (520 to 710 ml) of mom's milk or formula at this age, meeting approximately one-third to one-half of their caloric needs.

Experts advise that babies should not drink pasteurized cow's milk at this age, and we agree due to its increased risk of anemia, iron deficiency, gastrointestinal bleeding, and allergies and intolerance. Fresh, raw, unpasteurized milk, from a trusted grass-fed source, however, does not carry such risks. Even with this high-caliber dairy, one year is the appropriate age to offer cow's milk to drink, unless it is part of a recipe for homemade formula (see chapter 3).

FLUCTUATING APPETITE. Be aware that your baby's appetite can fluctuate, and his likes and dislikes can change. If he's not eating much, choose foods that pack the most nutrient-dense punch in the smallest quantity, namely Super POWER foods like organ meats, fish eggs, grass-fed raw butter, and raw yogurt.

Recipes to Optimize Immunity

Popular snack foods like cereal and crackers are typically introduced at this age. They often become instant favorites, with babies preferring them over more nutritious options. These products usually don't offer many nutrients and aren't worth eating; you'd be better off allowing your child to become hungry enough (within reason) to accept more nutritious offerings.

Between 10 and 12 months, you can introduce beets, cooked berries, fish, coconut water, and raw cheese. For a more complete list of acceptable foods at this age, see the Food Introduction Timeline on page 255.

Stewed whole chicken, bone-in pork, or beef roasts are choices that include bones, connective tissue, fat, skin, necks, and feet. Eating meat on the bone, down to the bone, helps guarantee you get critical nutrients that support intestinal and nutritional health, and therefore immune strength. You can also use Vital Amines or unbleached, unrefined gelatin (including Great Lakes Gelatin) in soups, stews, sauces, and baked goods as an additional source of gelatin.

MASHED NOT-POTATOES

Since white potatoes are part of the nightshade family—which can cause inflammation—we don't recommend them yet. Either taro (a tuber) or cauliflower (in the cruciferous family of vegetables) can be used to make a mashed potato–style side dish. Part of Polynesian cuisine, taro must be well cooked prior to consumption in order to reduce the calcium oxalate content. Taro has small amounts of vitamins and minerals as well as some antioxidant value.

MASHED CAULIFLOWER

1 crown cauliflower

Ghee or other Fabulous Fat (see page 38) to taste

Celtic sea salt to taste

Steam the cauliflower until mushy. Drain the water well. Purée with the butter or ghee and sea salt until desired consistency.

YIELD: About 1 cup (225 g)

MASHED TARO

2 to 4 taro roots

Ghee or other Fabulous Fat (see page 38) to taste

Celtic sea salt to taste

Preheat the oven to 300°F (150°C, gas mark 2).

Bake the taro for 1 hour. When cool enough to handle, peel. Mash with fat of choice and sea salt.

Optional: Add coconut cream for varied texture, richness, and flavor.

YIELD: About 1 cup (225 g)

MASHED POI
(FERMENTED TARO ROOT)

2 teaspoons mom's milk or raw whey,

or

¼ cup (60 ml) water + ¼ tablespoon culture starter + ½ teaspoon non-centrifugal sugar (such as Rapunzel brand rapadura), allowing this mixture to rest for 20 minutes

1 cup (225 g) baked, peeled, mashed taro

Mix ingredients in a glass bowl and place in a Mason jar on a counter, sealed, for 24 hours. Serve as a side dish to meat.

YIELD: About 1 cup (225 g)

NOTES

⊙ Taro can replace potato in many recipes.

⊙ Rapadura is a mineral-containing sugar, found at health food stores or online.

PLAYFUL PANCAKES

Coconut flour is coconut flesh that has been dried and ground into a powder. It's actually a by-product of the creation of coconut milk. Higher in fiber (about 5 grams of fiber per tablespoon [7 g] of coconut flour) and with a lower glycemic index than grain-based flours, it doesn't spike your blood sugar as quickly. Baked goods are not necessarily healthy simply because they are made with coconut flour. Baked goods should always be an occasional treat, not an everyday staple. Coconut flour does not require presoaking or preparation to neutralize antinutrients.

COCONUT FLOUR PANCAKES

½ cup (56 g) coconut flour

¼ teaspoon Celtic sea salt

4 large, or 5 to 6 small, farm-fresh organic, pastured eggs

1 mashed, ripe banana

¼ cup (55 g) coconut manna/butter (2 tablespoons [28 g] coconut oil can be substituted), melted

¼ cup (55 g) homemade stewed apples, *optional* (See recipe for apples and pears in chapter 5.)

¼ cup (60 ml) coconut milk, mom's milk, homemade formula, or some combination

4 to 6 tablespoons (55 to 85 g) grass-fed butter, ghee, or coconut oil for cooking

Grass-fed butter, ghee, or coconut butter for spreading on warm pancakes

In a medium bowl, combine the coconut flour and sea salt.

In a large bowl, whisk the eggs, mashed banana, melted coconut butter or coconut oil, and stewed apples, if using, together. (Melt the coconut butter or coconut oil in a small saucepan over low heat or place the jar of coconut butter or coconut oil in warm water.)

Add the dry ingredients to the wet ingredients; stir with a fork until well combined. Add the milk slowly until the desired consistency is reached. The coconut flour will thicken the batter as it mixes with the wet ingredients.

Heat a griddle or frying pan with the butter, coconut oil, or ghee until it sizzles.

Using a large spoon or small scoop, add a little batter to the pan. Cook for about 3 to 4 minutes. You may not see many bubbles forming on the top, so carefully check the underside of your pancake before flipping and then flip. Cook on the other side for 1 to 2 minutes until cooked through.

Serve warm. Spread with butter, ghee, or coconut butter if desired.

NOTE

⊙ Try substituting homemade raw curd (see Curds and Whey recipe, page 106) for the banana for a different base flavor.

YIELD: About 12 small pancakes

SIMPLE BANANA PANCAKES

3 large ripe bananas

1 large farm-fresh, organic, pastured egg

2 large farm-fresh, organic, pastured egg yolks

Pinch of Celtic sea salt or Himalayan salt

½ teaspoon ground cinnamon

3 to 4 tablespoons (42 to 56 g) ghee or coconut oil for cooking

Mash the bananas in a small bowl. Add the egg and egg yolks, and mix together. Add the sea salt and cinnamon and stir.

Heat a griddle or frying pan over medium heat with the ghee or coconut oil until it sizzles. Spoon the batter onto the hot, greased griddle (be liberal with the fat) and spread. It should spread easily.

Cook a couple of minutes, checking under the edges for doneness. Once it starts to brown, flip and cook on the other side until cooked through.

YIELD: About 12 silver dollar-size pancakes

NOTES

⊙ When your baby is over a year, if desired, you can add some non-grain-based flour like a mixture of tigernut flour or arrowroot starch. Following grain preparation protocols to reduce phytic acid and antinutrients is recommended. At that point, you can also use whole eggs. Both these additions will give your pancakes a more classic pancake look and texture.

⊙ Coconut flour is very dense, so recipes with coconut flour typically need more wet ingredients, particularly eggs, to prevent them from getting crumbly and dry.

SCHMALTZ AND GRIBENES

Rendered chicken fat is called "schmaltz" in traditional Jewish cooking. Gribenes are a bonus "by-product" of making schmaltz (as are "crispins" in lard rendering). You can sauté chicken liver with schmaltz and gribenes to round out the nutritional value of the dish. Animal fats, such as schmaltz, offer a buffet of important fatty acids that are good for supporting the immune system.

SCHMALTZ

1 pound (455 g) chicken skin and fat

Rinse the chicken skin and fat. Chop into ½-inch (1 cm) pieces. Using kitchen scissors makes this easier. Fry the pieces in a skillet over low heat for 15 minutes.

Remove the pan from the heat and drain the liquid fat through a mesh strainer, reserving the strainer contents. The golden oil is the schmaltz; put in a clean jar and save for liver or vegetables.

YIELD: 1 cup (235 ml)

GRIBENES

1 large onion, chopped

Celtic sea salt and pepper to taste

Put the contents of the strainer (the chicken skin and fat remnants) back into the frying pan. Add the onion and sauté for about 20 minutes (pieces will darken, but should not blacken). Season with sea salt and pepper. You can eat the gribenes as a salty snack.

YIELD: ½ cups (280 g)

NOTES

⊙ Schmaltz is liquid at room temperature and solid when cold. Use it to sauté foods like liver, add it to liver to make chopped liver, or just eat with gribenes.

⊙ Use gribenes as a topping for salads or other dishes (for you), or serve as a great snack for your baby.

UNNECESSARY ANTIOBIOTICS. Antibiotics are non-discerning when it comes to obliterating bacteria. The issue is that most bacteria is beneficial. From birth, the body works hard with friendly bugs to create a hierarchy and layering of health-providing bacteria and yeasts. Since most of our microbiome is good bacteria, when antibiotics mow down all bugs, they disproportionately do away with more good than bad. In nearly sterilizing the gut, antibiotics create a vacuum where good bugs were, and bad bacteria can move in and take over. Antibiotics are very useful in limited situations; unfortunately, they are still over-prescribed. Bad microbes, like yeast and clostridia, can cause a huge range of problems, from GI symptoms, food cravings, obesity, and ADHD to mood and psychological disorders like anger, anxiety, and depression. By letting your children practice using their immune system, you will ultimately make them stronger, which means that doctors shouldn't prescribe, and parents shouldn't request, antibiotics when an illness is viral (as opposed to bacterial), nor should antibiotics be started before a culture result confirms a bacterial infection. If and when antibiotics are needed, high-dose probiotics and fermented foods are the best thing that you can do to help restore flora and minimize overgrowth of bad bugs. Choosing organic, pastured chicken and animal foods are important to avoid the antibiotics animals are often given as part of industrialized, containment-based agriculture practices.

BERRIES GALORE

In a few months, you can introduce raw berries, but until then, they must still be cooked because this makes them easier for babies to digest them. Start with strawberries and blueberries at this age. Add blackberries, raspberries, marionberries, juneberries, and fresh mulberries around 15 months of age. Dark purple berries are rich in resveratrol, a powerful antioxidant, anticarcinogenic, and anti-inflammatory compound, which supports the immune system.

1 cup (145 g) diced ripe strawberries

1 cup blueberries, (145 g) fresh or (155 g) frozen

⅓ cup (75 g) coconut oil or grass-fed organic ghee

Cook the berries and coconut oil or ghee in a small saucepan over medium-low heat until the berries are soft. Stir occasionally and mash the fruit or purée it off the heat.

Once the berries are cooled, either on the counter or in the refrigerator, they can be served with a spoon.

NOTES

⊙ You may notice some seeds (from raspberries and strawberries) or the skins of blueberries in your baby's diaper afterward. These can be hard for a baby to digest and often just pass right through their systems.

⊙ The remaining berry compote will make great Gelatin, Jam, Jigglers, and Custard (page 132).

YIELD: 2 cups (475 ml)

BRIGHT RED BLAST GUMMIES

Gelatin contains trace minerals and coveted amino acids that are used to build your baby's growing body with connective tissue, muscle, and sinew, which help keep our cartilage, skin, and bones healthy. Amino acids are also used to build antibodies, hormones, neurotransmitters, and enzymes. One of the amino acids in gelatin, glycine, has been shown in human trials to improve sleep quality. Glycine has also been associated with decreases in anxiety and calming the mind. For excellent information on gelatin recipes and health benefits, we recommend referencing *The Gelatin Secret: The Surprising Superfood That Transforms Your Health and Beauty* by Sylvia McCracken.

7 tablespoons (16 g) grass-fed gelatin (such as Great Lakes gelatin)

⅓ cup (80 ml) freshly squeezed lemon juice or freshly squeezed orange juice or blend

Pinch of Celtic sea salt

½ cup (75 g) organic strawberries and/or raspberries

½ cup (75 g) organic blueberries

¼ cup (56 g) peeled, boiled, drained, and mashed beets

In a small bowl, sprinkle the gelatin over the lemon juice and a pinch of sea salt and stir. Allow to sit while the gelatin absorbs the liquid, at least 5 minutes.

In a saucepan over low to medium heat, cook the berries until mushy, about 20 to 25 minutes. Reduce the heat.

Use a food processor or an immersion blender to mash the beets. Mix the beets and berries together; purée additionally if not smooth.

Stir in the lemon juice and gelatin mixture and continue stirring over low heat (without reaching a boil) until the gelatin is completely dissolved—it will be thick and of a syrup-like consistency.

Once dissolved, remove from the heat and quickly pour into molds or a large glass baking pan (greased with coconut oil).

Put in the freezer for 10 minutes to harden. Remove and pop out of the molds or cut into squares if needed.

NOTE

⊙ This recipe is adapted from Sylvie McCracken's *The Gelatin Secret: The Surprising Superfood That Transforms Your Health and Beauty*.

YIELD: 4 to 10 gummies, depending on the molds

COLOSSAL KIDNEY DISH

Kidneys, like liver, are a rare staple for most families, but that isn't ideal. Offal (organ meats) are more nutrient dense than any other foods, including muscle meat and plant foods. Weekly, or even monthly, including organ meats into your family's cuisine is a wonderful gift. Kidneys contain important retinol (the usable and beneficial form of vitamin A), heme iron, and B vitamins, just to name a few.

4 lamb kidneys or 2 calf kidneys

1 cup (235 ml) lemon juice (fresh squeezed/puréed preferred) or apple cider vinegar

1 teaspoon Celtic sea salt

1 tablespoon (14 g) lard or other fat

½ to 1 cup (120 to 235 ml) homemade beef stock

1 teaspoon gelatin dissolved in ¼ cup (60 ml) mom's milk, formula, or Souper Stock (page 45), *optional*, plus more liquid as needed

Cut the calf kidneys in half and carefully remove any tubes and their lighter color centers. If using lamb's kidneys, quarter them. Soak them for 2 to 3 hours in a bowl with 1 cup (235 ml) of lemon juice or vinegar and sea salt, placed in the refrigerator.

Heat the fat in a skillet, drain the kidneys, and sauté until just brown, about 1 to 2 minutes. Add the broth and sea salt and then raise the heat to a simmer, but do not boil. Add the gelatin and milk, if using; simmer for 10 to 20 seconds. Overcooking will result in tough meat.

Cool slightly. Purée, adding mom's milk, formula, or Souper Stock if necessary to get to the right consistency for your baby.

Store in a covered container in the refrigerator for 7 days or freeze for up to 4 to 6 weeks.

YIELD:
8 to 12 baby servings

COCONUT BANANA MARROW LOAF

This no-rise bread recipe contains spices you are able to give to your baby at this time: cinnamon and cloves. However, you might want to introduce these spices with just mashed banana, one at a time, to make sure your baby does not have a negative reaction to either. The treasure in this recipe is the marrow. Bone marrow was consumed by early man, evidenced by anthropological findings of broken animal skulls and larger bones. This recipe is inspired by the Coconut Flour Banana Bread by The Coconut Mama.

Coconut oil for greasing loaf pan

¾ cup (84 g) coconut flour

½ teaspoon aluminum-free baking soda

½ teaspoon ground nutmeg

1 teaspoon ground cinnamon

½ teaspoon ground cloves

¼ teaspoon Celtic sea salt

⅓ cup (29 g) shredded organic, unsulfured, unsweetened coconut

4 medium bananas (ripe)

3 to 4 tablespoons (45 to 55 g) bone marrow, additional
3 to 4 tablespoons (45 to 55 g), *optional*

⅓ cup (75 g) coconut butter, warmed

4 farm-fresh, organic, pastured eggs

Preheat the oven to 325°F (170°C, or gas mark 3). Grease a glass or ceramic loaf pan with coconut oil.

In a bowl, mix the coconut flour, baking soda, nutmeg, cinnamon, ground cloves, sea salt, and shredded coconut. Set aside.

In a small bowl, mash the bananas, bone marrow, and coconut butter.

In a large bowl, whisk the eggs until frothy. Add the mashed banana mixture and combine. Add the dry mixture and mix well.

Pour into the greased bread pan. Sprinkle extra shredded coconut and cinnamon over the top of the loaf if you desire.

Bake for 70 minutes. Remove from the oven and insert a knife or a toothpick into the loaf. If it does not come out cleanly, return the bread to the oven for another 10 minutes. Repeat until done.

Store in the fridge for up to 2 weeks or the freezer for up to 2 months.

Use the additional marrow, warmed, as a spread, sprinkling with sea salt and/or cinnamon.

NOTE

⊙ Marrow or foods containing marrow should be consumed soon after cooking or be refrigerated.

YIELD: 1 loaf

FERMENTED DILLS

This recipe makes fermented/brine pickles and relies on both salt and beneficial bacteria during the fermentation process. These pickles taste great, are easy to make, and are full of probiotics. Probiotics support chelation of heavy metals (detoxification), nutrient absorption, digestion, and immunity.

5 pickling cucumbers, 4 to 6 inches (10 to 15 cm) long (or 1 to 2 dozen gherkins), whole or sliced

2 tablespoons (30 g) Celtic sea salt (the finer the grain, the easier to dissolve)

3 cups (700 ml) filtered water

⅓ cup (80 ml) raw whey (if unavailable, use 1 tablespoon [15 g] extra sea salt)

2 cloves garlic, crushed

1 teaspoon dill seed

1 bunch of fresh dill

1 tablespoon (5 g) peppercorns, *optional* and not to be consumed

1 bay leaf, *optional* and not to be consumed

Wash the cucumbers and then soak in cold, iced water for 20 minutes.

Stir and completely dissolve the sea salt in the water, add the whey, and set this brine aside.

Place the garlic, dill seed, fresh dill, and any of the optional ingredients into the bottom of a quart (950 ml) Mason jar. Place the cucumbers into the jar, engineering them in to fit as many as possible. Pour the brine mixture over the cucumbers to completely cover them. The top of the liquid should be at least 1 inch (2.5 cm) below the top of the jar.

Cover tightly and keep at room temperature for 5 to 7 days (or fewer if sliced). Taste at this point and transfer to the refrigerator for cold storage or allow to continue fermenting to reach the desired taste, up to 14 additional days. Once moved to the refrigerator, they can be stored for up to 6 months.

NOTE

⊙ Oak leaves, grape leaves, or horseradish leaves all contain tannins and adding a few leaves prior to fermentation will make a crunchier pickle.

YIELD: 1 quart (950 ml) jar of pickles

SWEET POTATO CHIPS AND PLANTAIN CRISPS

Sweet potatoes are root vegetables that are rich in color, flavor, and nutrient value. They are filled with retinol-precursor beta-carotene, as well as vitamin C, manganese, copper, vitamins B5 and B6, and biotin. Plantains are not root vegetables, but are tropical starches that are good sources of carotenoids, vitamin C, B vitamins, potassium, magnesium, and copper. Very starchy, plantains should not be eaten raw, particularly green plantains.

SWEET POTATO CHIPS

2 to 3 tablespoons (28 to 45 ml) melted coconut oil, bacon grease, lard, or duck fat, plus more to grease baking sheet

1 large or 2 small organic sweet potatoes

Celtic sea salt or Himalayan salt to taste

Preheat the oven to 300°F (150°C, or gas mark 2). Lightly grease a baking sheet.

Scrub and dry the sweet potatoes. Slice as thin as possible, using a mandoline, vegetable peeler, or knife and aim for consistent thickness. In a large bowl, drizzle the fat and sea salt over the slices and toss lightly to distribute the fat evenly. Place the chips on the prepared baking sheet, without overlapping. Salt lightly. (More salt can be added right after they come out of the oven if desired.)

Bake for 1 hour or until crisp. Use tongs to flip the chips once or twice during baking time. Store in an airtight container in the refrigerator or pantry for up to 1 week.

YIELD: 2 to 3 cups (68 to 102 g)

PLANTAIN CRISPS

2 to 3 tablespoons (28 to 45 ml) melted coconut oil, bacon grease, lard, or duck fat, plus more to grease baking sheets

3 medium plantains, green or yellow

Celtic sea salt or Himalayan salt to taste

Preheat the oven to 325°F (170°C, or gas mark 3). Lightly grease 2 baking sheets.

Peel the plantains and slice very thin. Toss the plantain slices with the fat, and lay out on the prepared baking sheets. Sprinkle with the sea salt.

Bake for 20 minutes, and then flip each chip with tongs. Bake for another 10 minutes.

Remove the more well-done chips as they start to brown, especially if some are thinner than others.

Store at room temperature for up to 1 week.

YIELD: 2 to 3 cups (75 to 112 g)

NOTES

- Try these cooking methods with other root vegetables, particularly yucca, but taro root, carrots, and beets can also make tasty chips if they are sliced very thin prior to cooking.

- These do not have to get overly crispy for baby; they can remain soft, although thorough cooking is advised. Thicker slices will stay softer and not get as crispy. The fat and heat will make a delicious treat that won't scratch the palate.

- Younger babies will do better with thicker, less crispy chips.

- Alternatively, the plantain chips can be fried in a skillet in the hot oil, grease, or lard.

ACORN SQUASH AND SAUSAGE

Acorn squash, along with pumpkin, spaghetti squash, and butternut, are all part of a group of "winter squash," which have thicker, tougher rinds to protect them longer. Squash is a good source of vitamin C, fiber, and carotenes (which are fat-soluble antioxidants and precursors to retinol, true vitamin A) and may reduce the risk of heart and respiratory diseases, cancer, diabetes, and arthritis.

1 acorn squash

1 tablespoon (14 g) coconut oil

1 clove garlic, finely chopped

1 pound (455 g) grass-fed sausage or ground pork (ground beef can be substituted)

Pinch of Celtic sea salt

4 ounces (120 ml) Souper Stock (page 45)

Preheat the oven to 350°F (180°C, or gas mark 4).

Slice the acorn squash in half and remove the seeds. Place open-face down in a 9 × 13-inch (23 × 33 cm) baking dish with a small amount of water and bake for 30 minutes.

Meanwhile, melt the coconut oil in a skillet. Add the garlic and sauté for 5 minutes.

In a separate skillet, sauté the sausage with a pinch of sea salt. Add the sautéed garlic. Cook until no pink remains in the meat and ensure that the meat remains minced throughout the cooking process. Use a spatula to break up the meat if needed.

Allow the squash to cool slightly. Scrape out the cooked squash and discard the outer shell.

Purée the squash, cooked sausage mixture, and broth.

Alternatively, based on your baby's readiness, simply combine the cooked squash and sausage mixture as is.

Store in the refrigerator up to 1 week or in the freezer up to 3 months.

YIELD:
8 to 10 baby servings

NOTES

- *Adult adaptations:* Add ¼ cup (40 g) chopped onion to cook with the garlic and sausage. Mix 1 cup (225 g) homemade curds or yogurt cheese into the hot sausage mixture until it melts and is completely combined. Spoon the sausage mixture into the baked acorn squash halves. Return to the oven for 5 to 10 minutes to heat through. Or, scoop out the cooked squash and spread it on the bottom of a casserole baking dish. Top with the sausage mixture and return it to the oven to heat through, about 10 to 15 minutes.

- The sausage curd mixture can also be used to stuff mushrooms. Remove the stems, chop them, and add to the sausage during the sauté step. Spoon the stuffing mixture into the mushroom caps, brush with melted butter, and bake for 15 to 20 minutes at 350°F (180°C, or gas mark 4).

MOM-TO-MOM

When your baby begins eating more than one food at a meal, we advise including animal protein or at least an animal fat at each meal. Avoid making meals out of only fruits or only fruits and vegetables. Side dishes should be vegetables, ideally three times a day (i.e., one with each meal), and fruits no more than twice a day (e.g., snack and dessert).

SHAPE UP SWEETS AND SHIP OUT SUGAR

Getting Back to Nature's Basics

(12 TO 18 MONTHS)

Happy birthday to your baby! So much has happened during this first year. Your feeding practices have set a solid foundation for your baby's lifelong health—congratulations! But don't hang up the apron just yet; your work is far from over.

Your baby should still be eating a special diet rather than just smaller portions of what you might be having for dinner, unless your diet follows traditional-foods principles. At 12 months, 50% of her calories should still come from mom's milk or formula, with an average intake of 20 to 24 ounces (570 to 710 ml) of formula per day or with nursing at least 4 times per 24 hours. As you increase her solid food intake, limit—or preferably, omit—refined and processed sugars. If you don't, you're setting her up for developing 3C conditions, most notably diabetes and obesity.

At 12 months, many babies are indoctrinated into the world of adulterated foods, with sugar, white flour, trans fats, refined salt, colors, dyes, and flavorings. In this chapter, we'll keep you on the traditional-foods path.

Beware of Sugar

Rather than being a treat, research supports that sugar is *devastating* to health. Yet sugar intake has been drastically increasing over the last centuries and—notably—decades. Kids eat more sugar today than any generation of children before them.

The FDA, the U.S. Department of Agriculture's (USDA) Dietary Guidelines, the World Health Organization (WHO), and the American Heart Association (AHA) all formally recommend that,

for optimal health, people limit the amount of added sugars they consume in a day. The WHO specifically acknowledges a strong association between added sugar and increased cardiovascular disease in children and recommends reducing the intake of free sugars to less than 10% of energy intake, or less than 25 grams (6 teaspoons) per day, and *avoiding sugar altogether* for toddlers under 2 years old. If sugar were harmless, this wouldn't be necessary.

SUGAR HURTS DIGESTION

Sugar is scientifically proven to alter mineral balances. Imbalanced minerals are unable to function properly, as they rely on each other in specific proportions. Because minerals are helpers to enzymes, when minerals are imbalanced, enzymes don't function appropriately, and when enzymes can't do their job, digestion is significantly affected. When foods aren't digested, food allergies are likely to develop, which is why foods that are eaten with sugar are more likely to have allergies developed against them.

SUGAR IS A DRUG AND A TOXIN

It's hard to imagine cupcakes and apple juice being as toxic to the liver as alcohol, as well as a significant contributor to our most dreaded diseases. Yet, while sugar offers energy in the form of calories, it provides nothing to help us grow, heal, or support our body; it changes bodily functions; and its prolonged absence causes withdrawal symptoms. By definition, sugar is much closer to *a drug* than it is to food, particularly for those who have lower than normal levels of happy brain chemicals (neurotransmitters, including serotonin, endorphin, and dopamine).

Here's how and why:

1. Sugar gives pleasure differently than food; we celebrate and commemorate with it (as with alcohol for adults).

2. Sugar is addicting, according to research.

3. Going without sugar causes withdrawal, both emotional and physical, such as irritability, headache, tremors, and moodiness.

4. Sugar affects mood and behavior (disappointment without dessert; children ask and even cry for it distinctly more than for other foods, kids on "sugar high").

5. Ingesting sugar creates an emotional response (relief, pleasure, feeling better or less "down").

6. Sugar alters normal endocrine, metabolic, neurologic, and biochemical functioning.

7. Sugar consumption is often hidden from others (e.g., kids hiding candy wrappers under the bed, adults burying empty ice cream containers at the bottom of the garbage, candy bars stashed in sock drawers).

8. Sugar overconsumption can cause feelings of guilt and embarrassment.

9. Cravings arise when going without sugar or otherwise giving it up.

10. Sugar and drugs both stimulate the body via the very same neurotransmitters and biochemical mechanisms.

    ⊙ Prozac, Cymbalta, and SUGAR affect serotonin.

⊙ Morphine, opium, heroin, and SUGAR cause an opioid response.

⊙ Crack, cocaine, and SUGAR cause their high by affecting dopamine.

⊙ Caffeine, methamphetamines, and SUGAR trigger adrenaline and norepinephrine release.

When you give your child sweets, you are analogous to a dealer giving a fix. This is strong language purposefully; it is important that you understand the gravity of the situation.

Part of the continuous increase in sugar intake is related to the creation of high fructose corn syrup in the 1970s. Over the last 10 decades, as Robert Lustig, M.D., a pediatric neuroendocrinologist and professor, reports, daily fructose consumption has gone from 15 grams to 75 grams (that's like going from having 1 can of soda pop per day to having 5!). Your baby might not be drinking soda pop, but there are 26 grams (over 2 tablespoons!) of sugar in her 7-ounce (200 ml) *juice box*.

When you realize that *no* sugar is essential, any sugar your child consumes is too much. If you think moderation is still okay, you might want to reconsider your definition of moderation. Counting *all* sugars, including white flour, juice, and others (see sidebar on page 175), it's clear that "sugars" are not only *present* at every meal and snack but actually compose *the majority* of children's diets today. The reality is that just one 2-ounce (55 g) kid-friendly yogurt tube has more than 2 teaspoons of sugar (10 grams), a serving of typical breakfast cereal has 3 teaspoons of sugar (15 grams), and a pouch of fruit-flavored snacks has over 3 teaspoons of sugar (15 grams). Unless you make a serious effort to control and reduce sugars, your child will consume *far in excess* of moderation by just eating normal "kid" foods at every meal.

DEEP DIVE INTO THE WIDE WORLD OF NATURAL SWEETENERS

It is very important to strictly limit sweets, but those you do include should come from whole foods because they are able to offer some nutrient value, as opposed to most refined sugars that are devoid of nutrients. We do not advocate adding sweets or sweeteners to the diet, but where sweeteners are used, we recommend the following over standard options.

- Non-centrifugal sugar (NCS) is different than other sugars, in that it retains some nutrients during its processing from whole food, and is dehydrated whole sugar cane known around the world by various names, including panella, chancaca, piloncillo, jaggery, gurh, veli, gula merah, kokuto, rapadura, and dulce de panela (and can be purchased online as Rapunzel brand "rapadura"), notably retaining trace vitamins and minerals.

- Whole-leaf stevia (SweetLeaf brand green powder or brown liquid), typically a green powder made from simply drying and grinding stevia plant leaves, has the following nutrients: selenium, potassium, manganese, vitamins B1, B2, B3, and C, posphorus, beta-carotene, silicon, and chromium (which has a positive impact on glucose tolerance factor).

- Carob (rather than chocolate) contains vitamin B2, calcium, copper, manganese, potassium, and fiber.

- Blackstrap molasses contains B6, potassium, magnesium, and manganese.

- Honey (raw, unheated, unfiltered) with comb contains royal jelly (has copper, calcium, iron, potassium, phosphorus, sulfur, silicon, B vitamins, and amino and nucleic acids) and possibly propolis (like royal jelly, has antiviral, antibacterial, and antifungal properties).

- Maple syrup (use pure, darker color syrups, made from sap collected later in the season, reported to have higher mineral and phenol content).

- Dates (can be depitted and blended with a little water to make a syrup) contain potassium, non-heme iron, B vitamins, and fiber.

Note: Muscavado, turbinado, demarara, and "organic raw sugar" are all refined sugars (and sugar in the raw isn't raw, either). As products of heating, clarifying (with chemical treatments), then dehydrating sugar-cane juice until crystals form, then separating crystals from syrup via spinning, these are highly processed products. Molasses is reintroduced with the refined sugar crystals in some cases to achieve the desired brown color.

Even nutrient-containing sweeteners cannot be given freely. Having nutrients moves sweetener into a category between CRAP (where refined sweeteners squarely sit) and occasionally OK; by occasional, think every few months. It's worth repeating: Even nutrient-containing sweeteners, such as NCS sugar, darkest color maple syrup, and raw honey should be consumed only sparingly, if at all.

Both sugar (sucrose) and high fructose corn syrup (HFCS) contain glucose and fructose. The damage of too much glucose has been studied and reported, including metabolic syndrome and risk of heart disease, diabetes, and obesity—all of which are related to the insulin response triggered by excess glucose. However, it is now known that fructose (previously thought of as a harmless "fruit sugar") also negatively affects insulin and goes straight to the liver, where it is turned into fat.

In addition to its effect on insulin, fructose damages the liver. The liver processes fructose similarly to how it processes alcohol; too much fructose results in fatty liver disease—a disorder commonly seen in alcoholics. According to Harvard Medical School's *Harvard Heart Letter* (September 2011), nonalcoholic fatty liver disease is found in 30% of the U.S. population and in 70% to 90% of those who are obese or have type 2 diabetes.

Note: Fatty acid liver disease can and does occur in thin people; thinking all is well because the scale says so is a false sense of health security.

Alongside this rise in fructose, and overall sugar consumption, is a steep rise in heart disease, obesity, diabetes, cancer, and other 3Cs *in children*. With the known dietary dangers of glucose and a new, better understanding of how fructose harms health, it is logical that sugar plays a major role in chronic disease in both children and adults today. Dr. Lustig warns, "High fructose corn syrup and sucrose are . . . *both poison in high doses*" [emphasis added].

SUGAR HINDERS IMMUNITY

Sugar is also guilty of weakening the immune system. Studies show that the immune system's key white blood cells are *crippled* by sugar for 4 to 6 hours after sugar has been eaten. This means that if your child has had candy before a play date and then is exposed to an infection, she's much less able to defend herself against contracting it. Sugar depletes B vitamins and other nutrients that are critical to immune system functioning and protection against infection. Worse, it displaces nutrient-dense foods, further reducing intake of nutrients needed to protect and *strengthen* immunity.

SUGAR IS NOT NUTRITIOUS OR NOURISHING

Russell L. Blaylock, M.D., neurosurgeon, author, and nutrition researcher, states, "Sugar is the biggest enemy we face in the world of nutrition and health." Yet sugar is becoming an increasingly large part of our diet, although it offers no nutritional value. The vitamins and minerals required to assimilate and digest it are absent (sugar is a nutritional vacuum), and so the body must take from its stored nutrients whenever sugar is eaten. Thus, sugar serves to deplete nutritional status and therefore diminishes health each time it is consumed.

Even in "moderation," sugar:

⊙ Falsely stimulates appetite

⊙ Causes inflammation

⊙ Causes tooth decay

⊙ Cripples your child's immune system for hours

⊙ Disturbs calcium and magnesium metabolism

⊙ Causes out-of-control behavior, difficulty focusing, and anxiety

- Elicits cravings with drug-like effects— possibly laying the path for future alcohol and drug addiction
- Feeds yeast, disrupting healthy bacteria in the gut, causing the gut to be leaky
- Feeds cancer cells
- Creates critical mineral imbalances
- Depletes nutrients such as B vitamins, zinc, chromium, and magnesium
- Reduces the body's ability to detoxify
- Inhibits proper enzyme function
- Predisposes to food allergies
- Fattens the body and the blood cells
- Worsens heart health
- Causes emotional instability
- Disrupts hormones and neurotransmitters
- Disrupts the endocrine system, increasing the risk of diabetes and metabolic syndrome
- Accelerates aging

According to expert sugar researcher Nancy Appleton, Ph.D., author of the best-selling book *Lick the Sugar Habit*, sugar has nearly 150 ways of causing disease and dysfunction. Known as an antinutrient, sugar is best classified as a chemical, drug, or poison.

Obesity and Diabetes

According to the CDC, childhood obesity has tripled in the last three decades and type 2 diabetes (formerly "adult-onset" diabetes) is a "sizable and growing problem among U.S. children." The best indicator for type 2 diabetes in children is excess weight. In 2016, the CDC reported that more than 1 in 5 children aged 2 to 5 are overweight or obese. Obese children

FOOD ABUNDANCE DOESN'T EQUAL NUTRIENT ABUNDANCE!

First-world children have many common nutrient deficiencies, despite many being overweight. When fed "empty" calories, the body is overfed but undernourished. This is very common in developed, industrialized countries.

William Sears, M.D., in *The NDD (Nutrition Deficit Disorder) Book*, warns that American children (regardless of their weight) are most commonly deficient in omega-3 fats, iron, zinc, magnesium, iodine, calcium, and vitamins B12, C, and E. Additionally, deficiencies in probiotics and the fat-soluble vitamins D3 (upward of 80%), K2, and A are significant problems as well.

Lack of these nutrients leads to the following:

- Lowered immunity and susceptibility to pathogens
- Increased vulnerability to the impact of dietary and environmental toxins
- Increased activity of carcinogens, dietary opiates, and pathogenic flora

This increases risk for all 3C conditions.

are twice as likely to get insulin-resistant diabetes. These two highly correlated conditions are likely both caused by diets based on refined grains and sugar.

Since the advent of the low-fat diet and thousands of "low-fat" foods, we are fatter and more diabetic than ever—and so are our children. In 2015, 20% of school-aged children were overweight, with 14% of 2- to 5-year-olds, 18% of 6- to 11-year-olds, and 21% of 12- to 19-year-olds. This is more than triple the rate in the 1970s according to the CDC. Our kids are overweight and obese, which accelerates and exacerbates myriad troubling health issues. This is not just a U.S. issue; data from the National Child Measurement Programme in English schools shows that for the 2016–2017 school year, approximately 10% of 4- and 5-year-olds and 20% of 10- and 11-year-olds in England are obese also.

Mother Nature doesn't ever provide calories without nutrients, but modern, man-made food is filled with such dietary abominations. *It is a new and bizarre phenomenon to be simultaneously overfed and undernourished.* Such calorie-rich, nutrient-poor diets are at the crux of the 3C conditions.

The trends for increasing obesity and diabetes in children are going nowhere but up, even with the low-fat diet fad. Currently, it is estimated that over 30% of babies will develop diabetes and close to 50% will be overweight or obese. Experts, like Joseph Levy, M.D., professor of clinical pediatrics at Columbia University Medical Center in New York City, now clearly acknowledge *carbohydrates*—particularly refined flour and sugar—are responsible. Dr. Levy states, "Many studies have confirmed that the liberal intake of carbohydrate is a major contributor to obesity."

Prevent Diabetes and Obesity with Super Nutrition

There's no way to sugarcoat it: Sugar makes people sick and fat. Here are some things you can do to protect your child against sugar's harmful effects.

MAKE SURE GUT FLORA IS ON TRACK. Studies demonstrate that the kind of intestinal flora in the body can influence metabolism and appetite and therefore contribute to metabolic disorders like diabetes and obesity, as well as eating habits, according to studies such as those conducted at Emory School of Medicine. Optimize your toddler's gut ecosystem by keeping sugar out of her diet because sugar feeds troublesome yeast and causes gut dysbiosis (microbial imbalance). Include lacto-fermented foods, fresh and cultured dairy, and probiotic supplements to help her intestinal health.

DEEP DIVE INTO AN OUTDATED NOTION: ALL CALORIES ARE *NOT* EQUAL

We've all heard it: "A calorie is a calorie is a calorie." Weight loss is a simple formula: You must burn more calories than you take in—it doesn't really matter what they are. However, this is an old and oversimplified view of how food works in the body.

Food is far more than just calories. Elizabeth Lipski, Ph.D., C.C.N., clinical nutritionist and author of *Digestive Wellness for Children*, explains that "food is *information* for our bodies and brains." Depending on the food, different neurotransmitters, hormones, and cellular messages are stimulated. The body "reads" food and does different things with it depending on what it is, how much energy and nutrients it provides, and what the current needs of the body happen to be. Foods that contain glucose and fructose, for example, send hormonal messages that trigger both fat storage and hunger more than other foods, says Robert Lustig, M.D., a pediatric neuroendocrinologist and professor.

EXERCISE FOR ENDOCRINE STABILIZATION, NOT CALORIE BURNING. Sunlight, fresh air, and exercise are all elements of a normal childhood. Get your child active and outdoors. Such activities are critical because they have a positive hormonal impact: they increase insulin sensitivity (the opposite of disease-related insulin resistance), and for that, they are protective against obesity and 3C conditions. Furthermore, physical movement and activity also naturally stimulate happiness neurotransmitters, making sugars less appealing, and raise HDL ("healthy cholesterol" carrier).

AVOID THE ALL-CARBOHYDRATE TRAP. Children's diets often tend to be all carbohydrates: grains, sugars, and fruit, with minimal vegetables and protein. Ensure either animal protein or animal fats, and fiber or both, are part of every meal. Truly balanced meals are not based on grains; they are based on the presence of animal foods and vegetables, with properly prepared carbohydrate foods and other whole foods as garnishes, digestive aids, and nutrient boosters.

Time to Stop Nursing or Bottle Feeding?

If you are still nursing at 12 months, we salute you. We know that breastfeeding can present evolving challenges such as teething (and biting!), countless distractions, and increasingly busy schedules. Further, social pressures are prevalent, and sadly many people feel it is excessive to nurse a baby beyond one year of age.

But what our modern society has forgotten is that your baby's sucking instinct goes well beyond 12 months, lasting *at least* until she's 2½. Weaning leaves your baby without a way to satisfy this instinct and doesn't confer immune benefits from mom's milk. Continuing to nurse beyond one year provides specific benefits to both mom and baby:

- Immune support—shortening the duration and lessening the frequency and severity of illness
- Optimal nutrition for your baby
- Fewer orthodontic problems
- Allergy prevention
- Continued bond and comforting mechanism
- Preferred hydration and nutrition during illness
- Earlier reading in boys and fewer speech problems
- A natural way to space pregnancies
- Calorie burning for mom
- Calming and loving hormones for mom and baby, resulting in reduced stress and anxiety for both
- Reduced breast cancer and rheumatoid arthritis risk for mom—the longer you nurse, the better the protection

When it is time to wean (which you'll realize as your child is less interested in nursing and as feedings are gradually and naturally missed), there are ways to best protect and ensure your baby's health during and after the transition to end nursing.

Because your baby's gut flora changes as she weans, it is of utmost importance to continue providing good probiotics to her. Sources of probiotics include lacto-fermented foods and raw and cultured dairy. If you are not providing such foods, then giving a daily probiotic supplement is helpful (typically a small dose once or twice a day is adequate). Additionally, once nursing has stopped, there are benefits to having a stored supply of breast milk in your freezer, especially for times when your child gets sick. Stored milk is also helpful for softening the impact of the cow's milk on the gut since you can intersperse your milk with the newly introduced cow's milk. Furthermore, whey can be made from pumped milk (see Homemade Mom's Milk Whey, page 106) and stored for 2 to 3 months. This whey can then be used for lacto-fermenting foods for your baby, enabling her to continue to benefit from your milk, both from its nutrients and from lacto-fermentation.

When you do decide to wean, one way to ease the transition is to simply avoid offering the breast or bottle, but not to refuse when asked. Gradually, delay or distract your child when she indicates she wants to nurse or have a bottle, which will lead to skipped feedings. Over 3 to 4 weeks, your milk supply will begin to diminish. According to William Sears, M.D., removing a feeding every 3 to 7 days is about as fast as is wise to wean—much faster, and you increase your chance of developing mastitis.

Protect Your Child with Natural Nourishment

Low in fat and high in sugar, typical toddler foods like juice boxes and crackers supply chemicals, antinutrients, allergens, and toxins, but what they do not supply is sufficient nutrition. There is a better diet for your 12- to 18-month-old. It includes natural fat, wise carbs, even smarter sweets, and appropriate big-kid beverages.

USE FAT FOR FUEL

Fat is the best basis of energy for children. Benefits of a fat-based diet include:

- Stimulating leptin, sending "I'm full" messages and reducing overeating
- Ensuring fat-soluble antioxidants, vitamins, and mineral activators will be absorbed
- Having antimicrobial, antiviral, and immune-supportive factors
- Keeping blood sugar balanced
- Helping intestinal function and slowing down digestion so more nutrients can be absorbed
- Providing nutrition for your toddler's growing, developing brain
- Promoting healthy skin and cells
- Making foods delicious!

Let your child enjoy butter on veggies and grains (that are properly prepared), whole milk, full-fat yogurt, red meat, and dark-meat poultry with the skin.

BE WISE WITHIN THE WORLD OF CARBOHYDRATES

As your baby's carbohydrate world expands with the introduction of greens, new fruits, smart starches, tubers, nightshades, nuts, and raw veggies, we have some cautions. We recommend *most* carbohydrate foods be green veggies, fewer simple starch veggies and nuts, and even fewer from seeds, tubers, and fruits. Fewer still should come from grains and legumes, with fewest from whole-foods sweeteners. Within these categories of plant foods, be varied. Of the 50,000 edible plant foods on the planet, only 15 crops provide 90% of the world's food, and just 3 make up *60%* of the caloric intake of the world: rice, corn, and wheat.

A BETTER WAY TO SOOTHE THE SWEET-TOOTH MONSTER

Here are tips on avoiding refined sugars in your child's diet and how to incorporate naturally sweet *whole foods* that are better than processed, refined sugars.

DON'T INTRODUCE REFINED SUGARS. Without the experience of refined sugars, children will never feel deprived. For the first several years, you are in control of your child's diet, and there is no need to have refined sugar. Further, Dr. Lipski points out that children's "digestive systems cannot handle . . . sugars other than lactose until the age of three."

USE WHOLE-FOODS SWEETENERS. Often natural sweeteners contain nutrients that help glucose tolerance and sugar metabolism, such as chromium, magnesium, and B vitamins. (See page 175.)

USE EVEN THE NATURAL SWEETS SPARINGLY. Be discerning when you decide what calls for an out-of-the-ordinary sweet treat, offering whole fruit on a daily basis for meeting the sweet needs of the taste buds. Reserve any concentrated sweets (even from whole foods) for very special occasions.

CONSUME WITH CONTROLLERS. Fats, fibers, and protein reduce the impact of skyrocketing blood sugar and insulin that result when sweets are eaten alone. Keeping blood sugar steady is ideal for overall health, metabolic stability, and emotional and behavioral consistency. Providing plenty of fat and protein, along with carbs that naturally contain fiber, helps combat spikes in sugar levels. And omega-3 fats in cod liver oil and fats from grass-fed animal foods (like butter and raw cheese) are good examples of fats that help improve insulin sensitivity.

DON'T PROMOTE SELF-MEDICATING WITH SUGARS. Parents and caregivers often soothe, comfort, distract, and quiet children with sweets and treats. Understanding that using sugar as solace or reward builds unintended associations and results in health risks, we recommend eliciting oxytocin, endorphin, serotonin, and dopamine effects rather through comfort, back rubs, cuddling, holding, playing, laughing, and other activities that do not involve sugar.

NATURAL AND NUTRITIOUS BIG-KID BEVERAGES

Typical dietary changes at age 1 include switching your baby from formula to pasteurized cow's milk. But cow's milk isn't all it's campaigned to be. (See page 182.)

Comparing the Many Forms of Milk from Fresh to Highly Processed

NUTRIENTS & IMMUNE FACTORS	RAW MOM'S MILK	RAW COW'S MILK	PASTEURIZED COW'S MILK	COMMERCIAL INFANT FORMULA
Antimicrobial enzymes	Active	Active	Inhibited	Unavailable
Biodiverse probiotics	Active	Active	Destroyed	Added
Essential fatty acids	Active	Active	Damaged	Added
Lactase-producing bacteria	Active	Active	Destroyed	Unavailable
Delicate proteins	Active	Active	Destroyed	Altered
B12-binding proteins	Active	Active	Inactive	Inactive
Bioavailable vitamins	Active	Active	Inhibited	Inhibited
Bioavailable calcium	Active	Active	Inhibited	Inhibited
Bioavailable phosphorus	Active	Active	Inhibited	Inhibited
Phosphatase enzyme	Active	Active	Destroyed	Inhibited
Oligosaccharides	Active	Active	Diminished	Unavailable
Lymphocytes	Active	Active	Inactive	Unavailable
B-lymphocytes	Active	Active	Inactive	Inactive

SAY NO TO BEAN, GRAIN, SEED, AND NUT "MILKS." Soy, rice, hemp, and almond milk are poor substitutes for human milk or homemade formula due to their low nutrient value, low fat content, synthetic nutrients, degree of processing, and various sweeteners and additives. Even coconut milk, though great for recipes, isn't sufficient as a replacement for mom's milk. Best alternatives to mom's or cow's milk are goat, sheep, or camel milk (preferably grass-fed, organic, and raw from trusted sources). Homemade almond milk is an option too, but it's best to limit non-animal-based "milk" so as to not supplant more nutrient-rich foods and liquids in your child's diet.

REAL MILK. Real, unpasteurized, raw milk from cows or goats eating grass out on pasture is the ideal weaning beverage for your child. (See page 24.)

LACTO-FERMENTED BEVERAGES AND OTHER HEALTHFUL DRINKS.

Lacto-fermented beverages include kombucha, unpasteurized sauerkraut juice, Farmhouse-brand gut shots, coconut kefir (from coconut water or coconut milk, page 138), and homemade ginger ale, apple cider, and homemade

PATTERN	12 TO 18 MONTHS
Early AM	Early morning nursing and breakfast
Midmorning	Snack and possibly nursing
Midday	Meal
Afternoon	Nursing or bottle (before nap)
Evening	Meal
Nighttime	Nursing or bottle (before bed)

Super Nutrition Food Categorizations for 12 to 18 Months	
SUPER POWER	**PURE**
• Anchovies, sardines • Lacto-fermented beverages and sides • Liverwurst • Raw dairy	• Organic fruits and veggies • Organic, pasture-raised eggs • Organic, pasture-raised meats
OKAY	**CRAP**
• Fruits/veggies, nonorganic • Nonorganic trim meats • Nonorganic eggs • Nonorganic butter	• Rice cakes • Fishie crackers, cereal, cookies, candy • Juice (even 100% organic)

orangina. Souper Stock (page 45) can always be used as a nutritious beverage, as can unsweetened coconut water or coconut milk; for additional, occasional beverages, we recommend the excellent book *Nourishing Traditions* by Sally Fallon for more recipes—including homemade rice milk and almond drink.

Recipes without Refined Sugar Risks

Your baby's carbohydrate-digestion capabilities are improving. She can now handle some raw veggies and uncooked non-tropical fruits, as well as a few starches. Enzymes from mom's milk or homemade formula; raw and cultured dairy; lacto-fermented fruits, veggies, and beverages; and Souper Stock all aid digestion, so don't stop feeding these to her.

FEEDING AT 12 TO 15 MONTHS

Between 12 and 15 months, you can introduce whole eggs, honey, tomato, citrus fruits, cooked leafy greens, and liverwurst. Natto is a great finger food for continued fine-motor skill development (see page 190).

FEEDING AT 15 TO 18 MONTHS

Between 15 and 18 months, you can introduce soaked and sprouted nuts and seeds, lacto-fermented beverages, a few more raw veggies, and limited carob.

LIVERWURST

Liverwurst is a most nutritious convenience food. Because unhealthy liver can contain toxins, it is of paramount importance to get clean liver. We've found the very best quality and taste comes from www.uswellnessmeats.com, from which liverwurst comes frozen. Place it in the refrigerator for 24 hours to thaw. (Eat within 1 week of defrosting.) Slice and serve! It tastes great with sliced avocado and perhaps even some mustard. Liverwurst is a great on-the-go snack with a small cooler pack.

COD LIVER OIL

Cod liver oil was discussed in chapter 4. Now that your baby is 1 year old, you can increase the dosage to 1 teaspoon of high-quality cod liver oil. See Resources, page 260, for preferred brands.

CREAMED SPINACH AND GREENS

Raw leafy greens are inappropriate for a baby this age, as they are hard to digest and contain oxalic acid (oxalates) that block calcium and iron absorption, can irritate the mouth and intestinal tract, and lead to formation of calcium-oxalate kidney stones. Cooking helps neutralize much of the oxalic acid, so all leafy greens, like spinach, served to your baby must be well cooked and softened. Greens are rich in phytonutrients, vitamin C, vitamin K1, and beta-carotene (the rich red color is outshone by green chlorophyll).

1 bag frozen or 1 bunch fresh, organic leafy greens (kale, spinach, collard, or mustard greens, etc.)

4 cups (950 ml) Souper Stock (page 45)

2 tablespoons (28 g) coconut oil or ghee

1 clove garlic, minced

¼ small onion, finely chopped

½ teaspoon grated nutmeg, *optional*

⅓ cup (80 ml) raw cream or coconut cream

⅓ cup (33 g) freshly grated raw Parmesan or other raw, grass-fed cheese

Celtic sea salt

Remove the center stems from the greens and chop the leaves.

Bring the stock to a boil in a saucepan and drop in the leaves.

Cook until the leaves are soft and bright green, 3 to 5 minutes. Transfer to a large bowl of ice water to cool. Remove the leaves from the water, drain, and squeeze out the excess water.

Melt the oil in a large skillet. Add the garlic and onion. Sauté for 5 to 7 minutes, until the onion is translucent. Sprinkle in the nutmeg, if using, and stir.

Add the cream to the skillet and bring to a boil, whisking often. Stir in the greens; reduce the heat to low. Simmer, stirring often, until the greens are very tender, about 15 minutes, depending on the greens.

Slowly sprinkle the Parmesan cheese over the top. Continue to stir until the cheese is melted.

Season to taste with sea salt.

NOTE

⊙ Beet leaves and radish leaves are also great choices. They are healthy and too beautiful to waste.

YIELD: 2 baby and 2 adult servings

LAMB'S LIVER SHEPHERD'S PIE

We don't include many potato dishes, as they are abundant in the Standard American Diet. However, using potatoes with their peel can be acceptable. Potatoes do contain potassium, which supports healthy blood pressure, and manganese, which is good for bone and nerve health.

2 cups (220 g) coarsely chopped potatoes, unpeeled

3 tablespoons (42 g) coconut oil, ghee, or (45 ml) olive oil, divided

2 teaspoons Celtic sea salt, divided

1 pound (455 g) lamb's liver, sliced (chicken liver can be substituted)

2 cups (240 g) finely chopped celery

½ pound (225 g) organic, pasture-raised bacon, chopped

1 cup (71 g) sliced mushrooms

1 cup (150 g) sugar snap peas (without pods)

1 cup (130 g) chopped carrot

1 red onion and 1 yellow onion, finely chopped

3 tablespoons (12 g) chopped parsley

1 tablespoon (4 g) chopped oregano (fresh preferred)

1 tablespoon (8 g) arrowroot starch, *optional*

2 teaspoons crushed coriander seeds, *optional*

2 cups (475 ml) Souper Stock (page 45)

Preheat the oven to 350°F (180°C, or gas mark 4).

Place the potatoes into a saucepan of boiling water. Cook for 10 to 15 minutes until soft. Drain well. Purée with 2 tablespoons of the coconut oil (28 g) or ghee (30 g) and sea salt to taste.

As the potatoes are cooking, heat the remaining 1 tablespoon (14 g) coconut oil or ghee in a skillet. Add the liver slices and cook until brown, about 5 to 10 minutes, depending on thickness. Remove the liver, divide the amount in half, and transfer each half to a separate glass or ceramic pie dish.

To the heated skillet, add the celery, bacon, mushroom, peas, carrots, onion, parsley, and oregano. Stir. Cook until the bacon is crispy, about 10 minutes.

Add the remaining salt, optional arrowroot, and coriander. Add the Souper Stock and stir together.

Pour half of the mixture over the liver slices in each pie dish and then cover each evenly with half of the puréed potatoes.

Bake for 45 to 50 minutes.

Optional: Brush 1 tablespoon (14 g) melted ghee over the top to inspire a golden "crust" after baking.

NOTE

⊙ Cauliflower can be used in place of potatoes.

YIELD: 2 shepherd's pies, or 6 to 8 servings

DELICIOUS DESSERT ARRAY

Nature makes many sweets to satisfy a sweet tooth, but these treats come with nutrients that support assimilation of sugars and the glucose tolerance factor, including chromium, magnesium, and B vitamins. It is very challenging to keep refined sugar completely out of your child's diet. We urge you to make every effort to do so. Using whole fruit in various ways is healthy and sure to satisfy!

FRUIT DIPPED IN A COCONUT "SHELL"

½ cup (112 g) coconut butter

10 large ripe strawberries or other dippable fruit

Remove the lid and place the jar of coconut butter in a pot of warmed water on the stove. Stir the coconut butter as it begins to liquefy. If it doesn't melt after 10 minutes, add a teaspoon or so of coconut oil and continue to heat.

Once the coconut butter is melted and stirred, pour approximately ½ cup (120 ml) into a warmed glass dish. Dip each strawberry into it, up to its green stem. The coconut butter will cling to the berry. Remove and set on parchment paper–lined cookie sheet.

Continue dipping all the berries and place in refrigerator or freezer until hardened.

YIELD: 10 dipped strawberries

ENZYME BLAST PUDDING

1 cup (235 ml) coconut cream

1 cup (175 g) fresh ripe mango chunks (about 2 mangoes) (can also use guava, papayas, or apricots)

1 cup (146 g) diced avocado (about 2 avocados)

In a blender, add the coconut cream, mango, and avocado. Blend on high speed until smooth.

Pour the mixture into individual serving bowls. Chill for several hours in the refrigerator to firm up and set. Top with a few fresh mango slices or other fruit.

YIELD: 3 cups (675 g)

FRUIT ICE CREAM

1 teaspoon gelatin

1 tablespoon (15 ml) freshly squeezed lemon juice

1 cup (weight will vary) frozen fruit, such as cherries, strawberries, or peaches

2 farm-fresh, organic, pastured egg yolks, lightly beaten

1 cup (235 ml) raw cream or coconut cream

Sprinkle the gelatin into the lemon juice and allow 5 minutes to bloom.

Heat the gelatin with the lemon juice until dissolved.

Place the fruit and egg yolks in a food processor with the gelatin mixture and purée. Add the cream and stir together.

Consume immediately or store in a shallow container, covered, in the freezer up to 1 month.

YIELD: 2 cups (280 g)

CANTALOUPE SORBET

3 cups (480 g) chopped ripe
cantaloupe, frozen

1 pinch of Celtic sea salt

Remove the rind, chop,
and freeze the cantaloupe
overnight.

Purée with the sea salt in a
food processor until smooth.

This is best consumed
immediately.

For storage, transfer the sorbet
to a shallow container, cover,
and store in the freezer. Best
if used within 2 days.

YIELD: 3 cups (450 g)

NOTE

- Swap 1 cup (160 g) of
  cantaloupe for 1 cup (150 g)
  of chopped, seeded, frozen
  watermelon. You can also try
  honeydew, mango, or papaya.

HOMEMADE NATTO

We appreciate Dr. Mercola's contributions to the wellness community and we attribute the following recipe to his website's vast array of helpful information: www.mercola.com.

Generally, soy is a no-no in the diet. See chapter 3 for more information on the very real dangers of soy. Natto, however, is an exception. This is in the form of fermented soybeans, which are predigested, and it contains additional enzymes, making it easier to digest and helps improve the process of absorbing nutrients. It also aids in the production of more good bacteria in your gut, which helps with the health of your gut and immune system.

The number one reason, however, that we include natto in this book is due to its very high content of powerful vitamin K2. This is the MK-7 form of vitamin K2, and we also promote foods rich in the MK-4 form of vitamin K2, which are animal-based foods. We feel natto should be consumed in very small quantities, no more than once or twice per week.

Natto can be made in small batches or purchased (as from Rhapsody) and separated into small servings and stored frozen for a few months. Your baby can practice his pincer grasp on this sticky and interesting-smelling food that is staple for Japanese babies.

Please note that those with an underactive thyroid cannot tolerate high amounts of soy, especially fermented, with regard to its goitrogenic (thyroid-blocking) effects of both isoflavones and genistein. Eat very sparingly if you have hypothyroidism.

Sally Fallon Morell states in *Nourishing Fats: Why We Need Animal Fats for Health and Happiness*: "The main role of K2 is to place calcium where it belongs in [hard tissues such as] the bones and teeth, and prevent it from going where it does not belong, in the soft tissues, such as arteries and kidneys."

1 pound (455 g) organic soybeans, small bean variety

0.1 gram *Bacillus natto* bacteria powder (such as Dr. Mercola's Kinetic Vegetable Culture Starter)

Wash the soybeans and soak them in water to cover for 1 day.

Then, steam the soybeans for 3 to 6 hours. You should be able to easily crush them when they are done. Drain.

In a small bowl, mix the *Bacillus natto* bacterial powder with 2 tablespoons (28 ml) of the water used for steaming, once it has cooled. Stir until dissolved. Pour this mixture over the drained soybeans. Toss the beans to coat with the mixture.

Transfer into flat casserole dishes so the layer of soybeans is not too thick. Cover the pans with cheesecloth, which must be secured to the edges with clips or a rubber band around the edges.

Place in a turned-off oven, but turn the oven light on. The ideal fermentation temperature is 99 to 108°F (37 to 42°C). You can measure this with an ovenproof food thermometer

After 24 hours, place in your refrigerator for another day prior to eating.

The natto should be smelly, stringy, and sticky.

Store in the freezer for up to 3 months.

NOTES

⊙ Use organic soybeans; if they are not organic, they are likely to be GMO.

⊙ You can order organic soybeans from brands like Rhapsody Natural Foods and store in the refrigerator, or separate into serving sizes and store in the freezer for a few months.

⊙ Other sources of the amazing vitamin K2 are grass-fed dairy, emu oil, and cheeses (such as Gouda and Brie). These animal sources provide the MK-4 form of vitamin K2. Supplements, if taken, however, should be of the MK-7 (plant) form, as the MK-4 supplements are synthetic.

⊙ This recipe is adapted from http://recipes.mercola.com/homemade-natto-recipe.aspx.

MOM-TO-MOM

Offer no grains until at least 1 year of age, ideally 18 months. When you include grains, they should be whole (not refined, bleached, or enriched) and should ideally be gluten-free (not wheat, rye, or barley just yet). Make sure oats are organic (due to glyphosate). Soak, sprout, or ferment grains when possible. Avoid store-bought crackers, cereal, teething biscuits, bagels, or toast, as they can become addictive.

YIELD: 1 pound (454 g)

SAUSAGE CHEESEBALLS AND STEVEN'S FAVORITE SAVORY SAUCE

These are kid-tested and dad-approved favorites. (Your toddler may like the sauce as a stand-alone soup as well. Steven did!) You might want to double the recipe, as these are often high in demand in many households.

Pork from pastured sources can be a good source of important vitamin D. Pork can be substituted for chicken, turkey, fish, lamb, buffalo, or beef. If any ingredients below are new, test them individually with your child before providing the meal in totality.

SAUSAGE CHEESEBALLS

½ pound (225 g) ground sausage (or plain ground pork with additional seasonings and sea salt to taste)

½ pound (225 g) ground beef (with heart, kidney, or liver if available)

1 farm-fresh, organic, pastured egg

¼ cup (32 g) arrowroot starch

Dash of red pepper or paprika, *optional*

1 teaspoon Celtic sea salt

½ cup (120 g) grated raw, grass-fed, organic cheese

Organic lard or coconut oil for sautéing

STEVEN'S FAVORITE SAVORY SAUCE

2 tablespoons (28 g) grass-fed, organic butter, ghee, coconut oil, or lard

2 cloves garlic, minced

¼ small onion, finely chopped

1 large tomato, sliced or chopped

½ teaspoon dried oregano

½ teaspoon dried basil

1 teaspoon Celtic sea salt

½ cup (120 ml) Souper Stock (page 45)

To make the meatballs: In a large bowl, mix together all the ground meat. Add the egg, arrowroot starch, seasonings, and cheese. Knead all the ingredients together and form into 1-inch (2.5 cm) balls. In a large skillet over medium heat, sauté in warmed lard or coconut oil, turning frequently on all sides, until cooked through.

Alternatively, bake the meatballs on a baking sheet in the oven at 350°F (180°C, or gas mark 4) for 20 minutes or until cooked through.

To make the sauce: In a separate saucepan, warm the fat over medium heat and add the garlic and onion. Sauté for 3 to 5 minutes. Add the chopped tomato, oregano, basil, and sea salt. Add the Souper Stock and stir occasionally for 10 to 15 minutes.

Let the Sausage Cheeseballs cool. Cut them into bite-size chunks and drizzle them with Steve's Favorite Savory Sauce.

YIELD: 2 adult servings and 1 for baby

MEATS AND MARINADES

Marinating adds rich flavor to any dish, helps to predigest meat, and offers antioxidants and other protection against harmful heterocyclic amines (HCAs), polycyclic aromatic hydrocarbons (PAHs), and advanced glycation end products (AGEs) that form during cooking or grilling meat, all of which are related to cancer and/or aging of cells. Ironically, sugar increases HCAs, PAHs, and AGEs, and often in our SAD diet, it's used in the marinades!

DAVE'S MARINADE

¼ cup (60 ml) apple cider vinegar

½ cup (120 ml) olive oil

2 tablespoons (28 ml) tamari sauce

1 tablespoon (8 g) grated ginger

1 tablespoon (2 g) chopped fresh rosemary

2 cloves garlic, chopped

Mix all the ingredients together. Place meat in a zip-top plastic bag or glass container with a lid, pour the marinade over the top, and place in the refrigerator for 1 to 24 hours.

YIELD: 1 cup (235 ml)

NOTE

⊙ This marinade can also be used as a sauce. Heat it in a saucepan until boiling, reduce the heat, and let it simmer until it reduces by half. Only use marinade that has not been used to marinate raw meat.

Scientific research has found that antioxidants (including vitamins C and E) can reduce HCAs, and certain spices (including rosemary, thyme, pepper, oregano, sage, garlic, and brine) can reduce HCAs by 60%. Protection from PAHs comes from vitamin E and carotenoids (like beta-carotene), and notably, the absence of these nutrients, even without exposure to PAHs, can adversely impact healthy brain development. Acidic mediums (like lemon juice or vinegar) reduce AGE formation in cooking and grilling meat.

A toxin-fighting marinade contains three basic elements: an acid, seasonings, and an oil (optional). Acids—such as apple cider vinegar or homemade vinegar, unpasteurized pickle or sauerkraut juice, or fresh squeezed lemon or lime juice—should be raw. Oil—coconut oil, ghee, and on occasion, sesame oil or olive oil—should tolerate high heat. Seasonings—grated ginger, cilantro, garlic, onion, rosemary, dill, sage, mint, or others—should be as fresh as possible.

The longer you marinate the meat, the better.

TACO SEASONING FOR BEEF OR CHICKEN

Use this blend as a rub, as a seasoning when cooking meat, or as a marinade (add sauerkraut or lemon juice and an oil of choice).

½ tablespoon (3 g) turmeric

1 tablespoon (8 g) chili powder

1 tablespoon (7 g) paprika

1 tablespoon (7 g) ground cumin

1 tablespoon (7 g) onion powder

2½ teaspoons (8 g) garlic powder

1 teaspoon dried dill

2 teaspoons Celtic sea salt

⅛ teaspoon cayenne pepper

Mix all the ingredients together.

Use 3 tablespoons (28 g) for every 1 pound (455 g) of ground meat.

YIELD: Enough for 2 pounds (907 g) ground meat

LETTUCE WRAPS

1 pound (455 g) ground beef

2½ tablespoons (13 g) Taco Seasoning (at left)

6 to 8 lettuce leaves from butterleaf or romaine, for example, taking the largest outer leaves from 2 to 4 heads of lettuce

Brown the ground beef in a cast-iron skillet. Sprinkle the seasoning over the cooked ground beef.

Serve the seasoned meat wrapped in lettuce leaves.

YIELD: 6 to 8 servings

MOM-TO-MOM

Many of the items that we recommend for Super Nutrition must be of the highest quality, such as liver, lard, coconut milk, and fish roe. Unfortunately, these are not often found at your local grocery store; thus, online shopping is incredibly helpful. Keep two lists throughout the month—a shopping list and an online ordering list. Once a month, place your online orders. Try visiting www.uswellnessmeats.com and www.vitalchoice.com as a source of pastured, organic meats and organ meats, game, wild-caught seafood, and more.

SOAKED AND SPROUTED NUTS AND SEEDS

Sprouting nuts and seeds makes them much more digestible and nutritious. After nuts and seeds are sprouted and dried, they can be ground into flour for recipes or made into nut butters or crusts for quiche, fruit tarts, or other dishes.

For nuts, try pecans, almonds, or walnuts (these are different from peanuts, which are not actually nuts, but legumes). For seeds, try pumpkin, squash, and sesame.

SOAKED NUTS

Nuts (pecans, almonds, walnuts, or others)

Water (twice as much as quantity of nuts)

1 to 2 tablespoons (15 to 30 g) Celtic sea salt

Soak the nuts in water with sea salt for 12 to 24 hours, covered. Rinse well. Dry the nuts on cookie sheets lined with paper towels, switching the paper towels throughout the day; alternatively, dry in a warm oven (150°F [66°C] or the lowest setting on your oven) or use a dehydrator (the best and easiest option).

NUTS AND ALLERGIES

New research suggests that delaying introduction of nuts increases the risk of nut allergies. Allergies are due to an inability to digest well, along with low stomach acid, leaky gut, and gut dysbiosis due to sugar, low/no probiotic foods, etc. To actually reduce the likelihood that your baby develops allergies, soaking or sprouting nuts and seeds is strongly suggested, and the time of introduction should be based on each parent's discretion, but should consider health history (extra consideration should be given if your baby has other 3Cs, was born via C-section, had/has acid reflux, was not exclusively breastfed, or if you have a family history of allergies, OCD, learning disorders, etc.). (For additional information on allergies, see page 84.)

NOTE

⊙ This same process can be applied to seeds.

SPROUTED NUTS AND SEEDS

Soak nuts or seeds in twice as much water as nuts and 1 to 2 tablespoons (15 to 30 g) sea salt. Cover for 12 hours. Rinse and drain every 3 to 4 hours or just leave the mixture overnight. Rinse very well.

Place the seeds or nuts in a jar (find a sprouting jar at your health food store or online).

If you do not have a sprouting jar, secure cheese-cloth over the top of a Mason jar with a rubber band. Angle the jar, top down, in a dish-draining rack. Every 6 to 8 hours rinse 2 or 3 times by filling the jar with water and shaking, then draining.

When you notice sprouts (more obvious with seeds), move the jar into a well-lit area (but not direct sunlight) and continue to rinse well every 6 to 8 hours. Let sprouts grow for 3 to 5 days until you actually see a small sprout appear (be cautious during rinsing not to break it off, as this will cause spoiling during the sprouting process).

When complete, rinse very well. Dry on cookie sheets lined with paper towels, switching the paper towels throughout the day; alternatively, dry in a warm oven (150°F [66°C] or the lowest setting on your oven) or use a dehydrator (the best option).

YIELD: Will be equal to the amount of nuts or seeds used; typically 2 to 3 cups (about 200 to 300 g)

NOTES

- Mix 3 cups (300 g) of assorted, soaked and dried nuts (crushed or mashed to the right size for your baby), with 2 beaten eggs, 2 teaspoons cinnamon, 1 teaspoon each of vanilla extract and almond extract, and 1 teaspoon green stevia powder (just the leaves mashed and dried), optional. Mix well, and bake at 325°F (170°C, or gas mark 3) for 25 to 30 minutes. Makes a great snack or gift in a Mason jar around the holidays.
- Well-dried sprouted nuts and seeds can be stored in the refrigerator or cool pantry for 4 to 8 weeks.
- Sprouted nuts and seeds can be ground up and used as flour in many recipes or processed with additional oil into homemade nut or seed butters or spreads. The significance of sprouting is that the nutritional value has been increased, the digestibility improved, and the antinutrients minimized; the actual sprout itself isn't important.
- Brazil nuts, chestnuts, hazelnuts, pistachios, macadamia nuts, and pine nuts can also be used.
- Peanuts are actually legumes and shouldn't be soaked longer than 6 hours.

NUT FLOUR OR SEED FLOUR

Grind presoaked, dried nuts or seeds in a food processor or a coffee grinder to a flour-like consistency.

NOTE

- Nut flours should be stored in the refrigerator and consumed with a few weeks.

NUT BUTTERS

Nut butters like almond, sunflower seed, and cashew can be purchased, but those were not previously soaked and many have added sugars and damaged fats, and nut butters can also contain aflatoxins (due to mold that develops during storage), which are known to cause liver cancer. The National Cancer Institute states: "Aflatoxins are a family of toxins produced by certain fungi that are found on agricultural crops such as maize (corn), peanuts, cottonseed, and tree nuts. The main fungi that produce aflatoxins are abundant in warm and humid regions of the world. Aflatoxin-producing fungi can contaminate crops in the field, at harvest, and during storage."

2 cups (about 200 g) soaked and dried nuts

½ teaspoon Celtic sea salt, or more to taste

½ teaspoon almond extract, *optional*

2 tablespoons (28 ml or 28 g) oil (almond, coconut, or other)

In a food processor or Vitamix, mix together the nuts, sea salt, optional almond extract, and oil. Grind well. Store in the refrigerator in a Mason jar. Serve rolled into balls.

NOTE

⊙ Nut or seed butters should be consumed soon after grinding. Only grind what you're going to consume.

Store-bought major brands and organic brands of peanut and tree-nut butters are less likely to contain aflotoxins. Homemade is better. (Soaking is easier and less time-intensive than sprouting, but either method is recommended to improve the digestibility and nutritional value of nuts.)

YIELD: 1¼ cups (about 325 g) nut butter

ASHLEY'S RASPBERRY CAROB DESSERT

While recommended to be used sparingly for a sweet treat, carob is preferred to chocolate. It is a source of vitamin E, potassium, magnesium, calcium, anti-oxidants, and phytonutrients. It can satisfy a chocolate craving, but does not contain caffeine, which should be avoided by babies, children, and nursing and pregnant moms.

Add all the ingredients to a blender or Vitamix.

Whip together and serve immediately.

NOTE

⊙ This pudding-like texture can give baby practice with her spoon.

12 raspberries

2 tablespoons (15 g) carob

¼ cup (120 ml) coconut cream

YIELD: 1 to 2 desserts

INGREDIENT SPOTLIGHT: CAROB

Carob bean gum is also called locust bean gum. Be careful not to overdo it when using carob (made from the seeds of a legume tree); while it tastes great and doesn't contain cacao's caffeine (cacao is an extract from the seeds of a fruit tree), it does contain tannins (otherwise known as tannic acid), which are water-soluble polyphenols. Tannins do have some benefit, as they've been shown to shrink and strengthen blood vessel walls and have some antioxidant properties, but that can be outweighed when consumed in high doses by the fact that carob can be an irritant, can bind with minerals (such as magnesium), and can block vitamin B1 absorption.

ZUCCHINI BANANA BREAD

This healthy snack is particularly good warmed and buttered. It also makes a delicious "French toast." *Note:* This is a two-day recipe.

2 cups (256 g) cassava or (240 g) tigernut flour

2 tablespoons (30 g) yogurt

1 cup (128 g) arrowroot starch

½ cup (120 ml) water

¼ teaspoon baking soda

½ teaspoon aluminum-free baking powder

½ teaspoon Celtic sea salt

1½ teaspoons ground cinnamon

¼ teaspoon ground cloves

½ teaspoon ground nutmeg

3 farm-fresh, organic, pastured eggs

1 teaspoon vanilla extract

3 brown-spotted bananas, mashed

1 cup (90 g) grated zucchini

⅓ cup (75 g) coconut oil, butter, or ghee, melted

¼ cup (55 g) coconut butter, warmed

YIELD: 1 loaf

The night before baking, mix the flour, yogurt, arrowroot starch, and water until a thick liquid dough forms. Pour into a medium-size glass, stainless steel, or ceramic bowl and cover with a plate. Allow to sit at room temperature overnight.

The next day, preheat the oven to 325°F (170°C, or gas mark 3).

In another medium-size bowl, combine the baking soda and powder, sea salt, and spices.

In a large bowl, whip the eggs until frothy. Add the vanilla, mashed bananas, zucchini, coconut oil, and coconut butter. Mix until well blended. Fold in the flour mixture.

Grease a loaf pan with coconut oil and scoop in the dough. Bake for 25 to 35 minutes, or until a knife comes out clean from the center.

VARIATIONS

⊙ This can also be made into muffins.
⊙ Instead of zucchini and banana, use:
  » 2 cups (400 g) baked sweet potato, 2 cups (490 g) stewed apples, and ½ teaspoon vanilla extract
  » 2 cups (490 g) pumpkin, 2 cups (490 g) stewed pears, 2 teaspoons pumpkin pie spice, and ½ teaspoon orange extract

INGREDIENT SPOTLIGHT: CASSAVA AND TIGERNUT FLOURS

Cassava flour (or yucca) is a tuberous edible root, and tigernuts are small root vegetables indigenous to North Africa and the Mediterranean. You can substitute these flours 1:1 for traditional white flour, but soak them first to reduce antinutrients.

CAULIFLOWER ITALIAN DIPPER STICKS

We don't advocate refined flour and commercial yeast, so that leaves out most breadsticks and the like. However, using cauliflower allows you to re-create the idea of breadsticks. This recipe uses cheese to bind the cauliflower and add flavor. Consuming with raw mom's milk or other organic dairy will provide helpful enzymes, including lactase, for digestion.

1 medium head cauliflower

1 cup (115 g) raw mozzarella cheese, shredded, divided

1 farm-fresh, organic, pastured egg, slightly beaten

1 teaspoon dried oregano

1 teaspoon dried basil

½ teaspoon garlic salt

Coconut oil or ghee for greasing baking pan

½ cup (40 g) shredded raw Parmesan cheese

Cut the cauliflower into chunks, removing the core. Process in a food processor until it's a pearl-size consistency.

In a large saucepan, bring 1 inch (2.5 cm) of water to a boil. Add the riced cauliflower, cover, and simmer for 5 minutes.

Preheat the oven to 425°F (220°C, or gas mark 7).

Drain the cauliflower well. Place the slightly cooled cauliflower in a cheesecloth or a clean dish towel and squeeze to remove all the remaining water.

Place the drained cauliflower in a large bowl. Add ½ cup (58 g) of the mozzarella cheese, egg, oregano, basil, and garlic salt. Stir well.

Grease a stainless steel baking pan with coconut oil or ghee. Scoop the cauliflower into the pan and form it into an 8½ × 11-inch (21 × 28 cm) rectangle. Cook for 30 to 45 minutes, until golden brown and firm.

Remove from the oven and top with the remaining ½ cup (58 g) mozzarella and the Parmesan cheese. Bake for another 10 minutes, or until the cheese melts. Cut into strips lengthwise as "breadsticks" and serve with warm marinara sauce for dipping.

NOTE

⊙ Make your own marinara sauce by blending fresh tomatoes, Souper Stock (page 45), extra-virgin olive oil, and seasonings.

YIELD: Makes about 10 "breadsticks"

FISH "STICKS" AND MOM'S TARTAR SAUCE

Free of preservatives, white flour, and flavor enhancers, homemade fish sticks are marvelous and fun. The tartar sauce is a healthful addition, as well. Most of these recipes are adapted from *Nourishing Traditions* by Sally Fallon.

FISH STICKS

1 pound (455 g) wild-caught cod or other mild, meaty fish, cut into strips or chunks

1 farm-fresh, organic, pastured egg, beaten

½ cup (about 50 g) grated raw cheese like Parmesan, Romano, or asiago

¾ cup (96 g) arrowroot starch, tigernut flour, or cassava flour

½ teaspoon onion powder

½ teaspoon garlic powder

1 teaspoon Celtic sea salt

1 teaspoon dill, dried or chopped fresh

3 to 4 tablespoons (42 to 55 g) ghee or (39 to 52 g) lard

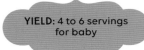
YIELD: 4 to 6 servings for baby

Dip the fish into the egg so it is coated on all sides. Place the cheese, arrowroot, and seasonings into a Mason jar or large zip-top plastic bag and mix well. Add the fish to the jar or bag and shake to coat the fish, a few pieces at a time. In a large skillet, sauté the coated fish in the fat over medium heat, allowing each side to brown to golden for 3 to 5 minutes. Flip a few times during the cooking process.

TARTAR SAUCE

1 tablespoon (15 ml) unpasteurized pickle juice (from homemade, Bubbies, or Gut Shot)

¾ cup (175 g) mayonnaise, based on avocado oil, if available (not soy or vegetable oil), or homemade (page 210)

½ cup (115 g) organic, pastured sour cream (raw preferred)

½ teaspoon dill, dried or chopped fresh

½ teaspoon Celtic sea salt

2 tablespoons (20 g) minced onion

¼ cup (34 g) finely chopped dill pickles

Mix all the ingredients together in a medium-size bowl. Use to top warm fish.

NOTES

⊙ Good choices include salmon, trout, anchovies, herring, sardines, and shad.

⊙ Purdue University also offers a free app that can help you track your seafood consumption and estimate your intake of omega-3s, mercury, and PCBs, a group of industrial pollutants that can harm your baby's nervous system.

DEEP DIVE INTO CHOOSING SEAFOOD WISELY

As our waters have become increasingly polluted, it is important to choose fish carefully. Monterey Bay Aquarium (www.monterey-bayaquarium.org, search "seafood watch") maintains a list of which seafood to buy or avoid, and the Environmental Defense Fund (www.edf.org, search for "seafood health alerts") suggests the number of times certain fish can be eaten per month to avoid toxic overload. Purdue University publishes a handy wallet card that tells you where most commercial fish falls on the mercury contamination scale and how much of each it's okay to eat.

Here are some general guidelines.

• The smaller the fish, the less toxic (sardines, anchovies, and fish roe are best) and can be eaten up to 3 times per week.

• The FDA warns pregnant and nursing moms to avoid shark, swordfish, king mackerel, and tilefish; we also suggest avoiding marlin, orange roughy, and big-eye or Ahi tuna.

• Lower-mercury seafood (salmon, shrimp, canned light tuna, pollock) can be consumed once per week, along with clam, crab, flounder, herring, haddock, oysters, scallops, sole, and whitefish.

• Albacore tuna has significantly more mercury than "light" tuna, so should be avoided, as should Chilean sea bass, bluefish, and grouper.

CELINA'S BENEFICIAL BEVERAGES

It is great to have healthy beverage alternatives to juice and soda pop, and these beverages serve as sources of nutrients, enzymes, and probiotics and as a digestive aid. Here are a few to try. These can also be frozen into ice pops in warm summer months or climates.

BERRY SHRUB

Shrubs are fun vinegar drinks that have been fermented so they provide great digestive benefits as well as nutritive benefits. Apple cider vinegar has so many benefits, entire books have been written on it alone. Shrubs go back to colonial days, when they were a popular way to preserve and enjoy the fleeting bounty of summer. Lisa Howard at TheCulturedCook.com has several additional recipes.

½ cup (85 g) sliced strawberries

½ cup (78 g) blueberries (thawed if frozen)

3 to 4 fresh mint leaves

2 cups (475 ml) apple cider vinegar

Crush the berries with a potato masher or the back of a spoon. Combine the berries, mint leaves, and vinegar in a wide-mouth quart (950 ml) jar. Allow to sit for 1 to 30 days, while the flavors infuse.

To serve, add 1 to 2 tablespoons (15 to 28 ml) to a glass of water or sparking water.

YIELD: 20 beverages

NOTES

⊙ Vinegar drinks can be made with almost any fruit, many vegetables, and unlimited combinations and can include various herbs and spices.

⊙ Only serve in small shot-glass size (1 to 2 ounces [28 to 60 ml]) servings at a time with a meal.

HOMEMADE GINGER ALE

Ginger is an excellent digestive aid that works great for nausea during pregnancy. This drink is the inspiration for the modern-day high fructose corn syrup–infused version. It is highly preferred and can be consumed for good health.

¾ cup (96 g) peeled and grated or chopped fresh ginger

½ cup (120 ml) fresh lime juice

¼ cup (48 g) Rapunzel brand rapadura or other whole-foods sweetener

½ teaspoon Celtic sea salt

¼ cup (60 ml) whey (see Homemade Raw Dairy Whey, page 107)

2 quarts (1.9 L) filtered water

Mix together all the ingredients in a 2-quart (1.9 L) jug. Leave at room temperature for 48 to 72 hours and then move to the refrigerator.

Strain into the glass when serving.

YIELD: 2 quarts (1.9 L)

NOTE

⊙ This will keep for several months in the refrigerator.

COCONUT LIME "SPRITZER"

Unsweetened coconut water contains blood pressure–lowering and alkalizing minerals. Adding digestive support with apple cider vinegar along with the antioxidants fround in citrus results in a refreshing and revitalizing beverage!

½ cup (120 ml) coconut water, either out of a can where cream has been used, made from fresh coconut, or purchased as unsweetened coconut water

Juice of 1 lime

Juice from ½ orange or grapefruit

1 tablespoon (15 ml) apple cider vinegar

Pinch of Celtic sea salt or pinch of whole-plant ground stevia (this is a green powder that has a sweet, grass-like scent), *optional*

Combine all the ingredients in a jar. Refrigerate until served.

YIELD: Three or four 1- to 2-ounce (28 to 60 ml) beverages for baby

HOMEMADE ORANGINA

This is a favorite beverage for children in France, though the commercial form has excessive sugar. Making your own at home makes for a more nutritious and still delicious alternative.

Juice of 6 oranges

1 teaspoon Celtic sea salt

2 tablespoons (60 ml) whey (see Homemade Raw Dairy Whey, page 107)

¼ teaspoon orange extract

3 cups (700 ml) filtered water

Place the all ingredients in a 2-quart (1.9 L) jar. Stir well and cover tightly. Leave at room temperature for 48 hours and then move to the refrigerator.

Stir before serving.

YIELD: 2 quarts (1.9 L)

GINGERBREAD MAN MILKSHAKE

This is a kid-tested favorite and a great "dessert" for a special occasion or holiday. The benefit of raw or rare animal foods is their unadulterated state of nutrition (undamaged vitamins and minerals), but they're most beneficial because of their enzyme content. Any animal foods consumed raw or rare must come from the purest sources, and meats, in particular, should be frozen a minimum of 14 days prior to raw or rare consumption.

Experts in traditional-foods nutrition say diets must always contain some raw animal foods (such as raw milk or raw eggs). Yolks add important amino acids and protein, making this smoothie a complete meal, as well as omega-3 fats and other vitamins and minerals. But most of all, a raw yolk adds a significant amount of enzymes.

½ cup (115 g) raw yogurt

¼ cup (60 ml) coconut cream

1 to 2 teaspoons blackstrap molasses

¼ teaspoon freshly grated ginger
(or ½ teaspoon powdered)

½ teaspoon ground cinnamon

1 small brown-spotted banana

1 farm-fresh, organic, pastured egg yolk

In a blender, combine all the ingredients and mix well. Consume immediately.

YIELD: 1 cup (235 ml)

NOTES

- ⊙ If you use a raw egg yolk, choose a farm-fresh, organic, pastured egg; otherwise, you need to soft-boil the egg (see page 99), leaving the yolk runny but warm.
- ⊙ Enzymes are destroyed by cooking, and enzyme content follows caloric content; therefore, animal foods in a raw or undercooked state are excellent sources of enzymes!

RAINBOW ROOT FRIES

1 yucca

1 sweet potato

2 medium beets

2 large or 4 small rutabaga

⅓ cup (75 g) coconut oil, ghee, or lard

2 to 3 teaspoons (10 to 15 g) Celtic sea salt

Root vegetables typically grow underground and serve as the root of their plant; they include carrots, horseradish, radishes, rutabagas, parsnips, and turnips. Often called roots, corms include celeriac, taro, and water chestnuts. Also generally seen as roots, onion and garlic are sulfur compound–containing bulbs. Rhizomes are also close to roots and include ginger and turmeric. White potatoes and yucca are tubers. Historically, root vegetables were never consumed raw. Often, they were harvested, stored in holes in the ground or root cellars, and cooked well, including in soups and stews, prior to consuming. Today, strong evidence exists that some of the vital nutrients found in many root vegetables—including carotenoids, vitamin C, potassium, magnesium, and dietary fiber—can help fight cancer, diabetes, obesity, and inflammation-riddled conditions.

Peel and julienne the root vegetables into slim sticks, or bigger if you desire.

Heat the fat in a skillet over medium-high heat until hot and a drop of water sizzles. Add the root fries in small batches. Use a splatter guard. Cook until slightly browned and then flip. Remove and let drain in a mesh strainer or on a paper towel.

Toss with sea salt and serve hot.

NOTES

- It is important to consume these fries, particularly yucca, with fat, fiber, and protein to slow down the blood-glucose spike that can be induced. We repeat purposefully: Carbohydrates should rarely, if ever, be consumed alone.

- Taro, turnip, and parsnip are other root vegetables that work well as fries.

- *Alternative:* Toss the root fries with bacon drippings, ghee, or warmed coconut oil and then sprinkle with sea salt. Place on well-oiled baking sheets. Roast for about 60 minutes at 400°F (200°C, or gas mark 6) until browned and softened, flipping the fries 3 or 4 times. Serve immediately.

YIELD: 5 to 7 servings

FRIED "RICE"

Cauliflower contains vitamin C, vitamin K1, potassium, manganese, phosphorus, selenium, sodium, calcium, niacin, folate, and fiber. Cauliflower, if consumed raw in high quantities, can block thyroid function, but if cooked, it is not a concern. In fact, cruciferous vegetables like broccoli, cauliflower, and Brussels sprouts have anticarcinogenic properties (as described in various studies, as well as in *Food Pharmacy* by Jean Carper). Further, this dish includes turmeric, both a cancer and an inflammation fighter!

1 head cauliflower

3 tablespoons (42 g) animal fat of choice

1 pound (455 g) meat—peeled shrimp, diced chicken, diced pork, sausage, fish, or ground beef

2 teaspoons ground turmeric

2 teaspoons minced garlic

1 small onion, chopped

1 bell pepper, any color, chopped

2 to 3 carrots, chopped

½ pound (225 g) pea pods

1 to 2 farm-fresh, organic, pastured eggs, beaten

2 teaspoons tamari sauce

¼ cup (25 g) chopped green onion

3 tablespoons (42 g) bone marrow, warmed and removed from bone, *optional*

Wash and thoroughly dry the cauliflower. Remove all the greens and cut the head into floret chunks. Discard the middle hard core.

Put the florets into a food processor. Depending on the size of your processor, you may need to do this in a couple of batches. Pulse the food processor several times until the cauliflower is the size of rice.

Once you have your cauliflower rice, set aside.

In a wok or large cast-iron skillet or tangine, heat the fat. Add the meat of choice, sprinkle with turmeric, and sauté until cooked to the desired doneness. Remove from the pan. Keep warm.

Add the garlic, onion, peppers, carrots, and pea pods to the hot skillet. Sauté until the vegetables soften, about 15 minutes.

Add the cauliflower and continue to cook 3 to 4 more minutes.

In a separate small skillet, cook the eggs until they are no longer runny.

Mix the cooked egg in with the vegetables. Return the meat to the pan and sprinkle the tamari sauce over all. Add the green onion and bone marrow, if using. Mix all the ingredients well and continue to cook until heated through.

YIELD: 4 to 6 servings

VARIATION

- A cup (235 ml) of Souper Stock (page 45) or coconut cream can be added to the fried rice at the end and then simmered for 5 minutes for a casserole-style dish.

NOTE

- Cauliflower can also be riced using a box grater using the medium-size holes. For the grater method, you will want to leave the florets attached to the center core so you can hold it while grating.

OLD-FASHIONED MAYO SALADS

In the last century, "salad" has taken on a new meaning relative to what traditional salads once were. Salads of our great-grandparents' era included leftover chicken, shrimp, or eggs mixed with mayonnaise—an emulsion of oil and eggs. Although mayonnaise can be used to make a salad dressing for today's lettuce-based salads, mayonnaise is now based on soy ("vegetable") oil, which is inflammatory and unhealthy on many fronts. Making your own mayonnaise or finding a product that is based on avocado oil or olive oil is recommended. Canola oil–based mayo is GMO and not the best choice. So many variations can be made with these simple salads, just by changing the ingredients, spices, and serving options.

HOMEMADE MAYONNAISE

(adapted from *Nourishing Traditions*)

1 teaspoon gelatin

1 teaspoon raw apple cider vinegar

2 farm-fresh, organic, pastured egg yolks, at room temperature

Celtic sea salt to taste

1 teaspoon garlic powder

1 teaspoon onion powder

1 teaspoon whey, *optional*

1 cup (235 ml) avocado or blended oil (such as Chosen Foods Chosen Blend— a mixture of organic high-oleic safflower oil, avocado oil, and coconut oil)

Add the gelatin to the vinegar in a small bowl and let sit.

In a food processor, combine the egg yolks, sea salt, garlic powder, onion powder, and whey, if using. Blend well. Add the gelatin and vinegar mixture.

Drop by single drop and with the motor running, add in the oil. You will see the oil emulsify—be patient.

When all the oil is fully emulsified, transfer the finished mayonnaise to a 16-ounce (475 ml) jar. Let the mayonnaise sit at room temperature, well covered, for 4 to 6 hours before refrigerating. The mayonnaise will last several months in the refrigerator and will become firmer in consistency with time.

YIELD: 1½ cups (337 g)

CHICKEN SALAD

2 cups (280 g) cooked and chopped chicken

⅓ cup (75 g) mayonnaise

½ cup (60 g) finely diced celery

½ cup (63 g) chopped green apple

¼ cup (25 g) sliced green onion

1 teaspoon ground turmeric

½ teaspoon Celtic sea salt

Mix all the ingredients and chill in the refrigerator.

Serve the chicken salad on a bed of lettuce. Or, serve with chunks of red, yellow, or orange bell peppers and let your child use them to dip and scoop the salad. This is also a good way to pack the chicken salad for a school lunch.

YIELD: 2 cups (450 g)

EGG SALAD

4 farm-fresh, organic, pastured eggs

¼ cup (60 g) mayonnaise

1 teaspoon yellow mustard

½ teaspoon garlic powder

¼ cup (25 g) sliced green onion

¼ teaspoon Celtic sea salt

Place the eggs in a saucepan and cover with cold water. Bring the water to a boil and immediately remove from the heat. Cover and let the eggs stand in the hot water for 10 to 12 minutes. Remove from the hot water, cool, peel, and chop or mash the eggs.

Place the chopped eggs in a bowl and stir in the mayonnaise, mustard, garlic powder, and green onion. Season with sea salt and mix well.

The egg salad can be served in an avocado half or half a tomato after scooping out the seeds. It can also be served with Cauliflower Italian Dipper Sticks (page 201).

YIELD: 1½ cups (337 g)

COCONUT BIRTHDAY CAKE AND FROSTING

This cake is delicious and is adapted from a recipe by Julie Matthews, autism nutrition expert and author of *Nourishing Hope*, a book we highly recommend. Coconut flour is dry, so there are many eggs in this recipe, which add positively to its nutrient profile. We recommend this cake, which uses honey, be a very special and rare treat. We've listed our versions of the Coconut Birthday Cake and Cashew Frosting, Julie Matthews's versions of the Coconut Birthday Cake and Cashew Frosting, and a recipe for Coconut Butter Frosting.

OUR COCONUT BIRTHDAY CAKE

2 to 3 tablespoons (14 to 42 g) coconut oil for greasing cake pans

¾ cup (84 g) coconut flour

⅓ cup (42 g) arrowroot starch

¼ cup (22 g) shredded, unsweetened, unsulfured coconut

¼ teaspoon sea salt

½ teaspoon aluminum-free baking soda

½ teaspoon ground cinnamon

1 small ripe banana

7 farm-fresh, organic, pastured eggs

⅔ cup (150 g) grass-fed ghee, melted

⅓ cup (113 g) melted honey

2 tablespoons (28 ml) vanilla extract

¼ cup (59 ml) coconut cream

Preheat the oven to 325°F (170°C, or gas mark 3). Grease two 8-inch (20 cm) cake pans.

Stir together the coconut flour, arrowroot starch, shredded coconut, sea salt, baking soda, and cinnamon in a large bowl.

Purée the banana. Beat the eggs and mix in the melted ghee, honey, vanilla extract, and coconut cream.

Blend all the wet ingredients together and then mix into the flour mixture. Thoroughly combine with a hand mixer, food processor, or Vitamix. Divide the batter between the prepared cake pans.

Bake for 40 to 45 minutes, or until a knife inserted into the center comes out clean.

Frost the cake after it has thoroughly cooled.

This is best if served the next day.

YIELD: Two 8-inch (20 cm) cake layers

OUR CASHEW FROSTING

1 cup (140 g) cashews, pre-soaked and drained

5 dates, pitted and chopped

¾ cup (175 ml) water

½ cup (112 g) warmed and stirred coconut butter

1 teaspoon vanilla extract

1 teaspoon almond extract

Dash of Celtic sea salt

Mix all the ingredients together in a food processor or Vitamix. Spread over the cooled cake to frost.

YIELD: 1 cup (240 g)

OUR COCONUT BUTTER FROSTING

¾ cup (165 g) coconut butter

2 tablespoons (28 g) ghee

1 teaspoon almond or vanilla extract

1 to 2 tablespoons (20 to 40 g) raw honey or maple syrup

¼ cup (56 g) crème fraîche

Warm a jar of coconut butter and a container of ghee in warm water.

Put the coconut butter, ghee, alond or vanilla extract, and honey or maple syrup into a Vitamix or use a mixing bowl and hand mixer. Mix all the ingredients together until well blended.

Add the crème fraîche and stir in by hand.

Spread on the cooled cake. The frosting will thicken if put into the refrigerator.

YIELD: 1 cup (240 g)

JULIE MATTHEWS'S COCONUT BIRTHDAY CAKE

1¼ cups (140 g) coconut flour

1 teaspoon sea salt

½ teaspoon baking soda

8 large pastured eggs

⅔ cup (160 ml) melted grass-fed ghee

1 cup (340 g) raw honey

2 tablespoons (28 ml) vanilla extract

Preheat the oven to 330°F (165°C). Grease and flour two 8-inch (20 cm) cake pans. In a large bowl, combine the coconut flour, salt, and baking soda. In a medium bowl, whisk together the eggs, melted ghee, honey, and vanilla. Blend the wet ingredients into the coconut flour mixture with a handheld mixer until thoroughly combined. Divide between the cake pans.

Bake for 35 to 40 minutes. Once an inserted toothpick comes out dry (a few moist crumbs), the cake is ready. Let cool in the pan, then cool on a rack. Frost after the cake is cool.

JULIE MATTHEWS'S CASHEW FROSTING

1½ cups (210 g) cashews

1 cup (235 ml) water

2 teaspoons vanilla extract

7 dates

Tiny pinch of salt

Mix all the ingredients in a blender on high speed to whip into a thick cashew cream. Spread on the cooled cake.

Top with fresh organic blueberries.

THINK OUTSIDE THE BOX OF MAC 'N' CHEESE

Convenience Foods Can Cost You Your Child's Health

(18 TO 24 MONTHS)

Between 18 and 24 months, your child might be able to express what he would like to eat. Also, toddlers are realizing their independence and need to have a sense that they are in control, even if it means simply being able to pick the apple over the banana. If you have provided only PURE and Super POWER foods, you can easily trust that his body knows what he needs and allow him to choose.

As we'll discuss, the foods you choose to feed your child at this age will impact health on many levels—not only physical, but mental and emotional as well. Providing adequate ingredients from nutritious foods is the recipe for a healthy, happy child! This fourth pillar (nutritious) of Super Nutrition will help steer your child through his next exciting milestones.

Dietary Influences on Tantrums and the Terrible Twos

Tantrums are expected and even somewhat accepted in childhood. Even in older children, behavioral issues, attention, mood, anxiety, and learning problems are also starting to seem quite normal. However, as we'll explain, diet can impact your child's mood, attention span, ability to follow directions, and how he manages his emotions. How much of children's "bad" behavior today is due to "bad" diet? Too much!

Diet can either contribute to mood and behavioral problems, or it can ameliorate—or even prevent—them. The typical toddler daily menu includes a breakfast of cereal or snack bars and juice or milk; a lunch of a white bread sandwich with jelly and sweetened peanut butter or a prepackaged meal, a cookie, and a juice box; snacks consist of cheesy grain-based crackers, chips, or "fruit" chews; and a dinner of pizza or pasta, accompanied by either juice or chocolate milk, and lastly dessert. This is a veritable diet of drinks and drugs! As such, behavior, mood, attention, and physical health are all negatively impacted.

Rather than being hardwired problems or just part of your child's personality, many mood and behavioral issues stem from excessive sugar, sugar-sensitive responses, or sensitivities to chemicals, such as dyes and preservatives. As reported in the *Journal of Attention Disorders*, sugar and other processed foods have direct effects on children's mental health.

We urge you to *just say no* to the drunken and drugged diet of typical toddlers. Highly processed sugar and refined-grain-based foods impact brain chemicals the very same way that street drugs, prescription drugs, and alcohol do.

HOOKED ON BAD-BEHAVIOR FOODS. The foods in typical toddler diets are habit-forming; kids become biochemically dependent on their drug-like foods. This is partly why your toddler vies (and cries) for sugary or flour-based foods. By giving in to these pleas, though, you act as an enabler.

DRUNKEN/DRUGGED DIETARY CONSTITUENT	WHAT IT CREATES	DRUG(S) THE EFFECTS MIMIC
Poorly digested grains	Dietary opiates, excitotoxins, and endocannabinoids	Morphine, heroin, and marijuana
Poorly digested pasteurized milk	Dietary opiates, excitotoxins, and endocannabinoids	Morphine, heroin, and marijuana
Sugar	Dopamine	Cocaine
Sugar	Endorphins	Morphine, opium, and heroin
Sugar	Feeds yeast (by-products are ethanol and acetylaldehyde)	Brain inebriation like alcoholic beverages
Sugar	Adrenaline and norephinephrine	Methamphetamine
Artificial sweeteners (aspartame), flavor enhancers (MSG, hydrolyzed vegetable protein), preservatives (carrageenan)	GABA, glutamate	Marijuana

ADDITIVES MAKE FOR A TROUBLED CHILDHOOD. Further sapping the nutrient quality of foods are the unnatural ingredients used to extend shelf life, affect "mouthfeel," make fake food's color or flavor more appealing, etc. These chemical additives can lead to hyperactivity and impact mood. By removing additives, you can help your child be calm, content, and able to concentrate rather than irritable, distracted, and hyperactive.

POOR DIET LEADS TO DISORDER DIAGNOSES. Both additives and sugar in typical toddler foods can significantly alter normal moods and behavior, leading to diagnoses of conditions such as attention deficit disorder, obsessive-compulsive disorder, learning disabilities, anger issues, anxiety, and even depression. For this reason, we suggest a trial of dietary intervention before turning to prescription drugs for treatment.

The Typical Toddler Diet

It is common to see toddlers eating predominantly highly processed "kid foods," including prepackaged meals, macaroni and cheese, microwavable dinners, fast food, juice, and even soda pop. In September 2015, CBS reported that, "About one-third of U.S. children and teens eat pizza or other fast food *every day*" [emphasis added]. While most parents would agree that this is not an optimal diet, many think "treats" and junk food in moderation is just fine, as they don't want to deprive their children. But this is *not* moderation! On the contrary, depriving your kids of this CRAP food is gifting them with better brain biochemistry and a better chance at overall optimized health.

While most toddlers are subsisting on CRAP foods, even those parents who focus on healthier foods can still end up with undernourished children. "Health" foods such as sweetened yogurt, whole-grain cereal, tofu, rice milk, probiotic-enriched juice, organic cereal bars, and low-fat foods are often just CRAP food in disguise and can lead to severe nutrient deficiencies and health and behavioral problems. Most are not nutrient-rich foods for growing children.

Many of the foods in toddlers' diets (such as whole grains and soy products) contain naturally occurring "antinutrients" that block digestion, absorption, conversion, and utilization of vitamins, minerals, enzymes, and hormones. Such foods, served under the guise of sustenance, can actually lead to nutrient deficiencies. They can also irritate the intestines, leading to tummy trouble like diarrhea, irritable bowel syndrome, gas/flatulence, bloating, and constipation.

A BETTER WAY TO NOURISH YOUR TODDLER

By avoiding processed foods, you will maintain your child's preferences for nutritious foods, creating a lifetime of good habits. The following are some other ways to protect your child's nutrition.

DON'T SWITCH TO SKIM FOR THE SAKE OF LOW FAT. Low-fat milk is processed milk. While the AAP and USDA dietary guidelines recommend switching from whole milk to low-fat at 2 years old, this move deprives your child of important fat-soluble activators (vitamins D, K, and A) in their natural form, as well as important protective constituents found in whole milk. Studies have shown that *fat*, particularly in milk, is protective against rickets, osteoporosis, other mineral-deficiency diseases, arthritis, joint pain, atherosclerosis, cancer, heart disease, and diabetes. (See page 220.)

DO FATS RIGHT. The easiest way to get the right fats, in the correct amounts and ratios, is to let Nature take care of it for you. Use animal-based foods that have been pasture raised because their fats will be appropriately proportioned. When using plant fats, choose coconut and red-palm oil as well as limited fruit oils such as cold-pressed olive oil and avocado oil. Occasional use of unrefined nut and seed oils, such as walnut and sesame seed oils, is fine. Small amounts of flaxseed oil can be used, though don't overdo, as polyunsaturated oils, even those with ALA (an EPA and DHA precursor) should be kept to a minimum (around 4% of fat intake), and should never be heated or cooked. Avoiding processed foods will minimize exposure to unhealthy vegetable oils.

CREATE CARB SAFETY BY KNOCKING OUT ANTINUTRIENTS. Historically, traditional cultures purposefully *prepared* grains, nuts, beans, and seeds before consuming them, spending significant time to soak, ferment, sprout, and leaven these foods. By doing so, they improved digestion and gut health; reduced gas, cramps, and intestinal irritation; and ultimately improved overall energy and decreased allergies and diseases. Such traditional preparation enhances digestibility by *neutralizing antinutrients* and *increasing enzyme activity*. It also increases nutrition worth by *increasing beneficial bacteria, nutrient content, and availability*.

At this age, your baby's digestive system can handle some grains. To make those grains (as well as seeds, beans, and nuts) the most nutritious and least irritating and inflammatory requires special, traditional preparation (see page 218 and recipes in this chapter).

First, focus on whole grains. Whole grains from nature come with a "whole" package of nutrients and thus are far less disruptive to the body than refined grains. Then consider variety. Our society relies heavily on wheat and corn as our staple grains, and both are highly allergenic, especially when eaten frequently. Many other grains such as amaranth, quinoa, teff, millet, sorghum, and buckwheat (a fruit) provide an array of nutrients, don't contain gluten, and can be less irritating to the gut.

Instead of basing meals on grains, make grains a garnish or small side dish. The healthiest meals are based on protein, fats, vegetables, and greens—with fruit and nuts as dessert.

A Low-Fat, Grown-Up Diet Is Not Best for Kids

At your child's 2-year checkup, his doctor may stress the importance of grains, fruits, and vegetables while avoiding animal fats. Avoiding animal fats and animal proteins means that vegetable oils will be the predominant fats in your toddler's new diet. But plant-based oils such as vegetable (soy), corn, cottonseed, sunflower, safflower, and canola are man-made, processed oils, with unhealthy omega fatty acid proportions, are highly processed and therefore damaged, and are inflammatory. They also lack cholesterol, which, as we discussed in chapter 4, is critical for your toddler's brain development and gut health, and they lack nutrients and specific fatty acids found uniquely in animal fats.

Consuming too much vegetable oil of any kind can cause organs and systems to flounder. These highly polyunsaturated fats cause inflammation and internal body "rusting" and aging. These vegetable oils are mostly made up of inflammatory omega-6 fatty acids. Because we all need a healthy balance between omega-3s and omega-6s, focusing primarily on vegetable oils means your toddler's fat ratio will be out of balance. This imbalance can disrupt cellular communication and can result in neurologic and psychological issues—aka: big-time health problems. To sum up, Williams Sears, M.D., and Martha Sears, R.N, succinctly state in *The N.D.D. (Nutrition Deficit Disorder) Book*, "The *healthier the fats, the healthier the cell membrane, the healthier the child*." Your child also gets these inflammatory fats by eating factory-farmed meats, as the animals are fed soy and corn (high in unhealthy omega-6s). Fat from grass-fed animals and wild-caught fish are higher in health-promoting omega-3s.

Oils higher in plant-based omega-3 (alpha linolenic acid [ALA], the EPA and DHA precursor), specifically perilla oil, as opposed to omega-6 (linoleic acid [LA]), such as safflower oil, were shown to result in fewer kidney, mammary gland, and colon tumors, as published in *Carcinogenesis*.

Not all omega-6s are bad for you, though, depending on their source and quantity. Chickpeas (garbanzo beans), nuts, borage oil, black currant seed, mom's milk, and evening primrose oil are sources of the particular kinds of omega-6s (arachidonic acid [AA] vs. linoleic acid [LA]) fats that are healthy in small amounts.

Experts, like Judy Converse (*Special-Needs Kids Eat Right*), R.D., warn that high intake of vegetable oils (with unhealthy omega-6s) are associated with:

⊙ Poor school performance

⊙ Problems in autistic and ADHD children

⊙ Misbehaviors: impulsive, aggressive, and angry

⊙ Mood swings: sad, angry outbursts; anxiety; and aggression

⊙ Dyspraxia (poor gross motor coordination)

⊙ Vision problems: decreasing acuity, dry eyes

⊙ Skin: dry, flaky, scaly "chicken skin"

⊙ Allergies: asthma, hay fever

⊙ "-itis" illnesses: dermatitis, bronchitis, colitis, and arthritis

⊙ Dyslexia

⊙ Poor learning (in animal studies)

As the word is spreading that polyunsaturated fat is now scientifically recognized as very dangerous to overall health, large agribusiness companies are pushing hybridized and genetically modified "high-oleic" breeds of seeds, such as safflower and sunflower, resulting in higher monounsaturated than polyunsaturated levels. Yes, monounsaturated and saturated fats together should make up 95%+ of your fat intake, with polyunsaturated below 5%, so on the surface, this seems like a good idea. However, these newfangled oils come from chemical forms of hybridization or genetic engineering, and they are products of heavy processing, resulting in a highly processed, chemical laden, free-radical-filled, and rancid end product that causes systemic inflammation on many levels. Better oils are always those that are cold-pressed, unrefined, organic, non-GMO, and virgin, such as olive and coconut oils. One study in the *Journal of Nutrition* demonstrated that high-oleic safflower oil (with and without vitamin E administration) pitted against coconut oil yielded "significantly more tumors than did the coconut oil group."

TRANS FATS. When hydrogenated, liquid oils are forced into solids at room temperature (think shortening or margarine). Hydrogenation causes polyunsaturated fatty acids (like those found in vegetable oils) to change on a molecular level, and they become trans fats. Of all fats, the man-made molecular monsters called trans fats are unequivocally the most unhealthy fats. They increase risk for cardiovascular disease, diabetes, and cancer; they cause inflammation and lead to obesity, infection, and illness. Further, babies born to moms who eat a diet high in trans fats have lower birth weights and their moms' milk is poorer in brain-building quality than that of moms who do not consume trans fats.

"GMO" COULD ALSO STAND FOR GENETICALLY MODIFIED OIL

Today's popular vegetable oils are also mostly made from genetically modified organisms (GMOs), which is yet another reason to avoid them. Soy, corn, canola (a man-made oil that stands for *Ca*nada *O*il *L*ow *A*cid), and cotton-seed oils are genetically modified. Oils labeled simply "vegetable oil" are soy-based. (For more information on soy and GMOs, see chapter 3.) Almost all oils used at fast-food joints, restaurants, cafeterias, schools, amusement parks, movie theaters, and other places from which you purchase ready-to-eat food are vegetable oils, so know that you are selecting GMO and inflammatory, damaged, risky oils as part of that plate.

TAKE THE SUGAR OUT, PUT THE PROTEIN, VEGETABLES, AND FAT IN

In her book *Little Sugar Addicts: End the Mood Swings, Meltdowns, Tantrums, and Low Self-Esteem in Your Child Today*, Kathleen DesMaisons, Ph.D., pioneer and expert in the field of addictive nutrition, shares the straightforward relationship: Food affects feelings and feelings affect behavior. She writes, "Changing your child's food can give you back his sweet and loving side." Avoiding refined flour and sweeteners, while also regularly including protein with vegetables (avoiding carb-only meals or snacks), "can help . . . [children] focus, contribute to weight loss, alter blood sugar levels, eliminate mood swings, and defuse rage." Defusing rage with loving embraces and distraction is particularly important in young toddlers who can't express emotions well.

CONTROL MOODS WITH MINI-MEALS

Going *too* long without food can negatively impact hormones and brain chemicals. Dr. DesMaisons warns in *Little Sugar Addicts*: "Junk foods, soda . . . and *missed meals* activate the worst of what sugar sensitivity sets up." The drop in blood sugar resulting from a missed meal or snack can lead to a meltdown.

Though it's best to avoid constant grazing, children are in need of more frequent meals and snack intervals than adults (children are typically hungry every 3 hours or so). According to Elizabeth Lipski, Ph.D., in *Digestive Wellness*, "Small, frequent meals keep children's energy levels even and their minds alert. Snacking reduces the incidence of children's tantrums."

However, snacking does not mean giving your child treats and processed foods. Better than thinking of them as snacks—too often associated with "treats"—think of them as "mini-meals," composed of animal protein, animal fat, and natural fiber-filled carbohydrates. Mini-meals are often parents' biggest challenge, as generally, the go-to snacks are refined flour based—and sugar filled.

Instead, try those listed below:

- Pemmican (a meat-based "power bar," see recipe on page 55).

- Liverwurst with cucumber and avocado slices

- Homemade nut butter (see recipe on page 198) with celery

- Raw cheese chunks and apple slices

- Raw yogurt and diced pears, peaches, or apricots

- Sardines or anchovies with a few berries

- Deviled eggs and carrots

- Olives or pickles with leftover meat

- Old-fashioned mayo salads (see recipe on page 210)

Decay and the Dentist

At 2 years old, it is typically time for your baby's first trip to the dentist! Although cavities and fillings are a very common part of childhood, humans are the only species with such rates of dental decay. For children, 1 in nearly 4 develop cavities in their primary teeth, according to the CDC, and 3 out of every 5 children ages 12 to 19 years old have cavities in permanent teeth.

Diet is a significant part of what causes tooth decay, and the dietary element that is worst for teeth is, of course, sugar. Studies from the *Journal of Dental Research* show that sugar *feeds* cavity-causing bacteria and pulls nutrients *away* from the outer portions of the teeth, making them malnourished and weak.

TODAY'S TEETH STARVE FOR MINERALS

Minerals are the building blocks of strong bones and teeth. Modern foods are mineral poor because the soil in which they grow has become nutrient depleted. Compared to nutrient values in food five decades ago, broccoli now has half the calcium and cauliflower has only 60% of the vitamin C. Without these nutrients, our teeth and bones suffer. The importance of minerals reaches beyond *dental* health, as teeth are "windows" to the rest of the body: When dental health deteriorates, so does overall health.

Of the few minerals children *do* get in their diets, many of them aren't usable. This is because minerals can only be used if "activated." They need specific fat-soluble vitamins to assist them: vitamins, A, D3, and K2, found in pastured-animal foods, fats, and seafood. Lacto-fermented food and drinks are the magic mineral activators.

A RECIPE FOR HEALTHY TEETH

Just as a diet based on Super Nutrition protects your child's *body*, it also protects his *teeth*. Studies in the *Journal of Dental Research* report that protein consumption does not lead to dental decay, because it doesn't feed the bacteria that cause cavities (nor does it disrupt minerals) as refined carbohydrates do.

According to the ADA, "Tooth decay occurs when foods containing carbohydrates (sugars and starches) such as milk, pop, raisins, cakes or candy are frequently left on the teeth. Bacteria that live in the mouth thrive on these foods, producing acids as a result. Over a period of time, these acids destroy tooth enamel, resulting in tooth decay."

Dental-health research experts, including Dr. Edward Mellan and Dr. Weston Price, have found that in addition to consumption of too much refined sugar, lack of minerals (particularly calcium, magnesium, and phosphorus), lack of fat-soluble-activating vitamins (A, D, K2, and E, but particularly vitamin D), and too much phytic acid (from grains and legumes) results in tooth decay.

Our Super Nutrition program eliminates refined and excessive sugar intake, highlights mineral-rich and fat-soluble vitamin content, and describes how to avoid or neutralize phytic acid and other antinutrients. Additionally, this program highlights the value of natural fats: saturated, monounsaturated, and limited polyunsaturated (the latter being predominantly body-ready omega-3s [EPA and DHA] and a little bit of arachidonic omega-6).

MOM-TO-MOM

With concern for dental health, doctors typically start recommending fluoride supplementation for babies at 6 months. We strongly disagree. As discussed on page 116, fluoride is a known neurotoxin that can harm brain function. Paul Connett, Ph.D., toxicologist and environmental chemist, states, "A variety of studies . . . have indicated that in communities with higher levels of fluoride, children have lower IQs."

A 2017 study out of Mexico that spanned 12 years further indicates that fluoride should be avoided even in pregnancy, as those with higher prenatal exposure to fluoride were more likely to have children with lower IQs.

Notably, dietary fat *protects* teeth! Researchers state that "most [diet and cavity] studies . . . indicate that the effect of [fats and] oils is to *reduce* cavities" [emphasis added]. Fats coat the teeth and prevent acid from eating away at enamel, while also facilitating tooth mineralization (vitamins that activate mineralization are fat-soluble, needing dietary fat to be effective).

According the National Institutes of Health, "Building your children's 'bone bank' account is a lot like saving for their education: The more they can put away when they're young, the longer it should last as they get older." Building strong teeth, bones, and bodies relies on minerals and their fat-soluble activators vitamins D3, A, and K2.

Regularly feeding your child foods rich in minerals and fat-soluble activators, while avoiding foods that deplete minerals and create imbalances (sugar, soy, unprepared whole grains, white flour, and vegetable fats), translates into a great investment in your baby's health account.

Recipes That Go Beyond Mac 'n' Cheese

Grain-based foods can expand the diet and menu for your toddler. The recipes we provide are healthy ways to incorporate these foods into your child's diet. We offer advice on how to prepare whole grains and whole-grain flours before using them in recipes, and these suggestions might—at first—seem daunting and too time-consuming. This method of cooking does take some forethought, but know that you are providing the best, most digestible and nutrient-rich foods for your growing toddler that won't have the harmful repercussions of "regular" toddler diets.

Always try new recipes twice. Sometimes the first time is just a trial run and the second time is a smashing success.

FEEDING AT 18 TO 21 MONTHS

Between 18 and 21 months, you can introduce gluten-free grains, raw greens, and higher-fiber raw vegetables. For a more complete list of acceptable foods at this age, see the Food Introduction Timeline on page 255.

FEEDING AT 21 TO 24 MONTHS

Between 21 and 24 months, you can introduce properly prepared gluten grains, properly prepared legumes, and shellfish. For a more complete list of acceptable foods at this age, see the Food Introduction Timeline on page 255.

WHOLE GRAIN PREPARATION

Cooking and fermentation increase protein content in grains and support removal of antinutrients (including polyphenols, phytic acid, and tannins); however, antinutrients in grains are best removed, while nutrition is best enhanced, through leavening, fermentation, soaking, or sprouting. Enhancing digestibility and nutrient value through these techniques speak to the pillars of our program.

GRAINS

1 cup (about 80 g) whole grains (these will look like seeds or kernels and can be found at health food stores or online)

2 cups (475 ml) warm/room temperature water

2 tablespoons (28 g) plain yogurt or (28 ml) lemon juice, raw vinegar, or whey (see Homemade Raw Dairy Whey, page 107)

Combine the ingredients in a glass or ceramic bowl. Stir the mixture. Cover and leave at room temperature for 7 to 24 hours.

Either prepare immediately in whole form (see Notes) or drain and dry for later grinding into flour (see directions at right).

YIELD: About 1 cup (236 g)

FLOUR

Drain soaked grains and dry with a dehydrator or on paper towel–lined cookie sheets (changing the paper towel several times). You can also use the lowest setting in your oven or toaster oven (150 to 170°F [66 to 77°C]).

Store *completely* dried grains in a glass container in the refrigerator or cool pantry.

To make flour, grind the dried grains fresh in a coffee grinder, grain mill, or Vitamix to yield the amount of flour you need for a recipe.

YIELD: About 2 cups (250 g)

NOTES

⊙ Whole quinoa does well in beanless chili: Soak 1 cup (173 g) quinoa in 3 cups (700 ml) water with 1 tablespoon (15 g) yogurt, (15 ml) whey, kefir, vinegar, or lemon juice for 12 to 24 hours. Rinse and drain. In 2 cups (475 ml) Souper Stock (page 45); to further increase nutrient content), bring the quinoa to a boil and then simmer, covered, for an hour. Mix with ground beef, garlic, a pinch of chili pepper, and cooked onion, zucchini, stewed tomatoes, and other vegetables of your choosing.

⊙ Whole millet makes a nice casserole-style accompaniment to meat: After soaking (as described above), drain, replace with fresh water or Souper Stock (page 45), and bring to a boil; then cover tightly and simmer for 45 minutes. Add butter and sea salt to taste.

DEEP DIVE ON PHYTIC ACID

Phytate, or phytic acid, is the main storage form of phosphorus and is found in plant tissues, including beans, seeds, nuts, grains, and tubers. This bound form of phosphorus isn't useful (except to multi-stomached animals, like many herbivores). This form of phosphorus also binds very easily with minerals such as calcium, magnesium, iron, and zinc, which renders them unusable by the body. Further, phytic acid hinders enzymes' ability to digest food, by inhibiting pepsin in the stomach and trypsin in the small intestine (both are required for protein digestion, and as we mention elsewhere, undigested proteins are allergenic proteins!), and blocks amylase, which digests starches.

STORE-BOUGHT FLOUR PREPARATION

Flour that is ground just before use in a recipe is ultimately most nutritious. Once ground, grain begins to oxidize and lose nutrients; therefore, grocery store flour, even if whole grain, is not as ideal. In many cases, however, the convenience of purchasing already-ground whole-grain flour is necessary.

Kamut, spelt, and whole-grain wheat flour can be used, but because they contain gluten, they are better postponed until 2 years of age. Gluten-free, organic flours are best.

1⅓ cups (about 160 g) purchased whole-grain flour (millet, brown rice, sorghum, teff, tigernut)

½ cup (120 ml) water or raw milk or ½ cup (115 g) raw yogurt (if using raw milk or yogurt, omit tablespoon below)

1 tablespoon (15 g) yogurt or (15 ml) whey, vinegar, or lemon juice

Stir the ingredients together in a glass bowl. Leave to soak overnight, covered, at room temperature. Use in the morning or store in the refrigerator for use later that day or possibly the next.

NOTES

⊙ Use this "wet" flour, measure for measure, in recipes for crepes, pancakes, muffins, and more.

⊙ You might need to reduce the liquid called for in your recipe, as the prepared-flour mixture will contain liquid.

MOM-TO-MOM

This might go without saying, but never should babies or children consume soda pop. It contains toxins (mineral-leaching, bone-weakening phosphorus), colorings, and excessive sweeteners with no nutritional value. Displacing calories or food/beverages with soda is a major disservice to your child and the intensity of sweetness will alter his or her palate and appreciation for Nature's sweets.

YIELD:
About 1 cup (235 ml)

SIMPLE BACON BRUSSELS SPROUTS

Brussels, Belgium, is the namesake of this cruciferous vegetable that is cousin to broccoli, cauliflower, and kale and looks like cabbage's baby brother. When cooked with fat, almost any other flavor can be added to make Brussels sprouts delicious. And, cooking makes them more nutritious; according to *The Journal of Nutrition* (2001), indole is an organic compound formed in cruciferous veggies when they're cooked. Indole is great because it helps destroy precancerous cells before they proliferate.

½ pound (225 g) organic, pasture-raised bacon

1 pound (455 g) Brussels sprouts, quartered (or food processed, depending on your baby's needs)

½ cup (120 ml) bacon grease/drippings

Celtic sea salt and pepper to taste

Preheat the oven to 375°F (190°C, or gas mark 5). Bake the bacon on a basic broiler pan (stainless steel is preferred) in the oven for 15 to 20 minutes, turning the bacon once.

While the bacon is cooking, quarter the Brussels sprouts.

Remove the bacon and the top of the broiler pan and set aside. Add the quartered Brussels sprouts to the bacon drippings directly in the bottom of the broiler pan.

Bake in the oven for 30 minutes until crispy.

Dice the bacon and sprinkle over the cooked Brussels sprouts. Season with salt and pepper.

MOM-TO-MOM

Avoid nitrates and nitrites. Found in most processed meat products, nitrates and nitrites convert to potent carcinogens called nitrosamines. Read ingredients and avoid food with "sodium nitrate." Since toxic nitrosamines can form in certain cooked foods during storage, don't store and reheat dishes of nonorganic carrots, beets, turnips, and spinach. *Fortunately, lacto-fermented foods and Souper Stock (page 45) neutralize nitrosamines!*

YIELD: 2 cups (256 g)

RICE AND BEANS PREPARATION

Though rice is low in mineral-blocking phytic acid, it is still a grain and can be made more digestible and nutritious through sprouting or soaking or a lengthened cook time before eating. Organic whole-grain rice can be short, medium, or long grain and should be colorful (not white): black, wild, or brown.

RICE PREPARATION

1 cup (185 g) long-grain, brown, black, or wild rice

2 cups filtered water

1 tablespoon (15 ml) whey, vinegar, lemon juice, or (15 g) raw yogurt

2 tablespoons (28 g) ghee, coconut oil, or other pastured animal fat

2 cups (475 ml) Souper Stock (page 45)

Combine the rice, water, and whey in a bowl. Stir. Cover and leave to sit on the counter overnight.

Drain and rinse.

In a skillet, sauté the rice in the fat and continuously stir the rice and ghee over medium-low heat. When the rice and liquid are cloudy, add the Souper Stock. Bring to a soft boil and simmer for 10 to 12 minutes. (Or follow cooking directions from the rice packaging, using Souper Stock in place of water.)

Reduce the heat to low, cover, and cook for about 2 hours.

To create resistant starch, which acts more as fiber than starch, cool the cooked rice for several hours or overnight in the refrigerator and then reheat batches to consume immediately.

Optional: Add 1 tablespoon (7 g) gelatin to the Souper Stock.

NOTES

⊙ TruRoots brand is available at health food stores and is already germinated (sprouted). You can simply follow the package directions or grind into sprouted brown rice flour.

⊙ Riced cauliflower can be used in place of rice in most recipes calling for rice.

⊙ Rice or cauliflower can be used in a chicken curry recipe with coconut and green apple chutney. Use ¾ pound (340 g) cooked chicken, 3 cups (585 g) prepared rice or (300 g) riced cauliflower with 3 tablespoons (42 g) ghee, 2 teaspoons turmeric, minced garlic, chopped onion, and sea salt to taste; mix 1 cup (235 ml) Souper Stock with 1 cup (235 ml) coconut cream or milk with 1 tablespoon (15 ml) tamari sauce (gluten-free, fermented soy sauce) for the sauce. Make the chutney with sulfite-free dried mulberries, chopped green apple, chopped pear, and unsulfured, unsweetened, shredded coconut to total 2 cups (500 g). Serve the chicken and rice with sauce, topped with chutney.

YIELD: 3 cups (495 g)

BEAN PREPARATION

1 cup (weight will vary) beans of choice
(split pea, kidney, navy, etc.)

2 to 3 tablespoons (28 to 45 ml) whey, vinegar,
lemon juice, or (15 to 45 g) raw yogurt

2 cups (475 ml) filtered water

In a bowl, soak the beans in the whey and water
(as specified below, as per type of bean).

Rinse and drain. Cook in a slow cooker for 4 to
8 hours in enough water to cover the beans; beans
will be ready to eat after 4 hours but can be cooked
longer (which might make digestion easier).

NOTES

⊙ *Black, brown, white, and kidney beans*,
soak for 18 to 24 hours.

⊙ *Lentils*, soak for 10 hours.

⊙ *Fava beans*, soak for 10 hours (be sure to discard
the liquid and remove the outer skin of the fava
beans before using in a recipe).

⊙ *Dried and split peas*, best soaked for 10 hours
with a pinch of baking soda.

SPROUTING GRAINS AND BEANS

In addition to the soaking method of preparation,
grains and beans can be sprouted. Sprouts are
very healthy in that their nutrient content and
digestability are vastly increased in sandwiches,
porridges, casseroles, and more.

Revisit the nut and seed sprouting directions on
page 197, following these guidelines: *Wheat,
rye, and barley*, rinse 2 to 3 times per day for 3 to
4 days; *buckwheat*, rinse 2 to 3 times per day for
2 days; *kidney, lima, and black beans*, rinse 3 to
4 times per day for 3 days; *lentils*, rinse 3 times
per day for 2 to 3 days.

Most grains and beans will develop tiny sprouts
when germination has been successful. When
sprouted, store in the refrigerator.

MOM-TO-MOM

"Sneak" Super POWER foods into what you're
serving to get your kids to eat foods that will
really impact their nutrition: Use Souper Stock
(page 45) in rich sauces over meats or when
cooking rice. Include fish roe in egg dishes or
minced-meat salads. Add extra eggs and gelatin in pancakes and other homemade baked
goods, and grate organ meats into ground beef.

MOM'S NUTRITIOUS MUFFINS (M'N'Ms)

These are not the M'n'Ms you are thinking of—these can be served to kids as snacks with best intentions and healthy results. Warm and slather with ghee or grass-fed butter for a weekend morning breakfast, or for a late evening treat! Make a big batch and freeze them for later.

2 cups (weight will vary) flour of choice, freshly ground preferred

1 tablespoon (15 g) raw yogurt, (15 ml) whey, or (15 ml) apple cider vinegar

2 cups (475 ml) coconut milk

1 teaspoon ground cinnamon

¼ teaspoon ground nutmeg

1 teaspoon baking soda

1 cup (86 g) unsweetened coconut flakes

½ teaspoon Celtic sea salt

1 farm-fresh, organic, pastured egg

1 teaspoon vanilla extract

2 tablespoons (28 g) ghee or coconut oil

⅓ cup (73 g) stewed apples and pears (refer to First Fruit Sauces recipe on page 111)

1 pear, coarsely chopped

2 apples, coarsely chopped

The night before baking, in a bowl, soak the flour with the yogurt and coconut milk.

The next day, preheat the oven to 350°F (180°C, or gas mark 4).

In a large mixing bowl, combine the flour mixture, cinnamon, nutmeg, baking soda, coconut, and sea salt. Set aside.

Mix the egg, vanilla extract, and melted ghee with the stewed apples and pears. Stir into the flour mixture and fold in the chopped fruit. Mix until all ingredients are fully incorporated.

Spoon the mixture into a greased or lined muffin pan. Bake for 25 minutes, until toothpick comes out clean.

Remove from the oven and allow to cool.

Enjoy the muffins warm or at room temperature.

Refrigerate in a tightly sealed container and reheat to enjoy later. You can store in a sealed container in the freezer for up to 3 weeks.

VARIATION

⊙ Add nuts to the existing recipe or try adding blueberries, banana, shredded carrot, or sweet potato.

NOTE

⊙ If you add 2 tablespoons (28 ml) of additional fat, the batter can be preapared as waffles, frozen, and then toasted for a quick, healthy treat.

YIELD: 20 mini muffins

NACHOS, GUAC, AND SALSA

Having "treat" meals for special occasions adds variety and fun to the family menu. Typical nachos can serve up GMOs, refined flour, rBGH cheese, and sugared salsa. However, Super Nutrition nachos pack in sprouted grains, raw cheese, enzyme-rich guacamole, and lacto-fermented salsa.

NACHO CHIPS

1 package (8 ounces, 224 g) sprouted corn tortillas

½ cup (120 ml) red palm oil or melted ghee or coconut oil

1 teaspoon Celtic sea salt

Cut the tortillas into wedges, wide strips, or quarters and fry in preheated oil; the oil must be hot and sizzle when sprinkled with water. Turn the tortillas over in the oil until crisp. Remove and place in mesh/wire strainer or on paper towels to drain. Sprinkle the chips with sea salt.

YIELD: 4 to 5 servings

NOTES

- If buying premade corn chips, look for corn that was treated with lime or where the ingredients say "masa" flour—masa indicates the corn flour was nixtamalized, which prevents B3 deficiency or pellagra.

- These are fun, but be cautious of the crispy chips breaking once bitten and having sharp edges for your toddler. Gauge when your child is ready to try these based on other foods being consumed. If chips aren't ideal, avoid them and add cooked meat or chicken and salsa to the guacamole for spoon-feeding.

GUACAMOLE

2 ripe avocados

2 teaspoons Celtic sea salt

1 teaspoon minced garlic

¼ cup (40 g) diced onion, *optional*

¼ cup (45 g) diced tomato, *optional*

1 teaspoon freshly squeezed lemon or lime juice

Peel, quarter, and mash the avocados. Stir in the sea salt and garlic. Add the onion and tomato, if using. Squeeze the lemon or lime juice over the avocado mixture and stir.

Serve immediately or cover tightly and store in the refrigerator for 2 to 6 hours.

YIELD: 1½ cups (338 g)

LACTO-FERMENTED SALSA

1 to 2 large or 3 to 4 small tomatoes, finely chopped

1 bunch of cilantro, finely chopped

1 small onion, finely chopped

2 cloves garlic, minced

½ teaspoon Celtic sea salt

1 tablespoon (15 ml) Homemade Mom's Milk Whey (page 106) or raw, organic, grass-fed homemade whey

In a mixing bowl, combine the tomatoes, cilantro, onion, garlic, sea salt, and whey. Stir and transfer to a clean Mason jar.

Shake and leave on the counter for 1 to 3 days. This will store in the refrigerator for up to 2 weeks.

YIELD: ¾ cup (195 g)

NOTE

⊙ This salsa recipe is adapted from Sally Fallon's *Nourishing Traditions*.

TO ASSEMBLE THE NACHOS

1 recipe Nacho Chips (page 232)

1 cup (225 g) cooked meat, such as ground beef or chicken

½ cup (60 g) raw, organic shredded cheese

1 recipe Guacamole (at left)

1 recipe Lacto-Fermented Salsa (at left)

Spread a layer of nacho chips on a baking sheet. Top with the cooked ground beef or chicken. Sprinkle the shredded cheese on top.

Place under the oven broiler to melt the cheese.

Serve with guacamole and lacto-fermented salsa.

YIELD: 4 servings

ALTERNATIVE PIZZA AND QUICHE CRUSTS AND "BREADS"

Pizza and quiche are fun, fabulous dishes that can combine many healthy ingredients, if they are made with attention to digestibility and highest quality ingredients, including vegetables. Many veggies can have their nutrients and antioxidants enhanced through cooking, and with fats added, their fat-soluble nutrients can be absorbed and utilized for myriad health benefits. Some veggies, however, have health-providing elements that can be reduced through cooking. Consuming mostly cooked veggies with some raw and some fermented is the best blend of vegetables!

QUICHE OR PIZZA CRUST

1 cup (112 g) coconut, (128 g) cassava, or (120 g) tigernut flour

1 cup (128 g) arrowroot starch

1 teaspoon Celtic sea salt

1 teaspoon onion powder

1 teaspoon garlic powder

3 farm-fresh, organic, pastured egg yolks

1 cup (235 ml) coconut milk

½ cup (112 g) coconut butter, warmed and stirred

Preheat the oven to 400°F (200°C, or gas mark 6).

Combine the dry ingredients in a medium mixing bowl.

In a separate bowl, whisk the egg yolks, coconut milk, and coconut butter. Pour the wet ingredients into the dry ingredients and mix with a whisk until no clumps are visible.

Allow the dough to sit for about 5 minutes to allow it to firm up a little. It will make a spreadable dough.

Spread the dough onto a parchment paper–lined baking sheet and bake for 25 to 30 minutes, until golden brown on the bottom. You can bake it a little longer to make it crunchier.

YIELD: 1 crust

NOTE

⊙ For a crunchier top, you can invert the cooked dough onto another flat pan and then add the toppings. This method is easier with the smaller sized pizza crusts.

Broccoli can be added to your pizza or your quiche. If you add to pizza, shred the broccoli in the food processor and add to your melted cheese right as it comes out of the oven. Raw broccoli will retain the proper structure and activity of the enzyme myrosinase if it never reaches temperatures between 100 and 118°F (38 and 48°C). The benefits of raw broccoli is that myrosinase breaks down glucosinates into sulforaphane. The journal *Carcinogenesis* reported in 2008 that sulforaphane might be able to stop precancerous cells, and other studies have shown that sulforaphane reduces *Helicobacter pylori* bacteria, which can lead to both ulcers and stomach cancer.

PIZZA

1 recipe Pizza Crust (page 234)

½ cup (122 g) tomato sauce

Toppings of choice, *optional*

1 cup (115 g) shredded, raw mozzarella cheese

Shredded broccoli (see box above), *optional*

Preheat the oven to 400°F (200°C, or gas mark 6).

Spread the dough onto a parchment paper–lined baking sheet. (For a crunchier crust, use a larger baking sheet and spread it thinner.) Bake for 25 to 30 minutes until golden brown on the bottom. You can bake it a little longer to make it crunchier.

Add the tomato sauce, toppings, and raw cheese and cook for an additional 10 minutes until the cheese is melted.

When the pizza is removed from the oven, sprinkle on a layer of shredded broccoli, if desired.

YIELD: 6 to 8 pieces

BREADSTICKS

1 recipe Pizza Crust (page 234)

2 tablespoons (30 ml) ghee

½ cup (40 g) shredded, raw Parmesan cheese

Preheat the oven to 400°F (200°C, or gas mark 6).

Brush the crust with melted ghee and/or sprinkle with Parmesan cheese and bake for 10 to 15 minutes or until golden.

Cut the crust into strips for breadsticks.

YIELD: 10 breadsticks

QUICHE

1 recipe Pizza Crust (page 234)

6 large farm-fresh, organic, pastured eggs

1 to 2 cups (weight will vary) chopped vegetables, such as broccoli, zucchini, mushrooms

½ cup (60 g) raw shredded cheese

⅓ cup (weight will vary) cooked meat, such as sausage, chicken, or ground beef, *optional*

Preheat the oven to 325°F (170°C, or gas mark 3).

Spread the dough into a pie pan and bake for 8 to 10 minutes.

Meanwhile, in a bowl, mix the eggs, vegetables of choice, shredded raw cheese, and optional meat of choice (cubed, diced, or minced). Mix well and pour into the baked crust.

Return to the oven and bake for 35 to 40 minutes or until a knife comes out clean when inserted in the center.

YIELD: 6 servings

NOTE

⊙ Crusts can be cooled and frozen for up to 2 months for later use.

CLOUD BREAD

Coconut oil for greasing baking sheet

4 farm-fresh, organic, pastured eggs

¼ cup (57 g) curds (homemade cream cheese, see page 106) or (50 g) organic, cultured, pastured cream cheese

3 tablespoons (42 g) ghee or coconut oil

¼ teaspoon aluminum-free baking powder

1 teaspoon onion powder

1 teaspoon garlic powder

1 teaspoon Celtic sea salt

For pizza or garlic bread, add 1 teaspoon dried oregano, *optional*

Preheat the oven to 325°F (170°C, or gas mark 3).

Grease a stainless steel baking sheet with coconut oil. (If using an aluminum pan, line with parchment paper.)

Separate the egg whites and egg yolks.

In a bowl, mix the yolks, curds, and ghee or coconut oil until smooth.

In a separate bowl, combine the baking powder, onion powder, garlic powder, salt, and oregano, if using, with the whites and beat until firm peaks form.

Carefully fold in the egg yolk mixture, retaining the fluff of the egg whites mixture.

Immediately spoon 12 to 14 spoonfuls onto the prepared baking sheet.

Bake for 15 minutes and then broil for 2 minutes.

YIELD: 12 to 14 rolls

NOTE

⊙ Cloud Bread (adapted from thebigapplemama.com) can also be used for pizza crusts, grilled cheese sandwiches, or can be eaten topped with homemade pâté (page 97).

RAW CHEESE BLINTZES WITH RASPBERRY SAUCE

For a fancier, fun dish, try these blintzes as a dessert or breakfast on a special occasion. The Fruit Compote and Raspberry Sauce can also be used in porridge.

FRUIT COMPOTE

1 apple or pear, chopped

1 cup (145 g) blueberries or strawberries (fresh or frozen)

1 plum, chopped with peel intact

1 kiwi, peeled and chopped

Juice of 1 lemon or lime

Combine all the ingredients in a medium saucepan over low heat. Simmer for 30 minutes to 1 hour.

This fruit compote can be used as a topping for crepes, cheese blintzes, or porridge (page 241), mixed in yogurt, or even made into a fruit gel (see page 132).

YIELD: 2 cups (500 g)

NOTES

⊙ This is an excellent use of fruit that is overripe. Any type of fruit can be used; the amounts listed and the variety of fruit are just suggestions.

⊙ Prepare the fruit compote prior to making the cheese blintzes.

CHEESE BLINTZES

½ cup (120 ml) cold filtered water

1 tablespoon (15 ml) raw whey or (15 g) raw yogurt

1 cup (128 g) cassava or (120 g) tigernut flour

1 cup (235 ml) raw milk or coconut milk, divided

3 farm-fresh, organic, pastured eggs

2 tablespoons (28 g) coconut oil

½ teaspoon Celtic sea salt

1 teaspoon vanilla extract

1 tablespoon (14 g) coconut oil, butter, or ghee (for frying crepes), plus more as needed

FILLING

1½ cups (337 g) coconut butter, warmed and stirred, or (375 g) organic, grass-fed ricotta cheese

½ cup (60 g) curds (separated from whey in raw milk, see page 107) or (115 g) grass-fed, organic, cultured cream cheese

1 lemon, zested

1 large farm-fresh, organic, pastured egg

1 pinch of Celtic sea salt

(continued)

To make the blintzes: In a bowl, mix the water and whey. Add the flour, stir, then add ½ cup (120 ml) of the raw milk. Allow to soak for 4 to 7 hours at room temperature. Move to the refrigerator for a longer soak.

Combine the eggs, remaining ½ cup (120 ml) milk, fat, sea salt, and vanilla and mix in a blender, Vitamix, or food processor. Blend until smooth; allow the batter to sit at room temperature while preparing the cheese filling.

To make the filling: In a bowl, whisk together the warmed and stirred coconut butter or ricotta, curds or cream cheese, lemon zest, egg, and sea salt. Cover and refrigerate.

Heat a 10-inch (25.5 cm) skillet over medium-high heat. Grease with coconut oil. Pour in about ¼ cup (60 ml) of batter and quickly swirl the batter around to thinly coat the bottom of the pan to make a crepe.

Cook until the surface looks dry, about 1 minute. Flip the crepe and cook for about 30 seconds. Repeat cooking the rest of the crepes. You can stack them on a plate as you go.

Spoon 3 to 4 tablespoons (45 to 55 g) of the cheese filling and fruit compote (page 237) on the edge of a crepe. Fold the short edge over, roll once, and fold in the sides and roll again, ending on the seam.

Preheat the oven to 325°F (170°C, or gas mark 3). Lightly butter a baking dish.

Melt more coconut oil in a skillet over medium heat. Cook the filled and folded blintzes, turning gently until golden brown on both sides. Transfer to the prepared baking dish.

Bake for 12 to 15 minutes to firm up the filling.

Meanwhile, prepare the raspberry sauce. Pour over the warm, baked blintzes.

Cool the blintzes for 10 minutes before serving.

YIELD: 8 to 10 Cheese Blintzes

RASPBERRY SAUCE

1 tablespoon (14 g) coconut oil, grass-fed organic butter, or ghee

4 cups raspberries, (500 g) fresh or (1 kg) frozen

Warm the coconut oil in a saucepan over low heat. Add the raspberries. Stir and mash until the fruit is liquefied, about 25 to 35 minutes.

NOTES

- ⊙ You can also substitute blueberries.
- ⊙ This recipe can also be made ahead of time and stored in the refrigerator until needed.
- ⊙ Sally Fallon's *Nourishing Traditions* has a nice raspberry syrup recipe for special occasions.
- ⊙ Cheese blintzes can be stored in the refrigerator for up to a week for later use.

YIELD: About 1 cup (235 ml)

MOM-TO-MOM

TIPS FOR CONVENIENCE. Homemade everything is best, but we are all very busy. A few time-saving options include ordering broth, liverwurst, pemmican, and rendered lard from U.S. Wellness Meats (www.uswellnessmeats.com). Also, coconut wraps (that contain only coconut manna, coconut milk, and coconut oil) can be a good option for a quick rollup of leftovers. Primal Kitchen avocado mayo is a time-saver, as are sprouted corn tortillas. Additionally, soaking grains, nuts, or seeds once or twice a month and using them as needed saves prep time. These are all likely better introduced for yourself or older children, as conveniences, but not staples.

WARM MARROW CUSTARD AND PORRIDGE BREAKFASTS

Yorkshire pudding is a gluten-free, nutrient-rich dish and is a variation of a traditional English recipe typically made with eggs, flour, and roast beef drippings. The recipe is adapted from Bone Marrow Custard by Sally Fallon Morell in her *Growing Healthy Children* presentation. In the style of *Goldilocks and the Three Bears*, porridge is an excellent way to enjoy prepared grains, like oatmeal. In addition, buckwheat groats, whole teff, and amaranth are also good for breakfast porridge. Nutrients in grains, such as vitamin E, are fat-soluble and grains are starches made of glucose, so consuming with fats slows down blood sugar spikes and supports absorption of nutrients.

YORKSHIRE MARROW CUSTARD

1 tablespoon (7 g) gelatin

1 cup (235 ml) farm-fresh raw cream or coconut cream

Marrow from 2 pounds (910 g) marrow bones

1 ripe banana, mashed

½ teaspoon ground cinnamon

½ teaspoon vanilla extract

2 farm-fresh, organic, pastured egg yolks

1 whole farm-fresh, organic, pastured egg

Celtic sea salt to taste

Coconut oil to grease ramekins

Preheat the oven to 300°F (150°C, or gas mark 2).

In a bowl, add the gelatin to the cream and stir. Set aside.

Cover the marrow bones with water in a saucepan. Bring to a simmer and scrape out the softened marrow.

Blend the marrow with the gelatin and cream mixture, banana, cinnamon, vanilla, egg yolks, egg, and sea salt to taste.

Pour into 4 greased ramekins (or lined muffin tins). Bake for about 20 minutes or until the custards are set.

YIELD: 4 servings

NOTES

- This is great to serve with meat dishes.
- *Alternative:* Omit the banana, cinnamon, and vanilla for a savory rather than sweet version.

OLD-FASHIONED PORRIDGE

1 cup (weight will vary) grains, such as steel-cut gluten-free oats or buckwheat groats

2 cups (470 ml) filtered water, divided

2 tablespoons (30 g) raw yogurt, (28 ml) raw whey (see options, page 106), or juice squeezed from ½ lemon with ½ teaspoon Celtic sea salt

½ cup (43 g) shredded, unsweetened, unsulphured coconut

In a bowl, stir together the grains, 1 cup (235 ml) water, and yogurt. Cover and leave out overnight, at room temperature.

In the morning, bring the remaining water to a boil and then add the grain mixture.

Stir and cook for 5 minutes, or until thickened to porridge consistency. Add in the coconut and stir.

YIELD: 2 servings

NOTE

⊙ Serve with ghee, stewed fruit, and cinnamon.

MOM-TO-MOM

GRAINS TAKE A TOXIC TURN WHEN TURNED INTO CEREAL. Boxed cereal is to be avoided, and "cereals" (grains) should be consumed only when properly prepared, as the processing, extrusion, additives, and sweeteners related to creating the cereal boxes that line grocery store shelves result in a very toxic option for your family. The Weston A. Price Foundation notes unpublished studies that show the toxicity of extruded grains (like breakfast cereal). In one case, rats eating just the cereal box lived longer than those eating the cereal! In another study, using puffed wheat cereal, rats fed the cereal and fortified water died in just 1 month, much sooner than the rats who were fed only water. This is likely due to toxins in the cereal.

SEAFOOD AND SAUSAGE PAELLA

Shellfish offer a unique and hardy blend of minerals, vitamins, and fat-soluble activators (vitamins A and D3). We recommend your child consumes it no more than once or twice per month because it can be contaminated with pollutants, but its benefits outweigh its risks. See page 203 for seafood suggestions.

½ cup (112 g) ghee, melted

4 tablespoons (60 ml) fresh lemon juice

1 teaspoon Celtic sea salt

¼ teaspoon black pepper

½ teaspoon dried oregano

½ teaspoon saffron

1 teaspoon ground turmeric

1 teaspoon grated ginger

1 cup (235 ml) Souper Stock (page 45)

2 medium leeks, chopped

8 asparagus spears, chopped

3 cloves garlic, minced

½ cup (50 g) chopped green onion

½ pound (225 g) ground breakfast sausage

2 salmon fillets (4 ounces, or 115 g each), cubed

8 shrimp, shells removed

8 clams or oysters, shucked

In a medium mixing bowl, whisk together the ghee, lemon juice, and seasonings. Set aside.

In a saucepan, heat the Souper Stock, add the leeks and asparagus, and simmer for 10 minutes.

In a skillet, brown the garlic, onion, and ground breakfast sausage. Remove from the heat.

Add the salmon, shrimp, and clams or oysters to the Souper Stock and simmer for 10 to 15 minutes. Mix in the ghee mixture. Add the browned sausage mixture and stir to combine.

YIELD: 4 servings

INGREDIENT SPOTLIGHT: SHELLFISH

Shellfish, along with seaweed, is an excellent natural source of the very important mineral iodine. Alternatively, organic dulse flakes, a seaweed, can be found at your health food store and easily added to many dishes. Consuming fish with cilantro helps reduce mercury and other toxins. Overall, the Super Nutrition program will provide antioxidants to support detoxification, as needed, when consuming fish.

Weston Price reported that indigenous peoples would travel great distances and suffer hardships to secure foods from the sea to prepare couples for marriage and child-rearing. Following are some ways to prepare them.

- **SCALLOPS:** Sear in bacon fat or coconut oil.
- **GARLIC BUTTERED SHRIMP:** Warm butter and minced garlic and cook shrimp until lightly golden.
- **COCONUT SHRIMP:** Dip shrimp in beaten egg and then dip in shredded coconut. Sauté in preheated butter or coconut oil.
- **OYSTERS ROCKEFELLER:** Make a mixture of Creamed Spinach (page 185), chopped bacon, and grated raw Parmesan cheese and top oysters on the half shell and bake for 10 to 15 minutes at 450°F (230°C, or gas mark 8).
- **LOBSTER AND CRAB:** Serve warm with drawn butter.

MEXICAN FRITTATA

Frittatas are egg-based, but differ from omelets in that they are initially cooked in an oven-safe pan on the stovetop and then transferred to the oven, and their delicious fillings are mixed with the eggs, rather than added separately and enfolded within cooked eggs.

½ pound (225 g) ground beef

1 tablespoon (15 ml) extra-virgin olive oil, (14 g) ghee, lard, or coconut oil

1 tablespoon (8 g) arrowroot starch and ¼ cup (60 ml) filtered water, *optional*

5 farm-fresh, organic, pastured large eggs

1 small tomato, diced

½ cup (80 g) chopped onion

¼ cup (4 g) chopped fresh cilantro leaves, plus additional to garnish

¼ teaspoon ground cumin

1 cup (150 g) chopped bell peppers (red, yellow, orange, and green)

¼ teaspoon powdered or freshly grated turmeric

½ cup (36 g) sliced mushrooms

⅓ cup (77 g) raw yogurt or kefir

Celtic sea salt

¾ cup (90 g) grated raw cheese

1 avocado, chopped

Preheat the oven to 375°F (190°C, or gas mark 5).

Brown the ground beef in a large cast-iron skillet or other ovenproof skillet with the oil.

If using the arrowroot, make a slurry by combining it with the water and stirring or shaking it in a closed container. Add the slurry to the ground beef.

While the meat is browning, in a large bowl, beat the eggs and add all the remaining ingredients except for the cheese and chopped avocado.

Pour the egg/vegetable mixture into the meat and cook until the bottom is firm. Flip, immediately top with the cheese, and move to the oven to bake for 10 to 12 minutes.

Remove from the oven and serve topped with the chopped avocado and homemade salsa (page 233).

YIELD: 4 servings

DEEP DIVE INTO THE HEALTH BENEFITS OF CARNITINE IN MEAT

Recently, it has become abundantly clear that the 70-year experiment we've undergone as a country in reducing animal fats to prevent cardiovascular disease has been a dismal failure. This campaign began in the 1950s and in earnest in the '80s because of a claim that animal-based saturated fat raised cholesterol, which clogged arteries, which led to heart disease. Thus, animal foods were bad for health. The scientific data was never there, but the media storm, backed up by well-intentioned medical professionals, convinced much of the world.

Today, the science cannot be denied, and animal foods and saturated fat and even dietary cholesterol cannot be shown to be bad for heart health, because they are not. Now, though, confused practitioners and reporters continue to seek a valid link, to no avail.

In 2014, two meta-analyses were conducted, and saturated fat was found to have no link to heart disease. In fact, meat has heart-healthy nutrients, including CoQ10 and carnitine.

In 2013, *Mayo Clinic Proceedings* reported that "L-carnitine significantly *improves* cardiac health in patients after a heart attack" [emphasis added]. Further, 12 months of L-carnitine results in a *reduction* of chronic heart failure and death. In *Heart Disease* journal, researchers stated that "carnitine therapy may be useful in the treatment of various cardiac diseases."

Animal studies have shown that L-carnitine can improve hypertension (high blood pressure); and still yet, carnitine has been shown to reduce the risk of as well as treat depression "whilst offering a comparable effect to established anti-depressant agents with fewer side effects," according to the journal *Psychosomatic Medicine* in 2017.

INGREDIENT SPOTLIGHT: CARNITINE

This frittata recipe calls for ground beef, which contains carnitine. In addition to benefitting cardiovascular health, it has also been shown to prevent and treat depression as well as antidepressants do, without the side effects. Additionally, carnitine helps ensure fatty acids get to cells' mitochondria for energy production and fat burning.

STUFFED PEPPERS

While this dish calls for cooked vegetables (unless stuffing raw peppers, as one option describes), your baby at this age can have some raw veggies in moderation. For example, you could accompany the stuffed pepper mixture with some raw veggies if your baby is ready. Tender greens (like butterleaf), carrots, cucumbers, and tomatoes are low enough in fiber to be enjoyed raw. These foods have great nutrient worth, as they are bright and colorful—indicative of their nutritional value. You can offer these individually or as a salad. Carrots, in particular, have beta-carotene enhanced through cooking; however, their polyphenols are destroyed by cooking, so having carrots both cooked and raw is ideal.

2 tablespoons (28 g) preferred fat (lard, ghee, bacon drippings, coconut oil, red palm oil, duck fat, tallow, etc.)

½ cup (53 g) finely chopped onion

3 cloves garlic, minced

1 small zucchini, chopped

2 medium carrots, shredded

½ bunch of radishes, shredded

1 small butternut squash, rind removed, seeded, and cubed small

3 medium beets, peeled and cubed small

1 cup (71 g) chopped cremini or portabella mushrooms

Celtic sea salt and pepper to taste

Spices, including oregano and basil, to taste, *optional*

½ pound (225 g) ground beef (can use a mix of ground heart, sausage, dark meat chicken, and/or liver)

1 tomato, chopped

1 cup (120 g) raw curds (see page 106) or (230 g) organic, grass-fed, cultured cream cheese

½ cup (60 g) shredded raw cheese, *optional*

3 large bell peppers

First, make the filling. Heat the fat in a skillet and sauté the onion, garlic, and all the veggies and mushrooms (except the tomato) until soft (about 20 to 25 minutes). Season with salt and spices, if using.

Brown the meat and add sea salt and pepper to taste. Add the tomato and sauté for another 5 minutes. Remove from the heat, mix with the veggies, add the curds, and mix well.

Preheat the oven to 350°F (180°C, or gas mark 4).

Cut the peppers in half and remove the stems and seeds.

Stuff the bell pepper halves with the stuffed pepper filling and bake for 20 to 25 minutes.

NOTES

◉ Make stuffed mini peppers. Put the stuffed pepper filling into about 10 small, non-spicy halved and seeded banana peppers for a smaller, bite-size version.

◉ Serve in bowls, topped with the optional shredded cheese.

YIELD: 3 servings

STUFFED PEPPER SALAD

If serving a salad, make a dressing, which will provide the digestive-stimulating acid and the fat to absorb fat-soluble nutrients in the raw vegetables.

Try a "ranch" dressing with whole-milk raw yogurt, mixed herbs and spices, and sea salt; or an "Italian" version with 2 parts warmed coconut oil or olive oil to 1 part raw apple cider or fresh-squeezed lemon juice; add sea salt to taste.

See the salad dressings in Amazing Everyday Paleo Salad (page 51) and make a large container each time you're running low rather than each time you make a salad.

QUINOA-STUFFED PEPPERS

Quinoa can be added to the stuffing mixture. The quinoa must be prepared 1 day ahead of time.

½ cup (87 g) quinoa

2 cups (475 ml) filtered water

1 tablespoon (15 g) raw yogurt, or (15 ml) whey, kefir, raw vinegar, or lemon juice

1 cup (235 ml) Souper Stock (page 45)

Soak the quinoa in the water with the yogurt for 1 day on the counter. Rinse and drain.

In a medium saucepan, add the Souper Stock and drained quinoa. Bring to a boil, reduce the heat to low, and simmer until the quinoa has absorbed all the liquid.

YIELD: ½ cup (87 g)

GOOEY BERRY COBBLER BARS

Homemade treats are superior to mass-manufactured, store-bought for several reasons including the following: you have full control of ingredients, with no dyes, food colorings, refined sugar, and other processed food terrors, no additives to increase shelf life, and of course, the secret ingredient of "love" put into the making and baking of such goodies. That being said, treats are treats, meant to be enjoyed occasionally, and should still contain nutrients and be prepared with an eye toward digestibility.

OATS

3 cups (240 g) oats (gluten free, steel cut, organic, preferred)

3 cups (700 ml) filtered water

3 tablespoons (45 ml) whey or (45 g) raw yogurt, (45 ml) raw kefir, or (45 ml) lemon juice

BERRY COBBLER

⅓ cup (75 g) ghee (softened) or coconut oil, plus more for greasing baking pan

2 cups (340 g) chopped ripe peaches, (322 g) pears, (330 g) apricots, or (340 g) nectarines

2 cups (145 or 150 g) fresh or frozen blueberries or blackberries

4 farm-fresh, organic, pastured eggs, well beaten/whipped

2 tablespoons (28 g) coconut butter (manna), warmed, *optional*

⅓ cup (80 ml) coconut cream

1 tablespoon (7 g) ground cinnamon

½ teaspoon ground nutmeg

1 pinch of ground cloves

½ teaspoon Celtic sea salt

1 teaspoon vanilla extract

¼ cup (60 ml) maple syrup or (85 g) raw honey

½ cup (weight will vary) chopped nuts previously soaked and dried (see page 196), *optional*

3 cups (240 g) oats, previously prepared, wet but drained

To make the oats: Soak the oats in the water with whey, covered, on the counter for at least 8 hours or the day before.

To make the cobbler: Preheat the oven to 350°F (180°C, or gas mark 4). Grease a 9 × 13-inch (23 × 33 cm) baking pan with ghee or coconut oil.

Place the fruit on the bottom of the baking pan.

In a medium bowl, mix together the eggs, coconut butter, coconut cream, spices, vanilla, sweetener, and nuts, if using. Mix into the prepared wet oats; stir well. Pour over the fruit and spread to evenly cover.

Bake for 65 minutes. Remove and cool.

Place in the refrigerator; when fully chilled, cut into bars.

NOTE

⊙ This can be served warm, but might not cut into bars as easily.

YIELD: 12 to 15 bars

FROZEN FRUIT POPS

Enzymes and probiotics are wonderful digestive aids that are reduced but not damaged by freezing. Though freezing reduces bacteria by 60% to 90% by some studies, there will be some remaining probiotic benefit. Further, enzymes' tertiary structures are not damaged by freezing (as they are by heat), though cold temperatures slow down their catalytic activity.

Enzymes are rarely discussed when considering the nutrient value of foods, but they are critical. Enzymes are proteins that take action to ripen food, and then to "predigest" it for us, and ultimately are accountable for food rotting. When considering a fast-food meal that sits on a counter not changing for years, it becomes clear that no remaining active enzymes are available, and the food is "dead."

The Standard American Diet is filled not only with "dead" (no-active enzymes) foods, but also difficult to digest (denatured proteins in highly cooked foods, extruded grain cereals, and ultra-pasteurized dairy products lacking lactase) foods. Historically, prior to mass industrialization of food, humans consumed raw and cooked animal and plant foods, as well as lacto-fermented foods and cultured dairy. As a result, the digestive system is set up to expect some digestive enzyme support in the diet. Recently, a condition termed exocrine pancreatic insufficiency has been becoming more prevalent, due to the inability of the pancreas (which makes digestive enzymes) to keep up with the digestion of foods that are not predigested through fermentation and do not supply their own digestive enzymes. Pancreatic insufficiency is treated with pancreatic enzyme replacement therapy (PERT).

Dr. Francis Pottenger's studies of fresh food and uncooked milk and meat, and its ability to preserve mental and physical health generation after generation, as opposed to cooked milk, cooked meat, and non-enzyme-containing foods with the potential to degenerate the species fully in four generations, is likely attributable in part to the enzyme content in uncooked, raw, fresh foods.

2 ripe bananas or 2 cups (290 g) chopped strawberries or (240 g) peaches

⅔ cup (160 ml) coconut cream or raw cream

⅓ cup (77 g) raw yogurt

1 tablespoon (8 g) carob, *optional*

Peel the ripe bananas and freeze overnight. Remove from the freezer and chop.

Put the banana chunks, coconut cream, yogurt, and carob (if using) in a blender and purée.

Place the purée into ice pop molds with sticks and eat as ice pops or freeze in a small carton and eat as ice cream, topped with unsweetened, organic, unsulfured shredded coconut or berries.

YIELD: 6 pops

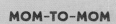

RECOGNIZING THE LINK BETWEEN JUNK FOODS AND JUNK MOODS. A large 2011 study, published in *PLoS One*, of more than 3,000 eleven-to-eighteen-year-olds, demonstrated that adolescents who ate highly processed and junk-food diets were more prone to episodes of depression and anxiety. Recent studies show polysorbate 80 and trehalose (chemicals commonly found in processed foods) are linked to mood and behavior disorders. The connection between chemicals in junk food and effect on mood occurs through the gut and the brain and is ultimately related to toxins' ability to impact gut flora, neurotransmitters, immunity, and inflammation.

Chemical toxins, such as those found in processed foods, disrupt the balance of healthy bacteria in the gut in favor of pathogenic flora, which cause not only illness in the body, but in the brain as well. Bad bug predominance, otherwise known as gut dysbiosis, has been shown to lead to anger, aggression, rage, and depression. Overall, gut dysbiosis, including overgrowth of yeasts and pathogenic bacteria, results in additional toxins being created, which contribute to mood and behavioral problems. Additionally, processed foods often contain excessive sugars and gluten-containing refined flour, both of which lead to an inability to fully digest proteins. Studies show toxins such as polysorbate 80 and carboxymethylcellulose lead to leaky gut and gut inflammation, which derail healthy digestion and mood regulation.

Together, chemicals, toxins, partially digested proteins, and byproducts of pathogenic gut flora can all reach the brain through a leaky gut and through their ability to cross the blood-brain barrier just as drugs and many medications do. *Both in the gut and in the brain, these same elements affect neurotransmitter levels and receptors, which are direct drivers of mood, perception, emotion, attitude, and behavior.*

By consuming more whole foods, studies show that children have less depression and anxiety. A diet of whole foods, rather than one of highly-refined carbohydrates and highly-processed foods, well serves the body *and* the mind. A more nutritious diet has been shown to reduce episodes of mental health problems, which should be both encouraging and worrisome. The level of mood and behavioral issues seen in children and a corresponding level of psychotropic drugs prescribed are both increasing. Those medications can have near-term and long-term side effects that are dangerous and possibly irreversible.

Rather than have discipline problems, risky medications, and unhappy families, changing the diet to a more nutritious one based on whole foods can work wonders and have long-term benefits. Particularly poignant is that 75% of psychiatric illnesses begin prior to adulthood but set a lifelong mental health trajectory; for example, once one has experienced depression, that person is likely to suffer with it again. By feeding your child well now, you'll take steps toward a better state of mental health throughout his entire life.

You can feed your child a diet free of junk food and can further positively influence stable mental health and contentedness through a diet rich in amino-acid-providing foods such as animal proteins, including red meat, which contains carnitine. (For more on carnitine, see page 245.) In addition, avoiding processed, chemical-laden foods and including complex carbohydrates found in greens, vegetables, nuts, and select seeds and grains, along with healthy, full fats and natural herbs and spices is important. Specifically, cilantro can act as a detoxifier and, according to the *Journal of Medicinal Food*, nutmeg has been shown to have an anti-depressant capability similar to raising dopamine and serotonin.

CAROB PUDDING PIE

This is a healthy, paleo-friendly treat. You can substitute pure, organic cacao, but there are tannins, phytic acid, and caffeine to contend with, and the bitterness requires additional sweeteners to overcome. Those who do not regularly consume refined sugar may find this quite sweet, but it is a pleasurable dish that can certainly be a true dessert—either as a pie or as a pudding.

PUDDING LAYER

2 ripe, organic bananas

1 ripe avocado

½ cup (112 g) coconut manna (coconut butter), warmed

3 to 4 teaspoons (8 to 10 g) carob

In a blender or Vitamix, add the bananas, avocado, coconut manna, and carob. Mix until smooth.

NOTE

○ You can enjoy this as a delicious, healthy pudding all by itself!

CRUST

½ cup (112 g) ghee, organic, preferably raw

1½ cup (150 g) chopped pecans, previously soaked and dried (see page 196)

½ cup (56 g) almond flour, made from presoaked almonds

2 tablespoons (28 g) coconut manna, warmed

1 tablespoon (14 g) coconut oil, plus more for greasing pie pan

Melt the ghee and pour over the pecans. Mix to coat. Add the almond flour and stir. Mix with the coconut manna. If needed, add a little coconut oil to get to a spreadable consistency.

Grease a glass or ceramic pie pan with coconut oil. Press the nut mixture into the bottom and up the sides.

Scoop the pudding layer over the nut crust, cover with berry compote (pages 163 and 239) or other mashed fruit, and refrigerate before serving.

VARIATION 1

- Mix 2 teaspoons gelatin with 2 tablespoons (28 ml) boiling water. Stir to dissolve the gelatin, let cool closer to room temperature, and then mix into the pudding layer and refrigerate for 1 to 2 hours until firm.

VARIATION 2

- Add kiwi wheels by peeling a kiwi with a paring knife and then inserting a spoon between the peel and flesh of the kiwi and rotating it to take the skin off. Slice the kiwi thin, layer on a tray, and dehydrate at low temperature for 6 to 12 hours. They should be dry, not wet, when done, and will be slightly chewy. You can serve them beside the pudding or pudding pie or as a wheel inserted in the top of each slice.

  If you do not have a dehydrator, you can also place these on a cookie sheet in the oven at the lowest temperature, checking them after about 4 hours. The amount of time will vary since not all ovens are the same.

AFTERWORD

"Life in all its fullness is Mother Nature obeyed."

—WESTON A. PRICE, D.D.S.

By the time your child is two years old, you've surely got an adorable little busy body. As she continues to rapidly learn and grow, her exploration of the world might now include more playdates with friends, outings, and even possibly preschool next year. While these new experiences will bring challenges of their own, we hope the suggestions and information gained from this book will help you create a strong and secure foundation. Continue to take pride in every small step forward you take to provide your baby with Super Nutrition, and know that your efforts are well worth it.

With the nutritional knowledge and commitment you now have, you can continue to positively influence your child's health destiny, steering her toward optimal health and the ability to live a full and rich life.

APPENDIX

FOOD INTRODUCTION TIMELINE

This timeline includes Super POWER and PURE foods that may or may not have been discussed in previous chapters. At each age, continue offering foods from the previous stages. With this excellent foundation, mixing in some OKAY foods, as needed, is acceptable. We of course caution you to avoid CRAP to every extent possible.

Note: You can shift the food introduction timeline by a month or two if nursing is going well and your baby is growing and developing as expected through visits with your pediatrician; in such a case, you would simply follow the introduction timeline below, but starting at 7 or 8 months rather than 6 months.

AGE	ALLOWABLE FOODS	CHAPTER
0–4 months	Mom's milk, homemade formula, and probiotics in special cases*; nursing moms: eat Super POWER foods and supplement with vitamin D, cod liver oil, 5-MTHF, B12, probiotics	2, 3
4–6 months	Egg yolk, cod liver oil, and liver in special cases*	3
6 months	Egg yolk, liver, Souper Stock, apple cider vinegar (cooked in stock) or diluted with filtered water, lard (from organic pastured animals), coconut oil (unrefined, virgin, organic), sea salt, unpasteurized sauerkraut juice (in special cases)	4
6½ months	Avocado, banana, sweet potato (lacto-fermented), taro (lacto-fermented), carrots (cooked in Souper Stock or lacto-fermented), kidney, heart, raw-dairy whey (for lactofermentation if not using mommy's way whey)	4
7 months	Fish roe, marrow, meats (poultry, lamb, beef—cooked in stock); veggies (carrots, pumpkin, squash—lacto-fermented or cooked in stock); fruits (apples and pears, cooked); sweet potato (cooked)	4
8 months	Tropical fruits (papaya, melon, cantaloupe, mango, watermelon, passion fruit, guava, pineapple, kiwi); gelatin, olive oil (extra-virgin, cold-pressed, organic), coconut milk, coconut cream, coconut kefir, coconut butter/manna, pork (bacon from pastured sources without chemical treatment, pork sausage from pastured sources); cooked vegetables (zucchini, parsnips, pumpkin, squash, carrots, mushrooms); fruits (nectarines, cherries, peaches, apricots, cooked); herbs and seasonings (cumin, garlic, ginger, turmeric, coriander, green cardamom, cinnamon, cloves, nutmeg, oregano, cilantro, basil, cumin, rosemary, mint, peppercorns—for flavor only)	5
9 months	Lemon zest, orange zest, curry powder, raw yogurt, raw kefir, ghee, oily fish (cooked), onion (cooked), leeks (cooked), olives, pickles (unpasteurized)	5
10 months	Coconut water, beets (cooked), filtered water, beet kvass, spinach (well steamed), herbs and spices (pepper, mustard seed, dill [ground], bay leaves [for flavoring only], onion powder), berries (strawberries, blackberries, raspberries, blueberries, mulberries, cooked), coconut flour	6
11 months	Paprika, fish stock, fish stews, deep-sea wild-caught fish (cooked), plantains (cooked), sweet potato (cooked), cultured dairy (curd, cream cheese, crème fraîche, from raw dairy), fats (bacon grease, duck fat, tallow, schmaltz), vegetables (cauliflower, rutabaga, cooked), raw cheese (sparingly), raw puréed apples and pears	6

(continued)

AGE	ALLOWABLE FOODS	CHAPTER
12–15 months	Baking soda, baking powder (aluminum-free), whole eggs, health sweeteners (raw, unheated, unfiltered honey; grade B, 100% pure maple syrup; blackstrap molasses; whole plant stevia), nuts (soaked), seeds (soaked), liverwurst, berries (uncooked), homemade juice and lactofermented beverages, raw dairy (milk, cream, sour cream, butter), citrus fruits (lemon, lime, grapefruit, orange, tangerine), non-grain flours (arrowroot flour/starch, tigernut flour, cassava flour), spices (almond extract [nonalcohol], vanilla, paprika, sumac, sage, red pepper flakes, chili powder), cranberries (cooked), oils (avocado, unrefined, high-oleic safflower, limited), fermented soy (as in tamari sauce), collard greens, kale, beet leaves, mustard greens, Swiss chard (well-cooked), raw puréed/chopped berries, pomegranate	7
15–18 months	Soaked brown rice, nuts (almonds, hazelnuts, walnuts, pecans, pistachios, macadamia, cashews, brazil, soaked and dried), sprouted seeds, nut butters, kombucha, beverages (ginger ale, homemade orangina), homemade mayonnaise, carob, raw veggies (tender greens, butterleaf lettuce, carrots, cucumbers, mint leaves, tomatillos, pimentos, mushrooms, green onion), cooked veggies (white potatoes, eggplant, turnips, peas), hot spices (chili, curry, paprika, cayenne pepper and other pepper, coriander, natto, mustard), carob, dates, flaxseed (ground), jicama, yucca, coconut flakes, asparagus, bacon	7
18–21 months	Properly prepared gluten-free grains, raw greens (except spinach, kale, and collard greens, which should still be cooked), pasteurized cheese (on occasion, only if raw is not available); gummies	8
21–24 months	Properly prepared gluten-containing grains, properly prepared legumes (peanuts, green beans, chickpeas), shellfish (lobster, shrimp, scallops, oysters, clams, mussels, sea cucumber, sea urchins, crab, prawns), raw onion, pasteurized cheese (sparingly if at all), raw tomato, Brussels sprouts	8

* C-section, eczema, other 3Cs, food allergies, parents with 3Cs: always accompany early feeding (before 6 months) with probiotic supplementation.

RECOMMENDED READING AND DOCUMENTARIES

Don't Stop Here. The following are books, DVDs, and websites that we have referenced throughout the book or that have positively impacted our views and understanding of food. While these are excellent sources of nutritional information, they aren't the only resources available. We provide them as a place to start, hoping that you will continue to build upon your solid foundation of traditional-foods knowledge. We encourage you to seek out even more information to support your crusade for better health for your family.

TRADITIONAL FOODS AND FOOD PREPARATION

Cure Tooth Decay: Heal and Prevent Cavities with Nutrition, 2nd edition, Ramiel Nagel and Timothy Gallagher

Deep Nutrition: Why Your Genes Need Traditional Food, Catherine Shanahan, M.D.

Eat Fat Lose Fat, Dr. Mary Enig, Ph.D., and Sally Fallon

The Grassfed Gourmet, Shannon Hayes

Healing Our Children, Ramiel Nagel

Nourishing Broth: An Old-Fashioned Remedy for the Modern World, Sally Fallon Morell and Kaayla T. Daniel

Nourishing Diets: What Our Paleo, Ancestral and Traditional Ancestors Really Ate (coming in 2018), Sally Fallon Morell

Nourishing Fats: Why We Need Animal Fats for Health and Happiness, Sally Fallon Morell

Nourishing Traditions, Sally Fallon

Pasture Perfect, Jo Robinson

Recipes for the Specific Carbohydrate Diet, Raman Prasad

Traditional Foods Are Your Best Medicine, Ronald F. Schmid, N.D.

Trick or Treat, Dr. Barry Groves

Truly Cultured, Nancy Lee Bentley

Vitamin K2 and the Calcium Paradox: How a Little-Known Vitamin Could Save Your Life, Kate Rheaume-Bleue

The Whole Beast; Nose to Tail Eating, Fergus Henderson

The Whole Soy Story, Kaayla T. Daniel, Ph.D.

Wholesome Home Cooking—Preparing Nutrient-Dense Foods, Katie L. Stoltzfus

Wild Fermentation, Sandor Ellix Katz

3C CONDITIONS AND CHILDREN'S HEALTH

Compromised Generation: The Epidemic of Chronic Illness in America's Children, Beth Lambert

Digestive Wellness for Children, Elizabeth Lipski, Ph.D., C.C.N.

Gut and Psychology Syndrome, Natasha Campbell-McBride, M.D.

Healing and Preventing Autism, Jenny McCarthy and Dr. Jerry Kartzinel

Healing the New Childhood Epidemics, Kenneth Bock, M.D.

The NDD™ Book, William Sears

Nourishing Hope for Autism, Julie Matthews

The Nourishing Traditions Book of Baby & Child Care, Sally Fallon Morell and Thomas Cowan, M.D.

The Nourishing Traditions Cookbook for Children: Teaching Children to Cook the Nourishing Traditions Way, Suzanne Gross and Sally Fallon Morell

The Puzzle of Autism, Dr. Amy Yasko and Dr. Garry Gordon

SUGAR ADDICTION

The Anatomy of a Food Addiction, Anne Katherine

The Hidden Addiction and How to Get Free, Janice Keller Phelps, M.D., and Alan Nourse, M.D.

Lick the Sugar Habit, Nancy Appleton, Ph.D.

Little Sugar Addicts, Kathleen DesMaisons, Ph.D.

Sugar Blues, William F. Duffy

Sugar . . . Stop the Addiction, Kelly Genzlinger, C.N.C.

Suicide by Sugar, Nancy Appleton, Ph.D.

GENERAL AND CHILDREN'S NUTRITION AND FOOD-RELATED HEALTH

A Compromised Generation: The Epidemic of Chronic Illness in America's Children, Beth Lambert

Could It Be B12?, Sally M. Pacholok, R.N., and Jeffrey J. Stuart, D.O.

Good Calories, Bad Calories, Gary Taubes

Healthy 4 Life Dietary Guidelines, The Weston A. Price Foundation

Our Children's Health: America's Kids in Nutritional Crisis and What We Can Do to Help Them, Bonnie C. Minsky

Real Food for Mother and Baby, Nina Planck

The Soy Deception, David Brownstein, M.D., and Sheryl Shenefelt, C.N.

The Truth about Children's Health: The Comprenhensive Guide to Understanding, Preventing, and Reversing Disease, Robert Bernardini, M.S.

The Vegetarian Myth, Lierre Keith

FRESH, RAW MILK

Milk Diet as a Remedy for Chronic Disease, Charles Sanford Porter, M.D.

Nature's Healing Gift (an eBook of personal raw milk testimonials), compiled by Laura Kozicki—http://www .realmilk.com/natureshealinggift.html

Pottenger's Cats, Francis Marion Pottenger, Jr., M.D.

Raw Milk Revolution: The Emerging Battle over America's Food Rights, David E. Gumpert

The Raw Truth about Milk, William Campbell Douglass II, M.D.

The Untold Story of Milk, Dr. Ronald F. Schmid, N.D.

ATTACHMENT PARENTING AND BABY CARE

The Attachment Parenting Book, William Sears, M.D., and Martha Sears, R.N.

The Baby Bond, Dr. Linda Folden Palmer

Continuum Concept, Jean Liedloff

THE TRUTH ABOUT FATS

The Cholesterol Myths, Uffe Ravnskov

The Coconut Oil Miracle, Bruce Fife

The Great Cholesterol Con, Anthony Colpo

Know Your Fats, Mary G. Enig, Ph.D.

The Queen of Fats, Susan Allport

VACCINE AWARENESS

A Shot in the Dark, Harrison L. Coulter and Barbara Loe Fisher

Callous Disregard, Dr. Andrew J. Wakefield

Dissolving Illusions: Disease, Vaccines, and the Forgotten History, Suzanne Humphries, M.D.

Evidence of Harm, David Kirby

The Sanctity of Human Blood: Vaccination Is Not Immunization, Tim O'Shea

The Vaccine Book: Making the Right Decision for Your Child, Robert W. Sears, M.D.

What Your Doctor May NOT Tell You about Children's Vaccinations, Stephanie Cave, M.D.

BREASTFEEDING

Breastfeeding a Toddler: Why on Earth?, J. Jack Newman, M.D.

Breastfeeding: Biocultural Perspectives, Patricia Stuart-Macadam and Katherine A. Dettwyler

The Breastfeeding Book, William Sears, M.D., and Martha Sears, R.N.

Mothering Your Nursing Toddler, Norma J. Bumgarner

The Nursing Mother's Guide to Weaning, Kathleen Huggins and Linda Ziedrich

The Womanly Art of Breastfeeding, La Leche League International

RESOURCES

Sources of Ingredients, Instructions, and Supplies for Homemade Formula

https://www.radiantlifecatalog.com/product/nourishing-traditions-kit-homemade-baby-formula/baby-child-care

TO FIND A TRUSTED SOURCE OF RAW MILK NEAR YOU

http://www.realmilk.com/real-milk-finder

VIDEO ON HOW TO MAKE HYPOALLERGENIC BABY FORMULA

http://www.thehealthyhomeeconomist.com/2010/09/video-hypoallergenic-baby-formula

RESOURCE PAGE FOR HOMEMADE FORMULA

https://www.westonaprice.org/health-topics/childrens-health/formula-homemade-baby-formula

HOMEMADE FORMULA TESTIMONIALS

https://www.westonaprice.org/health-topics/childrens-health/formula-homemade-baby-formula-testimonials

THE RECIPES

http://www.realmilk.com/formularecipes.html#chart

HOMEMADE FORMULA FAQS

For answers to frequently asked questions about milk-based formula, visit http://www.westonaprice.org/faq/faq-homemade-baby-formula

ONLINE COMMUNITIES

https://www.westonaprice.org/email-lists-and-forums

KEFIR STARTER

http://www.thehealthyhomeeconomist.com/resources/#starters

http://www.bodyecology.com, G.E.M. Cultures, 1-800-511-2660

YEAST

www.Iherb.com

RAW CREAM

Order sources found in the Weston A. Price Shopping Guide at www.westonaprice.org or realmilk.com

DOCUMENTARIES

Don't have time to read? Learn tons by watching!

- *Fresh*—http://www.freshthemovie.com
- *Food, Inc.*—http://www.takepart.com/foodinc
- *Healing Autism*, Kenneth Bock's DVD—https://uedata.amazon.com/Healing-Autism-Breakthrough-Approach-Kenneth/dp/B000P9G6ZE
- *InGREEDients*—www.ingreedientsmovie.com
- *King Corn*—http://www.kingcorn.net
- *Nourishing Traditional Diets: The Key to Vibrant Health*, DVD, Sally Fallon Morell
- *The Oiling of America: How the Vegetable Industry Demonized Nutritious Animal Fats and Destroyed the American Food Supply*, DVD, Sally Fallon Morell
- PowerPoint presentation on Real Milk—http://www.realmilk.com/ppt/index.html
- *Sweet Suicide*—http://nancyappleton.com/store
- *The Price Pottenger Story*—https://price-pottenger.org

- *Two Angry Moms*—https://www.angrymoms.org
- *The Industrialization of Giving Birth*—http://www.thebusinessofbeingborn.com
- Documentary regarding insights on the vaccine business—http://vaxxedthemovie.com
- *What's on Your Plate?*—http://www.whatsonyourplateproject.org

ONLINE INFORMATION AND RESOURCES

Traditional Foods and Real-Food Baby Feeding

For guidelines that support traditional foods and Super Nutrition, see the Healthy 4 Life Guidelines from the Weston A. Price Foundation, as opposed to the USDA MyPlate, MyPyramid, and Food Pyramid dietary guidelines that support the food industry and improper eating. Weston A. Price Foundation supplies shopping guides and a Healthy 4 Life book that can be ordered from their site.

- https://chriskresser.com—excellent blog on the truth about nutrition, food, and health
- http://community.westonaprice.org—discuss with a like-minded group living the traditional-foods lifestyle
- www.jamieoliver.com—revolutionary chef trying to change health by changing food, starting with children and school lunches
- www.ninaplanck.com—author of *Real Food for Mother and Baby*, informative site on "real food" for real people living real lives
- www.westonaprice.org/childrens-health/feeding-babies—more information on nursing and baby feeding
- www.westonprice.org—a comprehensive and amazingly abundant resource on traditional foods and nutrition related to optimal health and disease prevention
- www.westonaprice.org/soy-alert—for more about the actual effects of soy on health
- https://wellnessmama.org—from recipes to resources, lots of great information

3C Conditions and Children's Health

- www.dramyyasko.com—information on the biochemical problems related to the 3Cs, detoxification and methylation pathway information, genetic testing, and more
- www.epidemicanswers.org—a wonderful site outlining information on many 3C conditions, including autism

- www.healingthewholechild.com—Dr. Erlich's informative site, providing information, articles, and updates for Protective Nutrition
- http://nourishinghope.com—website of author Julie Matthews, discussing dietary treatment for autism
- www.nourishmd.com—informative articles and advice on "real-life" applications of healthy and traditional foods

Sugar, Autoimmunity, Hormonal, Thyroid, and Gluten-Free Information

- www.glutenfreegirltotherescue.com—acceptable recipes from a celiac and pretty much paleo teen
- https://www.glutenfreeliving.com/gluten-free-foods/diet/basic-diet—gluten-free ingredients and foods to avoid
- https//healingautoimmune.com—pantry list, quick start guide, food lists, and recipes to follow for the AIP (autoimmune protocol) diet
- www.hookedonjuice.com—for more information about the true risks of juice consumption
- Izabellawentz.com—Dr. Izabella Wentz provides information on causes of Hashimoto's Thyroiditis and practical advice to start feeling better through addressing root causes of autoimmune thyroid disease.
- www.kitchenconsultantkelly.com—information on great reads, kitchen overhaul advice for gluten free, paleo, traditional foods, AIP, and more
- www.nancyappleton.com—pioneering whistle-blower on the dangers of dietary sugars
- https://radiantrecovery.com—Kathleen DesMaison, Ph.D., discusses the realities and scientific basis of sugar addiction
- www.saragotfriedmd.com—author and Harvard-trained doctor with health insights
- suzycohen.com—America's most trusted pharmacist
- thyroidpharmacist.com—Izabella Wentz's site, author of *The Root Cause of Hashimoto's*

Vaccine and Antibiotic Information

- www.nvic.org—vaccine rights advocacy and information
- http://www.childrenshealthchoices.org/schedules—provides collection of alternative vaccine schedules

- www.pewtrusts.org/en/projects/antibiotic-resistance-project—takes a scientific look at factory farming and the use of drugs in farming
- www.cdc.gov/vaccines/vac-gen/additives.htm—list of all vaccines and their ingredients

Real Milk Information

- www.raw-milk-facts.com—information about raw, fresh milk
- www.realmilk.com—fresh milk information
- www.realmilk.com/raw.html—fresh milk information
- http://www.mercola.com/2004/apr/24/raw_milk.htm—fresh milk information
- http://www.usatoday.com/news/nation/tables/2006-08-06-raw-milk.htm—listing of which states allow raw milk sales

Sources for Food, Supplements, Ingredients, Books, Equipment, and More

FOOD AND SUPPLEMENTS

https://bodyecology.com—kefir starter, coconut kefir

https://grasslandbeef.com (was uswellnessmeats.com)—liverwurst, liver, beef stock, grass-fed meat, organs, and bones

www.mountainroseherbs.com or Frontier brand—stevia that is in whole form from dried and ground stevia plant leaves with no further processing (green powder)

www.pureindianfoods.com—a great source of grass-fed ghee

https://traceminerals.com/concentrace-trace-mineral-drops—for improving pH of filtered water

www.vitalchoice.com—fish roe and high-quality fish

www.wellnessresources.com—safest form of iodine, to be used through skin absorption

FOOD, EQUIPMENT, BOOKS, AND MORE

www.amazon.com—source of some ingredients for homemade formula and for dolomite powder (you must purchase U.S. Pharmacopoeia [USP] dolomite, to avoid lead)

www.babybullet.com—a useful tool in making baby food

www.krautpounder.com—a hand-carved wooden tool that fits in Mason jars to facilitate making your own lacto-fermented condiments

www.lalecheleague.org—1-800-LALECHE—breastfeeding support and information

www.ppnf.org—provides many books on traditional foods, holistic health, and some products

www.radiantlifecatalog.com—many items, including dehydrators, juicers, grain mills, pickling crocks, bath and shower water-filter systems, stainless children's dishes, stainless ice cube trays, gelatin, arrowroot powder, crystal ball bath dechlorinator, EvenFlo glass bottles, Bariani olive oil, VioLiv glassware, and Nourishing Superfood Kit for Homemade Baby Formula

www.reuseit.com—sustainable, responsible storage containers and more

www.happyherbalist.com—kombucha kits and more

COD LIVER OIL RECOMMENDATIONS PER WESTON A. PRICE FOUNDATION

Additional recommendations can be found at: https://www.westonaprice.org/health-topics/cod-liver-oil/cod-liver-oil-basics-and-recommendations

We do not advocate fermented CLO, but WAPF recommends it and many choose it.

In the United States:

BEST:

- Blue Ice high-vitamin fermented cod liver oil, if you choose fermented CLO
- NutraPro International virgin cod liver oil
- Rosita Real Foods extra-virgin cod liver oil

GOOD:

- Carlson soft gel cod liver oil super
- NOW Foods double strength cod liver oil
- Pharmax cod liver oil
- Sonne's cod liver oil
- Swanson double strength cod liver oil
- Twin Labs non-emulsified liquid cod liver oil

In Europe:

BEST:

- Blue Ice high-vitamin fermented cod liver oil, if you choose fermented CLO
- Funky Raw cod liver oil (UK)
- Healthcloud cod liver oil (UK)
- Green Pasture fermented cod liver oil
- Spain—Comida real cod liver oil, Ergomax
- The Netherlands—Rosita Real Foods extra-virgin cod liver oil
- Croatia—Green Pasture and soon Rosita cod liver oil
- Poland—Rosita Real Foods extra-virgin cod liver oil

GOOD:

- Health Span cod liver oil
- Goldshield cod liver oil

In Russia:

BEST:

- Holomed Nederland—Green Pasture cod liver oil

In Australia:

BEST:

- Blue Ice high-vitamin fermented cod liver oil, if you choose fermented CLO
- Green Pasture cod liver oil

In New Zealand:

BEST:

- NutraPro virgin cod liver oil
- Green Pasture fermented cod liver oil, if you choose fermented CLO

In Canada:

BEST:

- Blue Ice Royal fermented cod liver oil, if you choose fermented CLO
- Green Pasture fermented cod liver oil, if you choose fermented CLO
- Blue Ice high-vitamin fermented cod liver oil, if you choose fermented CLO

In Hong Kong (China):

BEST:

- Blue Ice high-vitamin fermented cod liver oil, if you choose fermented CLO
- Green Pasture fermented cod liver oil, if you choose fermented CLO

NOURISHING FOOD NEAR YOU

Fresh milk near you—http://www.realmilk.com/where.html and https://www.farmtoconsumer.org/raw-milk-nation-interactive-map

Local WAPF chapter—http://www.westonaprice.org/local-chapters/find-a-local-chapter, your local chapter will help with pastured animal foods, CSAs, and fresh, raw dairy

Produce-providing, local, seasonal CSA near you—http://www.localharvest.org

www.cornucopia.org—ratings for eggs, dairy, and other food-brand information

ORGANIZATIONS YOU MIGHT CONSIDER SUPPORTING

Farm to Consumer Legal Defense Fund—http://www.farmtoconsumer.org—support the small farmers treating animals, the Earth, and people right

The Institute for Responsible Technology—http://www.responsibletechnology.org—help raise awareness regarding the outrageous GMO liberties being taken

The National Vaccine Information Center—http://www.nvic.org—support those who are fighting for vaccine rights

The Price-Pottenger Nutrition Foundation—http://www.ppnf.org—support those who are preserving important research and information on traditional foods and health

The Weston A. Price Foundation—http://www.westonaprice.org—become part of the traditional-foods movement

SOURCES FOR MORE INFORMATION ABOUT VACCINES

"A Causal Association Between Haemophilus Influenzae Type B (Hib) Vaccine and Diabetes." *Autoimmunity*, May 2003; 36(3):123. https://www.ncbi.nlm.nih.gov/pubmed/12911277

"Acellular Pertussis Vaccines Protect against Disease but Fail to Prevent Infection and Transmission in a Nonhuman Primate Model." *PNAS*, Jan 2014; 111(2):787-92. doi: 10.1073/pnas.1314688110. Epub 2013 Nov 25.

"Aluminum in Brain Tissue in Autism." *Journal of Trace Elements in Medicine and Biology*, March 2018; 46:76-82

"Aluminum Neurotoxicity in Preterm Infant Receiving Intravenous-Feeding Solution." *New England Journal of Medicine*, May 1997; 336, (22):1557-1561

"AS03 Adjuvanted AH1N1 Vaccine Associated with an Abrupt Increase in the Incidence of Childhood Narcolepsy in Finland." *PLoS ONE*, 7(3): e33536. doi:10.1371/journal.pone.0033536

"Asymptomatic Transmission and the Resurgence of Bordetella Pertussis." *BMC Medicine*, DOI 10.1186/s12916-015-0382-8

"Autism after Infection, Febrile Episodes, and Antibiotic Use during Pregnancy." *Pediatrics*, Nov 2012; DOI:10.1542/peds.2012-1107

"Autoimmune/Inflammatory Syndrome Induced by Adjuvants (Shoenfeld's Syndrome): An Update." *Lupus*, June 2017; 26(7):675-681. doi: 10.1177/0961203316686406. Epub 2017 Jan 6.

"Common Variants Associated with General and MMR Vaccine–Related Febrile Seizures." *Nature Genetics*, 2014; 46:1274-1282

Dissolving Illusions: Disease, Vaccines, and the Forgotten History, 2013. Suzanne Humphries M.D.

"Duration of Pertussis Immunity after DTaP Immunization: A Meta-Analysis." *Pediatrics*, Feb 2015; 135 (2)331-343; DOI: 10.1542/peds.2014-1729. http://pediatrics.aappublications.org/content/135/2/331

"Evaluation of the Impact of a Pertussis Cocooning Program on Infant Pertussis Infection." *The Pediatric Infectious Disease Journal*, 2015;34:22–6.

"Flu Vaccination May Triple Risk for Flu-Related Hospitalization in Children with Asthma." *ATS*, 2009: American Thoracic Society International Conference: Abstract 561. Presented May 19, 2009.

"Immune Thrombocytopaenic Purpura: An Autoimmune Cross-Link between Infections and Vaccines." *Lupus*, May 2014; 23(6):554-67. doi: 10.1177/0961203313499959.

"Immunization with Hepatitis B Vaccine Accelerates SLE-Like Disease in a Murine Model." *Journal of Autoimmunity*, Nov 2014; 54:21-32 doi: 10.1016/j.jaut.2014.06.006. Epub 2014 Jul 16.

"Increased Risk of Noninfluenza Respiratory Virus Infections Associated with Receipt of Inactivated Influenza Vaccine." *Clinical Infectious Diseases*, June 2012; 54(12), 1778–1783, https://doi.org/10.1093/cid/cis307

"Influence of Pediatric Vaccines on Amygdala Growth and Opioid Ligand Binding in Rhesus Macaque Infants." *Acta Neurobiologiae Experimentalis*, 2010;70(2):147-64.

"Is Exposure to Aluminum Adjuvants Associated with Social Impairments in Mice?" *Journal of Inorganic Biochemistry*, April 2018; 181:96-103

"Measles Incidence, Vaccine Efficacy, and Mortality in Two Urban African Areas with High Vaccination Coverage." *The Journal of Infectious Diseases*, Nov 1990; 162(5):1043-8. PMID:2230232

"Pertussis Epidemic despite High Levels of Vaccination Coverage with Acellular Pertussis Vaccine." *Enfermedades Infecciosas y Microbiología Clínica*, Jan 2015; 33(1):27-31. doi: 10.1016/j.eimc.2013.09.013. Epub 2013 Nov 9.

"Residual Adverse Changes in Arterial Endothelial Function and LDL Oxidation after a Mild Systemic Inflammation Induced by Influenza Vaccination." *Annals of Medicine*, 2007; 39(5):392-9.

"Risk of Immune Thrombocytopenic Purpura after Measles-Mumps-Rubella Immunization in Children." *Pediatrics*, Mar 2008; 121(3):e687-92. doi: 10.1542/peds.2007-1578.

"Severe Tetanus in Immunized Patients with High Anti-Tetanus Titers." *Neurology*, Apr 1992; 42(4)761-764

"Tdap Vaccine Effectiveness in Adolescents during the 2012 Washington State Pertussis Epidemic." *Pediatrics*, Jun 2015, 135 (6) 981-989; DOI: 10.1542/peds.2014-3358

"Vitamin A Treatment of Measles." *Pediatrics*, May 1993, VOLUME 91 / ISSUE 5

Additional Links Referenced:

Tdap failure—http://www.cdc.gov/pertussis/pregnant/mom/vacc-effectiveness.html

Mumps vaccine failure—https://www.cdc.gov/mmwr/volumes/65/wr/mm6529a2.htm

Rates of Pertussis in Michigan, 2012—http://www.cdc.gov/pertussis/downloads/pertuss-surv-report-2012.pdf

Rates of Pertussis in Michigan, 2013—http://www.cdc.gov/pertussis/downloads/pertuss-surv-report-2013.pdf

Rates of Pertussis in Michigan, 2015—http://www.cdc.gov/pertussis/downloads/pertuss-surv-report-2015.pdf

Vaccine Injury Table 2015-2017—https://www.hrsa.gov/sites/default/files/hrsa/vaccine-compensation/pre03202017-vaccine-injury-table.pdf

ACKNOWLEDGMENTS

In the five years since the original version was written, my deep appreciation has not waned for all of those who contributed to the initial printing of this book, including the Weston A. Price Foundation and Sally Fallon Morell, and all other researchers, activists, authors, and parents who fight for the right to retain, procure, support, and choose traditional foods and healthy lifestyle and medical choices. Sincere gratitude to our family's farmers (and all pasture-focused, traditional farmers), without whom I could not properly provide optimal nutrition, raw dairy, and truly whole foods to my healthy, brilliant, socially well adjusted, athletic, and compassionate children. To my parents (Janet, Jim, Nancy, Dale, and Bob), I greatly appreciate your support and participation in our endeavor to raise the kids with commitment from us all to be sugar-free and following the traditional-foods approach (come holidays, birthdays, and all other celebrations), thank you. Mom and Mel, you were instrumental saviors in this revision, as was the "Lacrosse Test Kitchen!" To my husband and best friend: thank you for everything. Finally, many thanks to Marilyn (my most lovely agent) and all of the talented folks at Quarto, especially Jill, for their dedication to making this book beautiful and getting its reach to a global scale so it can help children around the world.

—K.G.

I must thank all of the parents who have trusted me to "practice" on their children—and the children themselves, including my own kids. You all taught me great lessons along the way. I hope and pray that I can continue to be a source of guidance, strength, and empowerment for all of you. Words can't express the gratitude I have for all of the doctors, naturopaths, acupuncturists, pharmacists, chiropractors, nutritionists (especially Kelly), dentists, and energy workers, friends, parents, and my family from whom I have learned and continue to gain such precious knowledge. I can't thank you enough! As you have been an inspiration and teacher to me, so too I hope I can be to others.

—K.E.

ABOUT THE AUTHORS

KELLY GENZLINGER, M.Sc., BBA, CNC, CMTA, has dedicated over a decade and a half to studying nutrients and foods and their effects within the human body, spurred by the nutrition-based medical conditions her children faced and from which they were able to recover. She is a traditional-foods advocate and is dedicated to promoting wellness for her family and children everywhere. An author, speaker, and certified nutritional consultant, Kelly is proud to have changed the lives of many through advice and education about whole, real, traditional foods. With both a master of science and an undergraduate business degree, as well as three professional certifications in holistic health and nutrition, she is an avid researcher. Kelly's first book, *Sugar . . . Stop the Addiction*, addressed the national crisis of excessive sugar consumption. She has been a featured speaker at wellness symposiums and a guest on cable shows such as *Diabetes Countdown* and *The Bottom Line*. She lives in southeastern Michigan with her husband and three well-nourished, well-loved, and thriving children.

KATHERINE ERLICH, M.D., is a board-certified pediatrician who spent her first eleven years after residency in a large, conventional pediatric practice. Combining her extensive clinical experience with her curiosity as to why kids get sick and how to help them really get better, Dr. Erlich opened Healing the Whole Child, PLLC, and now practices out of the largest holistic medical center in the Midwest, as well as in her private office in Franklin, Michigan. Dr. Erlich guides patients to better health through an individualized medical approach, integrating nutrition, holistic philosophies, and traditional medicine. Dr. Erlich has been featured on the news, and has authored articles printed in several publications. She frequently travels to Lansing to educate the government about serious environmental toxins, such as glyphosate. Dr. Erlich lives with her husband, two children, dog (Lucy), and parrot (Gracie) in Oakland County.

INDEX